Branding as Communication

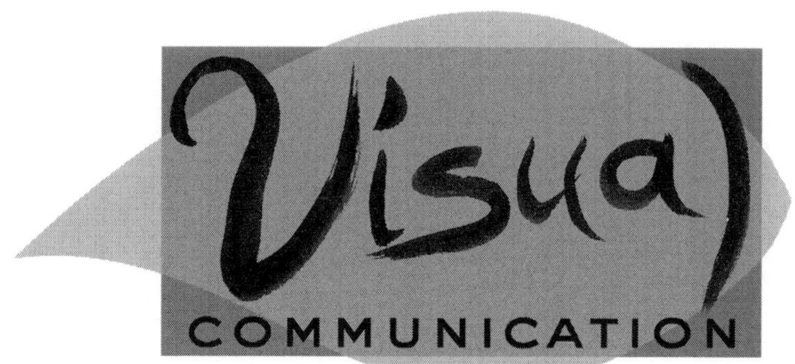

Susan B. Barnes
General Editor

Vol. 5

The Visual Communication series
is part of the Peter Lang Media and Communication list.
Every volume is peer reviewed and meets
the highest quality standards for content and production.

PETER LANG
New York • Bern • Frankfurt • Berlin
Brussels • Vienna • Oxford • Warsaw

Susan B. Barnes

Branding as Communication

PETER LANG

New York • Bern • Frankfurt • Berlin
Brussels • Vienna • Oxford • Warsaw

Library of Congress Cataloging-in-Publication Data

Names: Barnes, Susan B., author.
Title: Branding as communication / Susan B. Barnes.
Description: New York: Peter Lang, 2017.
Series: Visual communication; vol. 5 | ISSN 2153-277X
Includes bibliographical references and index.
Identifiers: LCCN 2015042699 | ISBN 978-1-4331-2804-2 (hardcover: alk. paper)
ISBN 978-1-4331-2803-5 (paperback: alk. paper) | ISBN 978-1-4539-1791-6 (ebook pdf)
ISBN 978-1-4331-3827-0 (epub) | ISBN 978-1-4331-3826-3 (mobi)
Subjects: LCSH: Communication in marketing.
Branding (Marketing) | Visual communication.
Classification: LCC HF5415.123 .B367 2016 | DDC 658.8/27—dc23
DOI 10.3726/b10498
LC record available at http://lccn.loc.gov/2015042699

Bibliographic information published by **Die Deutsche Nationalbibliothek.**
Die Deutsche Nationalbibliothek lists this publication in the "Deutsche
Nationalbibliografie"; detailed bibliographic data are available
on the Internet at http://dnb.d-nb.de/.

The paper in this book meets the guidelines for permanence and durability
of the Committee on Production Guidelines for Book Longevity
of the Council of Library Resources.

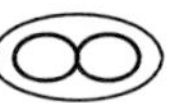

TABLE OF CONTENTS

INTRODUCTION

> *The momentous sign of the rise of image-thinking, and its displacement of*
> *ideals is, of course, the rise of advertising.... In fact it has meant a reshaping*
> *of our very concept of truth.*
> —Daniel J. Boorstin, 1987, p. 205

Fish don't know they are in water because they are surrounded by it, which makes it impos-
sible to see. Similarly, people are so surrounded by branding that it is something that we
do not notice. Today we live in a branded world. Branding influences many aspects of our
lives, whether we know it or not. The reason for this is part cultural, part emotional, and
part economic.

While window shopping at the airport, a travel bag captured my attention because it was my favorite color. The bag was simple and of lightweight material, the kind that is good for travel. The price was over $100, which was a surprise, because I had just bought a fancy leather bag the week before. That bag was Western style, with bronze leather handles, a huge buckle, and rhinestones. It cost $50 and was purchased at a Western clothing store on an Indian reservation near my home. This made me think: Why was the cloth bag so expensive?

In comparing the two items, my first observation was that I did not know the brand name of the Western bag. However, something very similar was on sale in a catalog for a higher price. (The Western bag is sold through a number of different outlets.) The cloth bag had a designer name and a tag with that name on it—something that lets other people know that you own so-and-so's bag. In contrast, it is the beauty of the design of the Western bag that attracts one's attention, not a name.

This experience reinforced for me the fact that "No-name" items are less expensive than branded ones, a concept central to the economics of branding. How do we know this? Is it read in a book or discussed on TV? In advertising courses I learned that the cost of advertising is incorporated into the price of a product. That is why a no-name can of fruit is less expensive than Del Monte or Libby's. Otherwise I learned this information in the course of cultural interactions.

Brands All Around Us

Brands surround us as we navigate our daily lives. A number of academics have attempted to make us aware of this fact, but we still need to be reminded. One reason why scholars have not focused on the communicative aspects of branding is because the term is often confused with the terms brandname, trademark, brand, and copyright, and many times they refer to the same thing. A brand is described as "a name, term, symbol, or design, or a combination of them which is intended to identify the goods or services of one seller or group of sellers" (Sacharow, 1982, p. 19). Tantillo (2010) states: "The formal definition of a brand is a 'name, term, symbol, or a special design that is intended to identify a product'" (p. 45). The purpose of the brand is to make it easier for a consumer to identify products and to differentiate them from those of other merchants. Levine (2003) argues further that a brand is never an accident.

However, terms used by scholars to describe branding, advertising, and commercial messages may seem arbitrary. Advertising terms are not consistent. Different scholars have used different terms to describe the influence of commercial messages. For example, Jacques Ellul (1973) describes commercial messages as "propaganda" rather than advertising or branding, a term that makes sense for a European scholar. In Europe, left-wing artists, especially those of the Bauhaus movement, embraced graphic design as a means of social reform. Visual design was viewed as an agent of social change—and thus a form of propaganda. Other scholars have used different terms. When deployed for political purposes, visual design can indeed be used as a form of propaganda.

In the United States, Daniel Boorstin (1987) coined the term "pseudo-events." Douglas Rushkoff (1999) refers to advertisers as "persuaders." Stuart Ewen (2001) argued that we live in a "consumer culture." Herbert Schiller (1989) used the term "commercial culture." Matthew McAllister (1997) contended that American culture has become a form of commercialization. In contrast to examining commercial culture, others have examined the images themselves. For example, Ernst Sternberg (1999) labeled branding the "economy of icons," and Gavin Fridell and Martijn Konings (2013) edited a text that examines how icons promote political agendas. These books examine how individual images persuade.

In 2007, the *Journal of Consumer Research* published an article entitled "Writing with Pictures" by Linda Scott and Patrick Vargas. The purpose of the article was to argue that images could communicate declarative statements. In contrast, the advertising literature on the impact of visual imagery on culture tended to describe images as sensory data. Scott and Vargas argued that advertising research needed to discuss visual images as a function similar to verbal language (an argument that has been made for years by visual communication scholars, especially Foss [1982, 1993]). Because of the academic confusion about whether or not images communicate messages, visual communication is a rather new topic of research. Scholarly and practical authors engaged in research on branding often come from a number of different disciplines that tend not to look at each other's literature. As a result, there is no common language in which to discuss the influence of visual communication, icons, or branding on individuals and society.

Boorstin (1987), for instance, identifies public relations and advertising procedures as pseudo-events. Pseudo-events are "the new kind of synthetic novelty which has flooded our experiences" (p. 9). Pseudo-events emerged with the graphic revolution: "man's ability to make, preserve, transmit, and disseminate precise images—images of print, of men and landscapes and events of voices of men and mobs—now grew at a fantastic pace" (p. 13). Boorstin claims that pseudo-events cost money to create and that they are planned events. For example, these are events that public relations firms and designers produce for commercial purposes. An example would be the branding of sports events. These events are often turned into news stories. Consider the controversy faced by Donald Sterling, the owner of the Los Angeles

Clippers basketball team, over racist comments he uttered. The story ran for days on CNN and involved Magic Johnson in the reporting. The owner of a basketball team does not influence politics, American culture, or individual lives, a fact that renders this a pseudo-event.

On the other hand, the legal dispute involving the Washington Redskins football team is news, because this story has legal and cultural consequences. The controversy that resulted in the taking away of the Redskins trademark or visual brand is newsworthy, because the trademark is offensive to Native Americans (Randazza, 2014). The government revoked the branding of the team. "This case was about a trademark, and the primary purpose of trademark law is to protect the public so that the public can accurately know the source or origin of goods and services" (Randazza, 2014). According to Native Americans, Redskins originally meant dead Indians. Native Americans have been fighting against the term "redskins" because they feel it is offensive to their children. Moreover, many people consider the term to be racially offensive. When is a sports team worthy of the same coverage as a war, murder, or natural disaster? Answer: when the team is involved in an issue that has cultural consequences. In contrast, when did entertainment become as important as a national election? Studying the impact of branding can help to answer these questions.

Ernst Sternberg (1999) identified branding as the economy of icons and how they create meaning. Each of the authors mentioned above described a different aspect of advertising and branded messages, but all of them have one thought in common: an acknowledgment that the rise of visual imagery as a means of communication corresponds to an increased use of cultural branding.

Boorstin warned us in 1987 that public relations firms manufactured many of the events broadcast through mass media and that those events weren't really news at all. A perfect example is the wedding of Kim Kardashian to Kanye West. CNN had it on the news as a major story. For numerous newscasts, reporters speculated on what designer created Kardashian's wedding dress. However, the answer to this "newsworthy" question was not answered with the same hype as the story. Today we are so accustomed to hearing entertainment news mixed in with world news that we accept these pseudo-events as being the same and real as actual events. This point relates back to the opening quotation of this introductory chapter. As argued by Neil Postman in *Amusing Ourselves to Death* (1985), how do we know the truth when reality is mixed with entertainment?

Following the entertainment argument, Stuart Ewen (1976/2000) argued that consumerism has become an idiom of social life and that we now live in a consumer culture. "The enormous growth of the advertising industry and the commercialization of art that it entailed took place along with the gradual depletion and demise of traditional expression and localized culture" (pp. 61–62). Ewen is correct that local cultures have blended into a national one. Every major city in the United States has a McDonalds, a Walmart, a Home Depot, and a Sears, which tend to look the same. While the landscape looks similar across the country, local news is stressed more on television than national events. A foreign graduate student once asked me why our news is about local happenings and not world events? The answer is that television stations capture better ratings with local stories than international ones. Many of these stories are pseudo-events. Moreover, marketers place stories about pseudo-events on satellite feeds for local stations to use as filler in their programming. Stories and images of products and services fill our news broadcasts on slow news days. Additionally, when sporting events are broadcast, numerous brands are often displayed.

Think about how many stadiums and sports teams are associated with a brand, or how many participants in the events wear clothing with recognizable logos. When Tiger Woods plays golf, what clothing brand is he wearing? Nike? When the National Basketball Association (NBA) makes a press statement, its backdrop displays a commercial logo along with its own—for example, the NBA logo alongside the KIA logo. Similarly, the Yankee brand is associated with Volvo. The visual association connects Tiger Woods with Nike, and the cars with the Yankees. There is no escaping the brands displayed in our mediated and physical environments.

In addition, corporate messages dominate communication in the United States. Schiller (1989) argued that corporations have infiltrated every aspect of our lives. This is especially true with the proliferation of branded images. Consequently, public expression has been overshadowed by corporate messages. The proliferation of commercial messages through advertising is so ingrained in our daily lives that we tend to ignore its influence on a conscious level. For example, advertising banners that circle a racetrack or hockey rink are reminders of a commercial culture. While we watch the sporting event, advertisers are always present in the background. On the Internet, many pages display logos and brands for other companies alongside the content. Often these images are for types of Internet software. Many sites include the Facebook and Twitter logos so as to promote these services as a means of communicating with the company. A manufactured product example is the slogan "powered by Intel" placed on different companies' products. By including the logos of other companies on a third-party creation, the branding is spread and made more recognizable.

Logos and branding are used similarly on many fashion items. Consider the number of T-shirts that display images of rock groups or brands of beer. In 1999, Sternberg described the economy of icons and how commercialization creates meaning. He described how consumers began to express themselves through possessions. Fashion is a clear example of this. Designer names and logos appear on all types of clothes and handbags. The status of wearing a designer label or holding a designer handbag are perfect examples of how this works. Just look around in public spaces and see how many women carry Coach handbags. It's easy to tell, because the "CC" logo is often embedded into the fabric of the bag. When Coach switched to making sneakers, the logo fabric identified the brand, turning casual footwear into a designer label.

Designer handbags are so much in demand that knockoff versions of these bags are available. In the course of my travels I have personally observed several instances of this. In the Caribbean, knockoff Coach handbags can be purchased at a fraction of the cost of the real item. Similarly, outdoor markets in Asia have handbags that duplicate those of famous designers such as Prada. On the street the bag has no logo, but after purchase, a fake label is attached to make the bag look very much like an original. The counterfeiters may also stamp the leather of the bag to read "Made in Italy," and the name of a designer can be embossed. These fakes look so real that only an extremely small tag saying "made in China" proves that the fake is not in fact a real designer handbag.

Douglas Rushkoff writes and creates video programs on how commercialized messages dominate culture. He argues that "It wasn't until the 1930s, 1940s and 1950s, as Americans moved toward movies and television and away from newspapers and radio, that advertisers' focus shifted away from describing their brands and to creating images for them" (Rushkoff, 1999, p. 171). Again, the rise of visual branding corresponds to the increased use of visual media. In addition to the rise of images, marketers at the turn of the century also shifted their focus from speaking to the intelligent mind to arousing the primitive one. In the Frontline special *The Persuaders* (2004), Rushkoff interviewed Clotaire Rapaille on his methods for uncovering the primal reptilian mind, the oldest and smallest remnant from our primitive past. Rapaille contended: "The reptilian always wins." Marketers are increasingly turning to the subconscious rather than the conscious mind to find methods for influencing consumers (as detailed in Chapter 5). Associative rather than logical thinking is part of the brand's message.

Another reason why branding may not be a scholarly subject is that most books written about the topic are from practitioners rather than scholars. These books often use a personal approach rather than a scientific one in describing how to create a branded product. David Ogilvy (1983) has described the brand image of a product or service as the "personality of the product." He argues that the personality is "an amalgam of many things—its name, its packaging, its price, the style of its advertising, and above all, the nature of the product itself" (p. 14). To support this idea, Ogilvy uses examples from advertising. Of course, many of these ad campaigns are from his own advertising agency.

Another example is the book *The Harvard Business Review on Brand Management*, a collection of essays based on case studies drawn from the experiences of people and companies (Harvard Business Review, 1999). Footnotes or references are sparse in these articles. Their format does not follow the general guidelines for an academic paper dealing with a topic in the social sciences, because it relies on observing actual examples rather than citing the work of others or conducting experiments. These differences in approach—case studies versus sourced scholarly works and research—demonstrate how different fields tend not to reference each other.

Branding books are based on observations about how brands perform in the marketplace. The academic approach to examining observations is ethnography. However, the creation of a brand is a team effort, and team members may represent different companies, making a study of branding difficult. Moreover, the number of consumers involved in the process makes the study of branding by means of an ethnographic method a complex endeavor.

As a result, the concept of branding is studied in the business school and generally ignored in the communication department. There is an irony here, because brands fill our natural and communication environments. Branding is a message that we cannot ignore in today's digital world. However, it is rarely examined as a communication message. Both images and words communicate information. Brands communicate information on both a logical and emotional level. Many times the emotional aspect of the message is ignored because it is more difficult to understand.

We currently have no single vocabulary for discussing branding. Moreover, different disciplines discuss the topic in different ways. By combining a scholarly approach with case studies and examples, this text attempts to bridge the worlds of communication and business. The goal is to merge these ideas into a coherent framework to enable discussions on the topic to take place in a variety of disciplines.

Examining branding from a communication perspective means that we need to look at both the logical and emotional messages communicated by a brand. This requires an examination of the history of branding, branding as communication, cognitive aspects of branding, emotional aspects of branding, and relationship branding. These topics and many more will be covered in this book.

References

Boorstin, D.J. (1987). *The image*. New York: Atheneum.

Elull, J. (1973). *Propaganda*. New York: Vintage.

Ewen, S. (2001). *Captains of consciousness: Advertising and the roots of the consumer culture* (rev. ed.). New York: Basic Books. (Original work published 1976).

Foss, S.K. (1982). Rhetoric and the visual image. *Communication Education, 31*(1), 55–66.

Foss, S.K. (1993). The construction of appeal in visual images. In D. Zarefsky (Ed.), *Rhetorical movement: Essays in honor of Leland M. Griffin* (pp. 210–224). Evanston, IL: Northwestern University Press.

Fridell, G., & Konings, M. (2013). *Age of icons*. Toronto, Ontario, Canada: University of Toronto Press.

Harvard Business Review. (1999). *Harvard Business Review on brand management*. Boston, MA: Harvard Business School Press.

Levine, M. (2003). *A branded world*. Hoboken, NJ: John Wiley.

McAllister, M.P. (1997). Sponsorship, globalization, and the Summer Olympics. In K.T. Firth (Ed.), *Undressing the ad* (pp. 35–64). New York: Peter Lang.

Ogilvy, D. (1983). *Ogilvy on advertising*. New York: Crown.

Postman, N. (1985). *Amusing ourselves to death*. New York: Penguin.

Randazza, M.J. (2014, June 21). Why Redskins decision is wrong. *CNN.com*. Retrieved September 12, 2016, from http://www.cnn.com/2014/06/20/opinion/randazza-redskins-constitutional/

Rushkoff, D. (1999). *Coercion: Why we listen to what "they" say*. New York: Riverhead Books.

Rushkoff, D. (2004, November 9). *The persuaders* [Video]. PBS Frontline special. Retrieved September 12, 2016, from http://www.pbs.org/wgbh/frontline/film/showspersuaders/

Sacharow, S. (1982). *Symbols of trade*. New York: Art Direction.

Schiller, H.I. (1989). *Culture, Inc.* New York: Oxford University Press.

Scott, L.M., & Vargas, P. (2007, October). Writing with pictures: Toward a unifying theory of consumer response to images. *Journal of Consumer Research, 34*(3), 341–356.

Sternberg, E. (1999). *The economy of icons*. Westport, CT: Praeger.

Tantillo, J. (2010). *People buy brands not companies*. New York: Five Titles Press.

· 1 ·

BRANDING SIGN AND SYMBOL

It is in symbolic, visual terms that the designer ultimately realizes his perception and experiences; and it is in a world of symbols that man lives.
—Paul Rand, 1985, p. 7

To examine brands in today's world, this text begins by discussing signs and symbols. Because visuals are important in the branding process, symbolic and Gestalt thinking are required in the meaning making process. Linguistic concepts such as connotation and denotation are also important ideas for understanding branded messages. Often a branded message can be read in several different ways. This raises the question of whether or not a brand is a sign or symbol—a focus of this first chapter.

A brand is not made in a factory. It is made in your mind on both conscious and subconscious levels. But how does this work? "Symbolic thinking is not the exclusive privilege of the child, of the poet or the unbalanced mind: it is consubstantial with human existence" (Eliade, 1969, p. 12). Symbols are discursive or rambling reason. They define aspects of reality that defy any other type of knowledge. Understanding images can be described through Gestalt theory, which argues that visual perception is the result of organizing visual elements or shapes into groups. Through association, the study of signs and symbols "enables us to reach a better understanding of man" (p. 12).

With associative thinking, understanding is not only about the nature of humans; it also relates to the different technologies humans have invented. "Differences between 'ideal-thinking' and 'image-thinking' are the differences between our thinking before and after the Graphic Revolution" (Boorstin, 1987, p. 197). "Instead of thinking that an image was only a representation of an ideal, we came to see the ideal as a projection or generalization of an image" (p. 201). With the development of technologies such as photography, film, television, and the Internet, our natural and mediated environments became vehicles for the dissemination of images. With digital technology, it became as easy to duplicate and share a picture as it is a word. Thus, in the Digital Age, the graphic revolution has become more prevalent. Currently, scholars are studying images and how they communicate in similar ways to language (see Barnes, 2011).

Connotative and Denotative

Borrowed from language, the ideas of connotation and denotation can be applied to brands. For example, the "W" of the Westinghouse logo is denotative, while the signs for Olympic sports are connotative. Connotative signs visually refer back to the referent; discursive signs do not. The W in Westinghouse relates to the word, not the products the company manufactures. In contrast, Olympic signage depicts actual things, as does a restroom or telephone sign. Comparing language to images, the word "cat" is denotative because the word is arbitrary. In Spanish the word is "gato." Any combination of three or four letters can be used to represent the small animal we call a cat. In contrast, a simple drawing of a circle, some triangles, and lines can be used to draw a cat. The triangles are used to create ears, the circle the outline of the face, and the lines the whiskers. Add some circles for eyes and a triangle for the nose, and most people would recognize the drawing as a cat. The lines create a representation of the animal. Simply stated, arbitrary signs are denotative. In contrast, signs that have a visual resemblance to the object they represent are connotative.

In photography, the denotation of a family photograph is the family itself. The connotative meaning is what an individual in the picture will associate with the taking of the picture. For instance, a family picture taken at a wedding will denote the husband and wife. The connotation for the wife may be that it is the happiest day of her life. Other family members will have different associations, such as "it was the day my hat blew off my head."

Every decision that a designer makes about a sign or symbol has a connotation. For example, using the Century Schoolbook typeface for a design relating to education has a connotation of grade school. Century Schoolbook is the typeface that is used in grade school textbooks. Although most people do not consciously recognize the font, they may have a feeling about it. As a result, connotation has much more to it than resembling an image. Every person may have his or her own connotation for a brand, and many of these connotations are based on feelings. Think about how many companies use the idea of sex to sell their products. Sex is a powerful motivator. Applying sexual connotations to a brand will often make that brand more popular.

Through the use of connotation, the images of brands influence us. For instance, what does the Nike swoosh mean to you? The symbol tries to convey the feeling of athletic success, because that is how the image in Nike's advertising campaign is depicted. How does wearing Nike shoes make you feel? At one point, the Nike logo meant expensive and hip. People would try to steal Nike shoes from others. Nike's price is part of its brand personality and the desire to own the product. How you feel wearing them is your own individual connotation.

Moreover, brands have specific denotations (the company) and personal connotations (personal experience). The denotation relates to the logical mind and the connotation to the emotional response. These distinctions are vital to an understanding of how branding works.

Signs

Signs can be both denotative and connotative. The theoretical foundation for understanding signs and symbols is based on the philosophical work of Langer (1957), Goodman (1976), and Peirce (1998); the visual communication research by Arnheim (1969), Barry (1997), Berger (1999), and Hoffman (1998); the cognitive research of Bruner (1966), Gardner (1983a, 1983b), and Pinker (1988, 2002); and the practical writings of Card, Mackinlay, and Shneiderman (1999), Meggs (1989), and Wileman (1980).

Signs can be used to help individuals understand information. For instance, public signs have been designed to enable literate and illiterate individuals to easily identify places and things in daily life. Signs also have historical origins. For example, in 1909, nine European countries developed a series of road danger signs. Later, between 1926 and 1949, intensive work was done on the creation of international road signs. Similarly, the road sign system designed in the United States has been adopted by other nations. Many public signs indicate services or facilities, including restrooms, coffee shops, telephones, airports, and train stations.

Modley (1976) stated:

> Today, in spite of increased literacy, many thousands of travelers are, in fact, illiterate in countries whose language they do not know.... There is, therefore, a need for graphic symbols to lead us to the nearest telephone, to help us claim our baggage or find an elevator.
>
> The number of these public [signs is] increasing rapidly. Some are accepted widely, some are not. There are even different symbols representing the same thing, and identical symbols standing for different concepts. Efforts are now underway to standardize the most important symbols into a "new universal language" through international efforts of careful selection, design, testing and education. (pp. vi–vii)

Peirce (1998) identified three different types of signs: iconic, indexical, and symbolic signs. Iconic signs resemble the things they represent. For instance, the icons on a computer screen are simple drawings that illustrate commands, such as the trash can or home page. Indexical signs make logical connections to the concepts they stand for. For example, maps represent a geographic location. In New York City, subway maps are a depiction of the underground train system. These maps—located in stations, on trains, and in flyers—assist passengers in finding their way through the city. Finally, symbolic signs have no representational or logical relationship to the object or concept they symbolize.

A discussion of whether or not brands are signs or symbols begins with a basic understanding of each. There is no single method for understanding these, and we can describe the ideas of signs and symbols by discipline. In philosophical terms, a sign is used as a method both for indicting things and representing them (Langer, 1957). Signs announce their objects to people, whereas symbols make people conceive or think about the object. A stop sign is clearly a sign because it tells us to stop the car. It is a sign that demands an action. By contrast, the logo for Pepsi-Cola is representative of the product. Although it is a representation, the company would like you to think about drinking the soda when you see the logo. However, branding is much more than the obvious representation of the product and its purchase. Brands also convey feelings. For instance, the "Pepsi Generation" advertising campaign tried to convey the idea that Pepsi is for a younger group of people, while Coke is for old folks. If you identify with being young, you drink Pepsi. The idea that Coke tastes better than Pepsi or vice versa is not considered, and people who say they can taste the difference are not believed. The key distinction between the products is branding.

Philosopher Nelson Goodman (1976) used the term *symbol* to cover "letters, words, texts, pictures, diagrams, maps, models, more" (p. xi). Although the alphabet is a denotative system that represents words, it is also visual. The typeface design and arrangement of the letters can create a branded image. Both words and images are visual. Goodman places symbol systems into two categories, notational and nonnotational. Notational systems can be broken down into smaller components that have meaning. For example, the words in a language represent people, places, and things. Words can be combined into sentences and sentences into paragraphs. Similarly, musical notes can be combined to create an opera or a rock song. Nonnotational symbols, by contrast, cannot be broken down. The smiley face is an example. If the dots that represent the eyes were removed from the circle, they would lose their meaning as eyes, because it is the relationship between the circle, semicircle, and dots that make up the idea of a face. Taking out elements changes the concept. Referring to the smiley face, Nystrom (2000) stated: it "brings to mind a human face, not because real human faces are composed of three black dots and a curve, but because the structural relationship between the dots and the curve in the symbols corresponds to the structural relationship among eyes, nose, and mouth that the mind abstracts from the sensory perception of human faces" (p. 28). Thus, a few simple elements can become the symbol of a face.

We do have many works that describe various symbol systems, such as Dreyfuss's *Symbol Sourcebook* (1972) and Cirlot's *A Dictionary of Symbols* (1971). Dreyfuss described symbol systems that derived from disciplines such as mathematics and safety. In contrast, Cirlot's book discussed mythological and ancient symbols. In addition, we cannot forget the books that have been written to explain dream images (Jacob, 1985; Miller, 1983; Robinson & Corbett, 1974). Authors have tried to decode these unconscious images of signs and symbols to help us understand what they mean on both the conscious and subconscious levels.

In communication research, "Signs are things which stand for other things" (Berger, 1999. p. 1). This is the same definition that Fromm (1951) used to define a symbol. A key difference is that Berger (1999) is describing a sign in terms of semiotics, the study of signs and symbols. According to semiotics, symbols are a sub-class of signs, because a symbol has cultural significance. Signs are denotative, while symbols are connotative; however, many authors mix up the terms. When studying signs and symbols, one needs to be aware of the context the author is using—philosophy, design, semiotics, and so forth.

In the context of graphic design, Meggs (1989) defines a sign as "a mark or language unit that stands for or denotes another thing" (p. 6). He also argues that the interpretation of a sign is dependent upon the context. For instance, Meggs (1989) discusses how the sign of a red circle is interpreted differently in various cultural contexts. People living in South Carolina use large red circles painted on buildings to indicate liquor stores. This sign was created because the owner of a liquor store told a painter working on the store that a sign could not be placed on the building. "The painter lit a cigarette, looked at the red circle on his Lucky Strike package, and suggested that he could paint a red circle on the building. Soon other stores copied this practice" (pp. 6–7). In this way an accidental symbol became a recognized sign for liquor stores in South Carolina. However, if a person from Japan visits South Carolina, he or she may wonder why the building has a Japanese sign. The red circle is a sign for Japan.

To cite another example, speaking about an apple in the context of food is different from talking about Apple in terms of computers. The capital "A" also indicates the name of a company rather than a fruit. The identification of a brand or trademark "can only be obtained by what men in the trade call 'strong penetration,' that is, insistent re-enforcement of the association" between the sign and the referent (Arnheim, 1969, p. 145). This is one of the purposes of advertising. Companies spend millions of dollars to create these associations between symbols and products.

Symbol

A number of different academics and designers have described symbols. Fromm (1951) states that a symbol "is something that stands for something else" (p. 12). Similarly, branding stands for a specific product or company, such as Coca-Cola with its swoosh and red can. Fromm goes on to state: "A symbol of this kind is outside ourselves; that which it symbolizes is something within ourselves" (p. 12). As Ogilvy (1984) argued, each brand has its own personality and emotional relationship to the consumer. "Symbolic language is language in which the world outside is a symbol for the word inside, a symbol for our souls and minds" (Fromm, 1951, p. 12). Advertisers use messages of persuasion to tap into the emotions of individuals. In the symbol system of branding, companies attempt to associate their brand with the inner feelings of a person, while simultaneously associating the symbol with a branded product.

As Rand (1985) states, "A symbol may be depicted as an abstract shape, a geometric figure, a photograph, an illustration, a letter of the alphabet, or a numeral" (p. 7). Classic brand examples are Arm & Hammer, with the photographic image of an arm and a hammer; Mr. Peanut, an illustration of a peanut with a top hat; letters such as the "W" for Westinghouse; and numbers that are used by the National Football League. (For the 50th year of the league, what were formerly Roman numerals were changed to numbers. The reason for the change was because the Roman numeral "L" did not look as good as the number "50." As a result, a 50-year tradition was changed because of the "look" of the Roman numerals.) Graphic designer Nigel Holmes (1985) describes a symbol as being "visually precise; it attempts to get the essence of an idea—either by being a literal, miniature drawing, or by being a non-literal, visual metaphor" (p. 11). Additionally, Holmes argues, "a symbol can give an identity to a subject and, by repeated use, can come to equal it" (p. 11).

Graphic designers attempt to create symbols that reflect the personality of an organization. They identify four different types of graphics: pictorial symbols, image-related graphics, concept-related graphics, and arbitrary graphics. Included in the category of pictorial symbols are 3-D models, photographs, computer graphics, and illustrations. These graphics are images that clearly represent the object or idea portrayed. In branding, the Quaker image on Quaker Oats packaging associates the name with the product. Similarly, Mr. Peanut illustrates the product being sold—peanuts.

In contrast, the next three categories move from concrete to abstract symbols. Image-related graphics have a relationship to the object. A great example is the Redskins sports team, because the image represents the name. The Redskins logo depicts the profile of a Native American with feathers. Image-related graphics could also be outlines, silhouettes, and profiles. After projecting an image, the outline can be traced to create a silhouette that is an image-related graphic. Using this technique eliminates the details; however, the outline is directly related to the object. For instance, many airline companies originally used silhouettes of airplanes, including the defunct Republic Aviation of Long Island, New York. Moving away from concrete images toward abstraction are concept-related graphics.

Concept-related graphics attempt to capture the essence of an object or service. These graphics are used to communicate an idea about services that are not tangible, such as banking or insurance. "You're in good hands with Allstate" uses the image of hands to convey the idea that the company will take care of your insurance needs. Travelers Insurance brands itself with an umbrella to convey a similar concept of being covered. Because it is difficult to remember the meaning of symbols, companies need to reinforce the relationship between the symbol and the organization through advertising and public relations. Graphic designers have also created books to standardize symbol use (Dreyfuss, 1972). Concept-related graphics tend to be easier to remember than arbitrary graphics.

Arbitrary graphics are abstract symbols with no visual resemblance to the object they represent. Letters of the alphabet, mathematical symbols, and trade symbols fit into this category. These symbols need to be learned, and a key concept in branding is establishing this relationship. In branding, when a company updates or creates a new logo, people need to be made aware of the change. This is done through repeated exposure to the company and the image. People will eventually think of the company when they see the image alone.

> As the world grows steadily smaller, the need for easy communication becomes increasingly acute, and man has apparently come full circle—from prehistoric symbols, to sophisticated verbal communication, and now back to symbols, to help us all live together in today's Tower of Babel. (Dreyfuss, 1972, p. 19)

In contrast to graphic symbols, Fromm (1951) contends that symbols are an expression of inner experiences such as a feeling or thought. Writing from a psychological perspective, Fromm identifies three different types of symbols—conventional, accidental, and universal. A conventional symbol has an inherent relationship between the symbol and object—that is, the flag of a country denotes that country. We learn these symbols through repeated experience. For example, advertising is how brands get repeated over and over again until the population knows them. Today brands are so familiar to people that a game has been created to identify them—*The Logo Game*.

The opposite of a conventional symbol is the accidental symbol. "There is no intrinsic relationship between the symbol and that which it symbolizes" (Fromm, 1951, p. 14)—for instance, making an emotional connection to a type of car, such as a Ford. A person may associate the car with an accident or happy event. When he or she sees the Ford, it will trigger the sad or happy feeling. There is no particular reason why someone would make this particular association; it generally happens by accident. Accidental symbols cannot easily be shared with others because the events need to be related to the symbol. These symbols are not generally used in symbol systems such as myths, fairy tales, or works of art because they are more individual, such as the red circle of Lucky Strike packaging used to identify liquor stores.

In contrast, myths speak to universal concepts that relate to some phenomenon of nature or humans. Myths are symbolic and the third type of symbol. Similar to conventional symbols, universal ones have an "intrinsic relationship between the symbol and that which it represents" (Fromm, 1951, pp. 15–16). For example, an empty, deserted city conveys the feeling of loneliness. However, the city symbol would not make sense to cultures that do not have cities. In contrast, many universal symbols are based on human experience. For instance, the one story that appears in practically every culture is the story of "boy meets girl." We can also use the phenomena of the physical world to express human emotions. Fire is a good example. It is constantly moving, while remaining the same. A fire can symbolize power, energy, and lightness. "The universal symbol is the only one in which the relationship between the symbol and that which is symbolized is not coincidental but intrinsic" (p. 17).

Another example of a universal symbol is the archetype. Archetypes are "universal and inherent patterns which, taken together, constitute the structure of the unconscious" (Jung, 1956, p. 228). Jung described archetypes as "the river-beds along which the current of psychic life has always flowed" (p. 228). Archetypes include the hero, the beautiful maiden, the trickster, and the wise old man. (Chapter 9 provides a more complete description of archetypes.) Themes such as the hero descending into a cave to save a precious object can be found in the stories of ancient myths and contemporary films. (Consider *Raiders of the Lost Ark* and *Star Wars* in terms of the hero plot.) In addition to films, archetypes can often be found in advertising. The hero can be a person who uses the product to solve a problem, or the product itself. The wise man image is used to add authority to a commercial for a product or service. Sometimes the wise old man takes the form of a child. These universal symbols influence people on an unconscious level. Archetypical figures are sometimes used in branding—for instance, Mr. Clean is a hero who solves cleaning issues. All of these symbols can be utilized to help identify products and services.

Branding

Is a brand a sign or a symbol? Barry (1997) contends that symbols "have abstract associations rather than experiential connections" (p. 118). For example, a stop sign is a clear indication of an action. Similarly, the sound of a fire alarm indicates a type of behavior and warns us of a potentially dangerous situation. In contrast, the symbol of a cross makes us think about the Christian religion. For some religions, the cross with Christ has a different meaning than one without. Christian churches are filled with images that represent different stories from the Bible. Additionally, the sign of the cross was used in hobo signs to mean that religious talk will get you a free meal (Dreyfuss, 1972). All of these images are used symbolically to represent an idea.

Today, a brand is both a sign and a symbol that has evolved into different roles. First, it indicates the company, product, or service (sign). Second, it symbolizes an action: purchase the product or service from the company depicted. Finally, current marketing wants us to associate a brand with a feeling (symbol). The point here is that brands not only point to a particular company; they also evoke a feeling in the receiver. In the early days of trademarking, the image represented a company. Early signs called trade cards represented specific companies and included the name of the organization along with a picture indicating the type of service performed. These cards were similar to the signs one would place in front of a store. (The evolution of trademarks into branding will be explored in Chapter 2.)

Verbally, all types of names have been used in branding. "Think of the power of the symbolic value of a strong name, and all that it implies—Rolls-Royce, Hilton, Chanel" (Sacharow, 1982, p. 23). These are all attitude- and behavior-inducing words. Socially, some of the earlier brand names would not be considered politically correct today, such as the Redskins described earlier. Brands that have letter logos are visual and are considered to be graphic images. Take, for example, the "W" for Westinghouse and the word Exxon for gas stations. Designers have visually created different fonts and elements to represent the W brand, while the Exxon letters remain the same across signage and advertising.

Branding is not an accidental symbol. Often it begins as a conventional symbol because companies and designers carefully construct the branded image. Through the widespread use of public relations and advertising, companies attempt to make their conventional symbols into universal ones. Brands such as Pepsi, Ford, and McDonald's have become more universal because their brands are recognized across numerous cultures. Brands are agents for social change (see Chapter 11), although the message is commercial rather than political. These symbols reflect the commercialization of culture and embody personal meanings for individuals.

Summary

Currently we have no single vocabulary within which to discuss branding. Moreover, different disciplines discuss the topic in numerous ways. By combining a scholarly approach with case studies and examples, this text attempts to bridge the worlds of communication and business. A goal is to bring theses ideas together into a coherent framework to enable discussions on the topic to occur in a variety of disciplines.

Branding serves the purpose of a sign and symbol. It both represents and evokes. Lately, the emotional influence of brands has been a focus of marketers (see Chapter 5). Once only a sign, technologies have helped to transform brands into symbols that we constantly encounter in our natural and mediated environments.[1] Moreover, the branding of culture marks a commercialization of society. Almost everywhere we look, a brand name or logo appears.

Exercises

1. Find examples of the following types of symbols: pictorial symbols, image-related graphics, concept-related graphics, and arbitrary graphics.
2. Write an essay about the brands you wear and how they make you feel. If you don't wear branded clothes, explain why.
3. Watch a sporting event and identify the different brands that you see displayed, especially in the background of the sport.
4. Pick brands that relate to your favorite drink, sports shoes, fast-food restaurant, and car. Describe how you feel about the brand and why you like it.

Note

1. The study of mediated environments is called media ecology, which is a humanistic approach to media and the type of messages it communicates. This perspective informs the author's thinking about technology and communication.

References

Arnheim, R. (1969). *Visual thinking*. Berkeley: University of California Press.

Barnes, S.B. (2011). *An introduction to visual communication*. New York: Peter Lang.

Barry, A.M.S. (1997). *Visual intelligence*. Albany: State University of New York Press.

Berger, A.A. (1999). *Signs in contemporary culture: An introduction to semiotics* (2nd ed.). Salem, WI: Sheffield Publishing Company.

Boorstin, D.J. (1987). *The image*. New York: Atheneum.

Bruner, J. (1966). *Towards a theory of instruction*. Cambridge, MA: Harvard University Press.

Card, S.K., Mackinlay, J.D., & Shneiderman, B. (1999). *Readings in information visualization: Using vision to think*. San Francisco, CA: Morgan Kaufman.

Cirlot, J.E. (1971). *A dictionary of symbols*. New York: Philosophical Library.

Dreyfuss, H. (1972). *Symbol sourcebook*. New York: Van Nostrand Reinhold.

Eliade, M. (1969). *Images and symbols* (P. Mairet, Trans.). New York: Sheed and Ward.

Fromm, E. (1951). *The forgotten language*. New York: Grove Press.

Gardner, H. (1983a). *Frames of mind*. New York: Basic Books.

Gardner, H. (1983b). *Creating minds*. New York: Basic Books.

Goodman, N. (1976). *Language of art*. Cambridge, MA: Hackett Publishing Company.

Hoffman, D.D. (1998). *Visual intelligence*. New York: W.W. Norton.

Holmes, N. (1985). *Designing pictorial symbols*. New York: Watson-Guptill.

Jacob, W.L. (1985). *Interpreting your dreams*. Coraopolis, PA: J. Pohl Associates.

Jung, C.G. (1956). *Symbols of transformation* (R.F.C. Hull, Trans.). Princeton, NJ: Princeton University Press.

Langer, S.K. (1957). *Philosophy in a new key* (3rd ed.). Cambridge, MA: Harvard University Press.

Meggs, P.B. (1989). *Type and image*. New York: Van Nostrand Reinhold.

Miller, G.H. (1983). *The dictionary of dreams*. Devon. UK: Blaketon-Hall Ltd.

Modley, R. (1976). *Handbook of pictorial symbols*. Mineola, NY: Dover Publishing.

Nystrom, C. (2000). Symbols, thought, and reality. *New Jersey Journal of Communication*, 8(1), 8–33.

Ogilvy, D. (1984). *Confessions of an advertising man*. New York, NY: Athene.

Peirce, C.S. (1998). *The essential Peirce*. Bloomington: Indiana University Press.

Pinker, S. (1988). *Visual cognition*. Cambridge, MA: MIT Press.

Pinker, S. (2002). *The blank slate*. New York: Penguin.

Rand, P. (1985). *Paul Rand: A designer's art*. New Haven, CT: Yale University Press.

Robinson, S., & Corbett, T. (1974). *The dreamer's dictionary*. New York: Warner Books.

Sacharow, S. (1982). *Symbols of trade*. New York: Art Direction.

Wileman, R.E. (1980). *Exercises in visual thinking*. New York: Hastings House.

· 2 ·

HISTORY OF BRANDING

*By sharpening our images we have blurred all our experience. The
new images have blurred traditional distinctions.*
—Daniel J. Boorstin, 1987, p. 213

*Branding was first developed when America went through the economic change of moving
into the Industrial Revolution. The replacement of handmade goods with manufactured ones
created the need for identifying products. When new technologies began to be developed,
these inventions supported the branding process in different ways. For instance, all new
communication methods helped to distribute branded messages to consumers.*

One of the original American brands, Cream of Wheat, is still in existence
today. However, marketing objects with branded inscriptions goes back to
ancient times. In the United States, branding began during the period in
which the economics of the country changed—that is, around the time of
the Civil War. Current concepts of brands as personalities were established in
the 1960s with the rise of advertising agencies. This chapter will discuss the
history of branding and how it evolved from associations with packaged goods
to global marketing. Moreover, the role of technology in the rise of branding
will be examined.

During the Stone Age, people used visual symbols to represent lifestyle situations. For example, primitive humans used pictures of animals to represent the hunting of animals for human survival. In today's consumer economy, brands represent the need and desire to purchase products and services that we perceive are needed for our continued existence. Thus, the use of symbols is inherently a human trait. Today desire has replaced need in a commercial culture where visual branding appeals to our emotions. However, the spread of visual imagery, which began in magical prehistoric caves, has moved into our daily lives to create mediated and non-mediated environments filled with branded messages.

From a media ecological perspective,[1] the history of visual technology corresponds with the history of branding. Every time a new visual communication medium was introduced into culture, companies, advertisers, and marketers found new outlets for the dissemination of branded announcements. As a result, there is a relationship between communication technology, symbols, and brands.

Ancient Brands

In ancient times, the cylinder seal was stamped onto pottery to mark ownership. The seal repeated the personal brand of the individual and was a technology that foreshadowed the future use of imagery. Today can think of the seal as a form of personal branding (see Chapter 8). The cylinder seal placed a unique private mark on an object. Similarly, personal branding is a unique presentation of self. Both represent the individual. As a result, we can argue that personal branding was used in ancient times.

While the origins of the use of symbols to represent people and objects is unknown, an early record of branding traces to the ancient city of Pompeii, which was destroyed by a volcanic eruption in 79 a.d. When it was excavated, symbols were found carved into the stone rocks that were used for streets signs. One of the distinct symbols was a graphic of an erect phallus. It is believed that this symbol directed people to the local brothel. The commercial nature of this concept could make Pompeii one of the earliest places to use branding.

Similarly, "Stonecutter's marks have been found in Egyptian buildings from about 4000 b.c." (Morgan, 1986, pp. 7–8). Egyptians also used livestock brands to identify personal property, evidence of which can be seen in

Egyptian wall paintings. People have used marks to identify their property since ancient times, and today brands indicate goods and services.

Medieval Brands

In medieval times marks were placed on paper, bread, and craft items in order to attract customers and to police infringements. "An English law passed in 1266 required bakers to put their mark on every loaf of bread sold" (Morgan, 1986, p. 8). Thus, marks were used to identify the quality of the product.

Similarly, English marks were placed on silver and gold products to help discourage fraudulent practices. Further, "typical marks were used by guilds on wine, knives, swords, drapes, pottery and precious metals" (Sacharow, 1982, p. 38). There were harsh punishments for people who counterfeited other artisans' marks. Marks were also placed on pottery and clay lamps. In addition, the Chinese placed them on porcelain.

In the late fifteenth century, the invention of the printing press enabled multiple copies of printed material to be produced. "The fact that identical images, maps, and diagrams could be viewed simultaneously by scattered readers constituted a kind of communication revolution in itself" (Eisenstein, 1983, p. 21). Eisenstein argues that the invention of the printing press changed culture, since—in terms of branding—it now allowed images to be reproduced for packaging. Printing brand labels on paper bags and advertising supported the new economy that was developing in the United States. For example, miniature illustrations were used as index newspaper advertising to identify goods and services.

Brands in the United States

By the time Europeans began to colonize America, the use of trademarks had been established. During the American Revolution, merchants used pictorial symbols to promote their products and services. These symbols acted as trademarks or branding for early businesses. During the 1700s and 1800s, technological developments such as the steam-powered press enabled publishers to print thousands of newspapers per hour. Advertising revenue, classified advertisements, and street sales generated income for many newspapers. These papers contained both words and pictures.

The increased use of visual images in newspapers created a demand for artists. The first advertisement for graphic artists appeared in 1834. The company, founded by a group of artists, was called the Boston Bewick Company. It took "orders for Wood cuts, Designs and Drawing, Maps and Charts, Cards of every description, Diplomas and Seals, Copperplate and Xyolgraphic Printing, Book and Job Printing" (cited in Hornung, 1947/1956, p. xiii).

This change in increased visual imagery corresponded with the Industrial Revolution. During this time, advanced printing technologies were developed that enabled printers to include more visual images. In the first stage of the mechanization of printing, the artist interpreted events and created illustrations to visualize those events. As technologies progressed, the photographic image could be transmitted through print. The invention of photography altered the image-making process because it directly duplicated and transmitted pictures to mass audiences. Artists no longer had to interpret news and events. These improved printing technologies and photography fostered an image revolution that transformed visual communication, art, illustration, and advertising. Further, during the Industrial Revolution, manufactured products replaced handmade ones.

During this period of transition in the American economy, branding became very popular. When individual packaged goods replaced bulk-packed products, manufacturers discovered they needed names and images to identify and promote their merchandise. In addition, in the 1840s, images were used more frequently and effectively in editorial and advertising communications because wood-engraved blocks could be locked together into a letterpress and be printed. Around this time, the product that pioneered branding concepts was patent medicines. These medicines were packaged in small bottles, and they had to be promoted because patent medicines were not necessities. These products created the idea that medicines could be used to kill pain. Names of these products included Swamproot Compound, Dr. Moog's Love Balm, Pitcher's Castoria, and Snake Oil. "No matter what such remedies were called, these new brewed-in-the-kitchen industries depended on cutting-edge advertising for their tonics" (Twitchell, 2000, p. 28). People needed to be convinced to buy these products. To make Lydia E. Pinkham's Vegetable Compound more personable, a picture of her face was used in newspaper advertising. Money was spent on advertising, and these revenues helped to finance newspapers.

Another early brand was Procter & Gamble. At first the company made candles that were shipped by boat to other cities in crates upon which was placed a star trademark. Merchants looked for the star on the crate and would refuse crates without it (see Morgan, 1986). The branding became a sign of quality, and the brand replaced knowing the individual who made the object. As the prevalence of packaged goods grew, so did the practice of trademarks.

"In the nineteenth century, trademarks were little pictures" (Holmes, 1985, p. 12). An example is the Shell Oil symbol, which "started out as a drawing of a real shell; it went through a number of changes before arriving at the simpler graphic arrangement of lines in use today" (p. 12). Another industry that used brand names was tobacco. Some companies developed creative names to sell their products—including, for example, Rock Candy, Black's Twist, and Lone Jack. They also experimented with picture labels and decorations to make the packages more attractive to customers.

Branding After the Civil War

Prior to the Civil War, people made their own clothes or had them made by a tailor. Forty years later, most clothing was ready-made and store-bought. Similarly, people bought their food from large bins rather than in small packages. The development of widespread branding began at the time of the Civil War with the identification of merchandise with specific names. Some of these changes occurred because distant companies replaced local businesses, and people no longer knew who made their products. Lithography, a printing process, kept printers busy supplying trade cards, cigar box labels, sheet music covers, Christmas designs, calendars, billboard posters, and advertisements. Culturally, this was the shift to the Industrial Revolution, were machines replaced local artisans. The brand names assured buyers that the source of the merchandise was reliable.

In this period new printing techniques also emerged. Photoengraving cut the cost and time required to produce printing blocks, and the reproduction of photographs was developed. In 1880, the first photograph was published in the *New York Daily Graphic*. By breaking the image into a series of small, various-sized dots, tones were created, as tonal values were simulated by the amount of ink printed in each area of the image. In 1885, this technique developed into the halftone process. Halftone is a term used to describe the intermediate tones between light and dark. The introduction of halftone printing changed the visual appearance of the printed page and enabled the integration of photographs and text.

From 1860 to 1920, factory-produced merchandise in packages replaced locally produced goods sold in bulk containers. This change in retail sales brought with it the widespread use of trademarks. Before products were packaged, people generally purchased items from local merchants who, in turn, knew who had created them. But with the widespread distribution of pre-packaged goods, individuals now needed to develop an identifying mark or brand. A new era of business, industrial progress, and advertising emerged. For instance, during the Philadelphia Centennial Exposition in 1876, scattered throughout the halls of the exhibition were colorful handbills, cards, folders, and announcements that represented a growing consciousness of sales. Around the same time, mail order businesses began printing catalogues, price lists, and illustrated folders. For example, the Sears Catalog, with its colorful copy and black-and-white illustrations, sold products across the nation. Most pioneer homes had a copy of the Bible and the Sears Catalog.

During the second half of the nineteenth century, marvelous inventions were being introduced: trains, electricity, improved printing techniques, photography, and motion pictures. All of these inventions created new outlets for the promotion of branding. In 1893, a foreman at a North Dakota flour mill created a hot cereal made from wheat kernels. The owners of the mill gave the foreman permission to make some sample packages of the cereal and ship them to New York City to see if it would sell. Someone suggested the name Cream of Wheat, and the name was hand-printed on the boxes. To give the box more visual appeal, an old printing plate of a black chef with a spoon over his shoulder was used in the packaging. The chef created a friendly personality for the product, and it became a success. Today we can still purchase packages of Cream of Wheat.

At this time, America was moving away from an agricultural economy and toward an industrial one. Visual communication played an important role in this economic change, including the development of the advertising system and the establishment of trademarks.

The Rise of Advertising

One of the earliest advertising agencies was N.W. Ayer & Son, the firm responsible for the hugely successful Uneeda biscuit campaign. Nabisco (The National Biscuit Company) made the biscuits and was instrumental in helping to develop advertising practices. Sacharow (1982) describes the trademark process as follows:

> The task fell to a young copywriter named Joseph J. Geisinger. He first thought of a fisherman, clad in a slicker, eating dry biscuits out of a dry package, an interesting concept which made the point that Nabisco products were always fresh and crisp. (p. 44)

At first the idea did not appeal to the National Biscuit Company, but then Geisinger's 5-year-old nephew dressed up in boots, an oil hat, and a slicker, with a box of biscuits under his arm. An advertising photo was taken and a concept-related graphic was created. The rest is history: the image was transformed into the logo, and the biscuit became a household word. Branding was now part of American culture.

Drawing on culture, companies used a variety of approaches to find symbols for their brands. For example, prior to the Civil Rights Movement of the 1960s, a number of brands utilized black stereotypes. Aunt Jemima pancake syrup is an example. Indians have also been used—consider the Redskins sports team described in the previous chapter. Other groups used in branding include the Chinese and Quakers (see Sacharow, 1982).

Animals have also been favorite symbols. Think about brands that have used horses, dogs, camels, cow, and lions. Metro-Goldwyn-Mayer's trademark lion is familiar to anyone who watches movies. Other well-known symbols are the Greyhound Bus Company's dog or Borden's Elsie the cow.

Names are also commonly used in branding. "The name is the hook that hangs the brand on the product ladder in the prospect's mind" (Ries & Trout, 2001, p. 71). Names such as Heinz, Procter & Gamble, Reynolds, and McDonald's relate to real people—Henry J. Heinz founded the Heinz Company; William Procter and James Gamble were the creators of their eponymously named company; and McDonald's was named after two brothers who owned a drive-in restaurant. Companies such as General Mills have used made-up names. Betty Crocker combined the surname of a board director with the popular name Betty. Dolly Madison ice cream is named after President James Madison's wife.

In 1896, Henry J. Heinz created the marketing slogan "57 Varieties" for his company's products. Heinz selected the numbers 5 and 7 because they were his family's lucky numbers. Moreover, the number 7 has an enduring significance as a lucky number for many people. At the time, the company was offering more than 60 products. The first product to use a slogan was horseradish, and it later became synonymous with steak sauce (Staff, 2014). Names, animals, and stereotypes have all been used to foster brand recognition.

Creating Brands

In the 1920s, America was developing a sophisticated style (see Baker & Blik, 1985). It was the golden age of Hollywood, and men wore top hats, tails, and spats. Women's evening gowns revealed female shoulders. Everyone knew Fred and Ginger and the wonderful manner in which they danced. The influential art style was Art Deco, a style of crisp, simplistic, black and white silhouettes. Brands used this style to create images for products and services. From clothing products to cake decorating, the top hat became an identifying image. Many art deco logos depicted actual objects and services, such as trains, planes, and automobiles.

As Ewen (2001) notes:

> By the end of the twenties, the corporate generals and the captains of consciousness had made significant inroads into America's social territories. Brand names had inserted themselves into the idiom of daily expression, prepackaged foodstuffs were increasingly the culinary fare of the population, the automobile—perhaps the archetypal commodity—was no longer merely an idiosyncratic mode of transport but an artifact of multidimensional significance within culture. (pp. 202–203)

The cultural appeal of branded products began to represent more than the item itself. People started to identify with the brands and assign them social values. For instance, the symbol of a Rolls Royce is different from that of a Ford. The car a person owned reflected the social status of the individual. Thus, branding became an integral part of society.

Branding and the Depression

During the Great Depression, the American financial system needed to be stimulated. President Roosevelt instituted the New Deal and the National Recovery Act to recharge the economy. Product design professionals were recruited to devise methods to create new consumer demand for products. Commercial artists began to redesign existing trademarks that captured the mood of the times. Charles Lindberg's 1927 flight across the Atlantic and the new aerodynamic shape of airplanes embodied speed and mobility as symbols for the new era. As a result, streamlining became the metaphor for creating trademarks and brands.

Many of these were image-related graphics. Aircraft companies, including the Karl Ort Aircraft Corporation, the Holler-Hirth Sailplane Corporation, and Ryan Airlines, used elements of airplanes in their trademarks (see Mendenhall, 1983). Up to this point in design history, trademarks had tended to be more concrete. Now, however, in addition to actual objects, trademarks began to use concept-related graphics and combinations of both. RCA Electron Tubes combined an image of an electron tube with the concept of electricity. Its trademark was a stylized version of a head with lighting bolts pointing toward the center of the head, where the tube was placed. Two companies that created concept-related graphics were the Prudential Insurance Company and the Zenith Radio Corporation. Prudential used the Rock of Gibraltar to demonstrate the strength of its insurance, a concept that is still in use today. Zenith stylized its name as lighting bolts. The lightning expressed the concept of electricity and radio messages traveling through the air.

Visually, themes of strength, progress, and determination represented American industry. These positive images helped to support economic recovery. For example, the image of lightning—used to create the trademark for the Zenith Radio Corporation, as mentioned above—was also used by the National Broadcasting Company (NBC). Thus, the role of branding began to influence not only American culture, but also its economics. Branding became an important aspect of the American economy.

Branding and American Economics

During the 1930s, modern engineering and America's growing industrial scene formed the foundation for the beginning of branding. However, as America emerged from the Depression, it plunged into the tumult of World War II. Artists turned away from depicting the virtues of the machine age and began to glorify American military power. Trademarks were altered to reflect patriotic themes, and government artists developed war bond promotions. The concept of branding emerged to describe trademarks, and more advertising agencies were founded. Those firms developed a network of agencies in and outside the United States.

Contributing to the change in visual communication were artistic movements such as the Bauhaus. The forces of engineering and technology shaped Bauhaus attitudes toward art, design, architecture, and crafts. Steam-driven machines were able to stamp, cut out, and fashion substances faster and more accurately than the human hand. The Bauhaus movement sought to upgrade design for an industrial society. As a result of World War II, a number of Bauhaus artists, including Herbert Bayer and Laszlo Moholy-Nagy, emigrated to the United States (see Wingler, 1984). Bayer became an advertising designer, and Bauhaus philosophies continue to be taught in American art schools today. Technology aesthetics thereby influenced visual design.

Television and Branding

Though television was invented prior to World War II, it was not until after the war that television networks were established. Branded advertisers sponsored radio programs. The term "soap opera" came from the sponsorship of programming by companies that manufactured soap. Following the sponsorship pattern, early television programs were also sponsored. It was not until later that the current system of multiple advertisements was established. In America, advertising revenues paid for programming production, which is why many stations include commercials within their programming content. These commercials provide opportunities for companies to publicize their branded messages.

The introduction of television marked a shift from a text-based to an image-based culture. As people began to spend more time watching television than reading newspapers or books, they tended to acquire information more from visual than verbal media outlets. This shift supported the trend of branding, because visual media can more easily express the personality of a product than printed words. Stephens (1998) describes television commercials as follows:

> Now, I know it is difficult for some of us to conceive of television commercials actually communicating any *information*. Sometimes their goal seems to be dazzle us with images to the point where we disregard what we do know—about the nutritional value of sodas, about the unlikelihood of a car or sneaker changing our social status, about the irrelevance to most of our lives of one or another brand of airplane engine. It is true that…the business of communicating belongs instead under the heading impressions (not in itself an unimportant category). But there are occasionally some honest-to-goodness facts in those commercials: thirty destinations to which General

Electric airplane engines fly, for instance. And this commercial does manage the considerable trick of introducing those thirty places to us, in pictures and in song, in only twenty seconds. (p. 154)

With the increased use of visual technologies came advertisers' attempts to create total marketing communication programs that managed and controlled the image of a product across all media. Additionally, corporate identity programs attempted to control the look and feel of all branded images.

Along with the growth in advertising came the development of visual communicators called graphic designers, or people who create the visual symbols and icons of industry. These icons are currently called brands. In the 1960s, many trademarks were considered old-fashioned and were consequently updated. As an example, the original Prudential Insurance Company's logo transformed over time from a graphic of the Rock of Gibraltar to an abstract and barely recognizable wedge. Mobil Oil lost its Pegasus image, and RCA abandoned Nipper, the dog who peered into the phonograph speaker (see Morgan, 1986).

The change in branding from animal and picture trademarks to more abstract ones illustrates a shift from concept-related graphics to arbitrary graphics. This shift also occurred because businesses began to diversify interests and expand their product lines. For instance, Procter & Gamble began as a candle company but later made laundry detergent, dishwasher detergent, toothpaste, and soap. As a result, the symbol of a specific product or service no longer applied to the company as a whole. In such cases, companies began to brand themselves with abstract symbols that people needed to learn through advertising.

Branding in the 1960s

One of the most influential figures in advertising during the 1960s was David Ogilvy, who said: "I do not regard advertising as entertainment or an art form, but as a medium of information. When I write an advertisement, I don't want you to tell me that you find it 'creative'. I want you to find it so interesting that you *buy the product*" (Ogilvy, 1983, p. 7). Moreover, the relationship between brands and advertising is that advertising should contribute to brand image. Ogilvy writes about brands as personalities, contending that "image is personality" (p. 14). Examples of brand personalities include Uncle Ben, Aunt Jemima, the Marlboro cowboy, and Old Grand-Dad.

The brand image or personality is a combination of physical and emotional factors. It gives the brand an aura, "differentiates it from, and makes it more desirable than, other products" (Douglas, 1984, p. 32). The name, the packaging, the advertising, and the established price of a brand create the value of the brand. Moreover, to establish a brand, the product itself must be of a high enough quality to stand up to comparison with the competition.

The 1960s were a time of a creative revolution. Culturally, many changes were taking place, including men walking on the moon, a new sexual freedom, the counterculture movement, and the Vietnam War. Advertisers wanted to appeal to younger consumers, known as baby boomers. Famous campaigns included Pepsi's "Think young" and the "Pepsi Generation" (agency: Batten, Barton, Durstine, & Osborn) and Coca-Cola's multi-ethnic song "I'd Like to Teach the World to Sing" (agency: McCann-Erickson). These commercials became essential to the "cola wars," or the battle between Coke and Pepsi.

Pop culture terms were incorporated into ads. More African Americans began to appear in commercials. Looser moral standards led to the creation of racier ads. For instance, Noxzema shave cream's 1967 commercial featured "The Stripper" theme and a sexy female model who urged the shaver to "Take it off, take it *all* off." This double entendre appealed to men. "Red-blooded American males heeded her call for Noxzema shave cream" (Staff, 2005, n.p.).

Humor, irony, and irreverence exemplified the style of advertising of the 1960s. One of the most famous campaigns was for the Volkswagen Beetle. Created by Doyle Dane Bernback (David Ogilvy's agency), the ads capitalized on negative perceptions in the headlines, including "Think Small" and "Lemon." Volkswagen created the small-car branded position. "Think Small," "perhaps the most famous single advertisement ever run, stated the position in no uncertain terms" (Ries & Trout, 2001, p. 122). Considered some of the most creative copy ever written, these advertisements turned negatives into a positive statement.

Branding and Culture

In the past, the concept of culture referred to entertainment, including poetry, opera, and ballet. Today the concept of culture includes socially transmitted behavior patterns such as arts, beliefs, institutions, and all other products of human work and thought. This includes advertising and branding. Branding has gone beyond the concept of selling a product to the idea of selling the brand. A perfect example is designer fashion. In the 1980s, the success of corporations depended on their brands. Companies such as Nike, Microsoft, and Tommy Hilfiger were selling the images of their brand rather than specific products. Marketing became more important than manufacturing. "Competitive branding became a necessity of the machine age—within a context of manufactured sameness, image-based difference had to be manufactured along with the product" (Klein, 1999, p. 8). Today people buy brands, not products, and brand images are everywhere.

Brands are currently pervasive throughout the world, not only through advertising outlets but also in our personal lives. Consequently, branding is part of contemporary culture. Klein (1999) contends that we live today in a branded world. Similarly, Tantillo (2010) argues: "I believe that marketing is involved in just about everything from our personal lives to our political lives to our consumer and professional realities" (p. 6). Economics supports this notion. In 1998, the United Nations Human Development Report stated that global advertising spending outpaced the growth of the world economy (see Klein, 1999).

As Hal Morgan (1986) contends:

> On a more personal level, trademark and package designs form an important part of our experience of being Americans. These are the symbols—the personalities—of the products we have bought, of the food we have eaten, and of the companies that we have relied on throughout our lives. (p. 13)

Branding is now an international phenomenon. No matter where you go in the world, you can find Coca-Cola. In major cities across the globe, people can purchase McDonald's hamburgers. Most young people wear Levi's jeans. The look and feel of today's global identity is the result of the influence of branded products.

Summary

Since ancient times, people have placed inscriptions on objects. Over time, these marks have been transformed into branded images. Technology has played a major role in the dissemination of branded visuals. The upheaval known as the Industrial Revolution transformed the production of goods, and with it came the increased use of branding, especially when manufactured items replaced handmade ones. Companies needed to create brand images to identify their products and services. Advertising became the method for identifying branded images with company names. Brand names and trademarks derived from a wide range of cultural associations, including animals, people, and cultural stereotypes. Eventually, brands became associated with cultural values. Today we can find the same brands distributed around the globe.

Exercises

1. Select a well-known brand. Using the Internet and advertising magazines, research the history of the brand and write up a report on your findings.

Pepsi-Cola	Shell Oil	Xerox
Coca-Cola	Ford	IBM
Procter & Gamble	Chevrolet	Kodak

2. Compare advertisements from the 1960s to ones that are more current. Examine the similarities and differences, including people in the ads, lifestyle images, and commercial message. (The commercials are available on YouTube.)

   > Examples: Compare Coca-Cola's "I'd Like to Teach the World to Sing" (1971) with the "Big Game" Commercial (2014) or any later commercial.

   > Or compare "The Pepsi Generation" (1963) commercial with Michael Jackson's "Pepsi Generation" commercial (2013).

3. Research and report on the "cola wars." How were the personalities of each product depicted?
4. Find a brand and describe its personality as if it were a person.
5. Make a list of the brands that you purchase and why you like them.

Note

1. Media ecology is the study of media environments or, broadly defined, the study of complex communication systems as environments. This perspective informs the author's thinking about technology and communication.

References

Baker, E., & Blik, T. (1985). *Trademarks of the 20's & 30's*. San Francisco, CA: Chronicle Books.

Boorstin, D.J. (1987). *The image*. New York: Atheneum.

Douglas, T. (1984). *The complete guide to advertising*. Secaucus, NJ: Chartwell Books.

Eisenstein, E.L. (1983). *The printing revolution in early modern Europe*. Cambridge: Cambridge University Press.

Ewen, S. (2001). *Captains of consciousness*. New York: Basic Books.

Holmes, N. (1985). *Designing pictorial symbols*. New York: Watson-Guptill.

Hornung, C.P. (1956). *Handbook of early advertising art*. Mineola, NY: Dover Publications. (Original work published 1947)

Klein, N. (1999). *No logo*. New York: Picador.

Mendenhall, J. (1983). *Symbols of power and progress: American trademarks 1930–1950*. New York: Art Direction.

Morgan, H. (1986). *Symbols of America*. New York: Penguin.

Ogilvy, D. (1983). *Ogilvy on advertising*. New York: Crown.

Ries, A., & Trout, J. (2001). *Positioning: The battle for your mind*. New York: McGraw-Hill.

Sacharow, S. (1982). *Symbols of trade*. New York: Art Direction.

Staff. (2005, March 28). 1960s creativity and breaking the rules. *Advertising Age*. Retrieved October, 22, 2006, from http://adage.com/article/75-years-of-ideas/1960s-creativity-breaking-rules/102704/

Staff. (2014, August 3). History of Heinz 57. *DFW Penny Saver*, p. 9.

Stephens, M. (1998). *The rise of the image and the fall of the word*. New York: Oxford University Press.

Tantillo, J. (2010). *People buy brands not companies*. New York: Five Titles Press.

Twitchell, J.B. (2000). *Twenty ads that shook the world*. New York: Three Rivers Press.

Wingler, H.M. (1984). *The Bauhaus*. Cambridge, MA: MIT Press.

· 3 ·

BRANDING AS COMMUNICATION

The new paradigm suggests that having a sensory experience, such as seeing an advertisement, creates feeling in the body first, as opposed to thought.
—Douglas Van Praet, 2012, p. 88

The branding communication process examines how people receive commercial information from brands. These messages are often created by an advertising agency to be communicated to the consumer. While an advertisement sends a message about the brand, understanding the branded message requires a deeper examination of the communication itself. Connotative rather than denotative messages can uncover the true message of the branded product or service and its personality. This chapter explores communication models for understanding branded messages.

Branding is a topic that is important to business programs but not generally discussed in communication courses. This is probably because brands tend to be visual, and visual communication is not always a course offered in many universities. Today we have no grand theory or model to describe the process of understanding visual messages, though many different models have been used to explain the visual communication process.

In advertising, authors often rely on basic rhetoric, and brand images can be described in terms of the rhetorical model. However, the analysis of a branded message is on a different level than the advertising communication.

In this way, rhetorical analysis can be used to identify several different meanings communicated through a single commercial message. Understanding branded messages can also be described through the Laswell model of advertising, which examines the denotative meanings of the messages. As a result, branded messages can be examined much like other types of communication exchanges are observed.

In the discipline of communication, a model is described as an object, event, process, or relationship. Models are an attempt to show how something works by representing its important features. In communication studies, models are designed to help us understand the relationships among parts of the communication process and enhance our understanding of how communication works.

Although models can help us understand the process of communication, they also have limitations. For this reason, several different models will be discussed here. By using more than one model, a greater understanding can be achieved. Communication is complex and dynamic; in contrast, models are static. They freeze the process they represent. As a result, no single model can accurately capture the entire communication process, because models do not represent motion and change. However, we can use models to represent communication in a general way and identify communication features and their relationships to each other. Moreover, we can design models to examine particular aspects of communication, such as understanding the message. In communication studies, the original rhetorical model developed in ancient times by Aristotle has been altered to meet the communication needs of today.

Rhetorical Model

Rhetoric is the art of persuasion. Originally, the rhetorical model was used to describe speech. Today we use it to examine mass media, advertising, and branding. The purpose of advertising is to persuade a person to buy and use a particular product or service. In contrast, the purpose of branding is to communicate the personality of the brand. Although currently commonplace, the concept of persuasion began in ancient Greece with the ideas of Aristotle and Plato. Both regarded communication as an art or craft to be practiced and studied. In Aristotle's view, communication was the means through which citizens participated in a democracy. People had to argue and discuss different views in order to make the right choices for their society. This concept is part of the foundation of American government—for instance, debating different perspectives to reach an agreement. From a face-to-face political perspective, communication is an orator or speaker constructing an argument to be presented in a speech to an audience. The goals of speakers are to inspire a positive image of themselves and to encourage the audience to be receptive to the message.

Rhetoric is envisioned as a triangular process—speaker, address, audience. Aristotle (2013) contended there were three aspects of public speaking—Ethos (speaker), Pathos (audience), and Logos (argument). Ethos is the source's credibility or the character of the speaker. Several factors influence ethos. These include how notable the person is within his or her field (such as a college professor, executive of a company, or minister of a religion) as well as whether or not the person has a vested interest in the topic or a personal bias.

"Ethos is often the first thing we notice, so it creates the first impression that influences how we perceive the rest" (Edlund, 2014, para. 1). There are two types of ethos: extrinsic and intrinsic. Extrinsic ethos is the character, expertise, education, and experience of the speaker as described above. An example of extrinsic ethos is a famous basketball player talking about basketball to another professional basketball player. In contrast, a college English professor does not have as much credibility when he is talking about basketball. One would expect him to talk about English literature, his area of expertise.

In advertising a brand, the message frequently uses doctors, medical studies, and customers to convince consumers that the product is the best one in the marketplace. A doctor recommending a healthcare product is more reliable than an actor. In some cases, actors are used when they suffer from the medical condition being advertised. For instance, a football player might recommend a drug for shingles because the player is speaking from personal experience. Another example is an actor recommending a weight-loss product because he or she used it to lose weight. Again, the actor is speaking from personal experience, which adds to the credibility of the message.

Ethos is the credibility of the speaker, and pathos is an appeal to the emotions. Pathos is how the audience feels about the message being communicated. Advertisers want to understand how audiences will respond to their messages and thus frequently test messages on focus groups to gauge an audience's response. Emotional messages are important to the success of a product or service. Brands need to know how people feel about them. (Emotional appeals are discussed in Chapter 6.)

Advertisers use the voice of the advertisement to create ethos. "Voice is the brand's image as expressed in language" (Felton, 2006, p. 78). This includes the headline and body copy of the advertisement. For instance, the "Think Small" Volkswagen headline used humor to sell the car. At the time, American cars were like streamlined jet planes, and the advertising made them sound like superheroes. In contrast, the Volkswagen "was small, ugly, non-obsolescent, and foreign" (Twitchell, 2000, p. 114). The advertising agency made a virtue of the reality of the car. "Think Small" displayed the Volkswagen as a postage-sized car in vast amounts of white space to make the viewer work to see it.

Later, when a new Volkswagen Beetle was introduced, another headline described it as "Less flower. More power." This headline makes a social reference to the hippie generation, because they were associated with the first generation of Beetles. Again the headline uses a humorous tone, meaning that the voice of this advertising is funny. The ethos is based on the idea that Volkswagen is making fun of its product and itself. Additionally, the Volkswagen ads directly and indirectly poked fun at American society. One reason for this may have been the difference between Volkswagen and most American cars. Humor was necessary to get people to pay attention to the product.

The car used humor to sell its message. In contrast, a cruise ship's communication—the headline "Civilization is advancing at a stately 18 knots" below a picture of the ship—was much more practical and serious. These different approaches to voice appeal to different groups of people. Volkswagen is an inexpensive and fun car. Its message is for people who are money conscious. Conversely, a cruise is more expensive and appeals to people who would have enough discretionary dollars to travel. Would a humorous headline work for a cruise ship? Or would a serious headline work for a Volkswagen advertisement? Such messages would probably depend on a creative strategy. In any case, the self-deprecating humor of Volkswagen helped to sell large numbers of cars and proves that the manner in which a company speaks to the consumer is vitally important.

Logos is the nature of the message being presented by the speaker to the audience. It is the appeal to the logical mind. It is how a company makes its argument to a consumer, including the type of evidence and support for the selling claims. Advertisements generally provide proof to support their statements. Such proof can be in the form of a visual or verbal message or both. An example is using before-and-after demonstrations. An advertiser spills wine on a carpet. A product is applied to the stain and it is removed. Or, clothes look white and bright after using a particular brand of laundry detergent. These messages are targeted to a particular audience.

Barry (1997) argued that advertising "messages are framed in the most subtle and effective way possible to reach the target audience (someone in a position to buy the product or act on the idea), to make them receptive to the message, and ultimately act on it" (p. 253). Advertisers know to whom they are speaking. The target audience for purchasing laundry detergent is different from the audience that would buy a Mercedes Benz car. A homemaker buys laundry detergent, while a successful businessperson buys a fancy automobile. Thus, addresses or logos need to be targeted to different groups requiring different types of messages.

Logos and pathos can influence ethos. How well the logic of the argument is made reflects on the knowledge of the speaker. The better the argument, the more credible the speaker. Pathos is also necessary. Speakers need to believe in the topic they are discussing, or actors need to convince the audience. How the receiver feels about the message is as important as the message itself.

Visual and verbal rhetoric draws the attention of the audience to the product. Advertisements are carefully crafted to appeal to the logic and emotions of the consumer. Spokespersons are selected to provide credibility for the message. In some cases a celebrity spokesperson is used because his or her celebrity makes an association with the product.

When we apply a rhetorical model to advertising, the process describes both the emotion and logic of the communication. Although the message of an advertisement may be clearly articulated, the emotional overtones may not. "The unconscious responds to the context or structure of a message not just the actual content, aware of how the information is delivered and not just what is said" (Van Praet, 2012, p. 17). When the consumer identifies emotionally with the advertising image and the product, the image can become intimately linked to the satisfactions inherent in the scenario. This is done without directly stating a causal relationship between the product and its social or emotional reward. For instance, beverages are often sold by showing groups of happy people having fun. It is implied that if consumers drink the product, they will also be entertained.

When we examine the rhetorical aspects of branded messages, the metaphors, gestalt, and indirect relationships of the elements in the message need to be considered. The headline or the body copy and the relationship between the text and images must be examined. Ries and Trout (2001) tell us that "words are triggers. They trigger the meanings which are buried in the mind" (p. 202). The juxtaposition of the words and image both attract the viewer and present cues for understanding the message. A deeper inspection of the ways in which the elements interact generally reveals the marketing message of a brand. Marketing can be described as "a two-directional relationship between seller and buyer that is predicated on satisfying needs on both sides" (Tantillo, 2010, p. 53). The marketing message may not be the same as the advertising message. Advertising is the method by which people discover a product. In contrast, marketing tells us what we will discover (see Levine, 2003). Thus an advertising message can work on two levels.

One method for uncovering the advertising message is to inspect the visual appeal of the communication. Foss (1993) presented a hypothesis of visual appeal when examining images. Visual appeal is "a novel technical aspect of the image [that] violates viewers' expectations; this violation functions both to sustain interest in the image and to decontextualize it" (p. 215). Simply stated, the image provides an unexpected yet familiar context in which to interpret the message. In the process of changing the context, the branded message may be revealed. For example, an advertisement uses impressionist paintings to show how vision can be clear when one wears glasses. (See the KelOptic advertisement example below.) One does not expect impressionism to be in focus, so using a realistic photograph in the middle of an impressionistic painting is unexpected. The message is one of clarity. Combined with the art, it links the promise of better eyesight to upper-class aesthetics (the association with the impressionist art).

Visual appeal, because it is more memorable, is a technique that can be used to better understand the marketing message. There are several types of messages that are communicated through an advertisement. The first is the advertising message, and it is easier to understand because it is created through the denotative, or obvious elements, in the advertisement. The second message is the marketing or branded message. It is communicated through a deeper understanding of how the elements interact with each other. In other words, the connotative meaning of the relationship between the items needs to be examined. In branding, the message of the advertisement needs to support the branded message of the product. Another way to look at this is to say that the advertisement needs to maintain the personality of the product or service. This is often done through an indirect method of communication. Thus the rhetorical method has two ways of being interpreted.

Laswell Model

The rhetorical model helps us to understand the main advertising and branded meaning of a message. In contrast, the Laswell model also explores the mediated aspect of sending and receiving an advertising message. The type of medium used to distribute the information is included. As a result, this model is designed to examine mass media. Moreover, the Laswell model asks about the persuasive purpose of the message. Rhetoric examines how a specific message is persuasive, while Laswell wants to explore its persuasive effect.

The American political scientist Harold D. Laswell created this early model of communication to examine political propaganda. The phrase he used is one of the most famous in communication research:

Who?
Says What?
In What Channel?
To Whom?
For What Effect?

Laswell used this formula to lend structure to his research method. The model assumes that the communicator has some plan for influencing the receiver of the information. Consequently, the message is a form of persuasion. The model suggests that there are a variety of outcomes or effects of communication, such as to inform, to entertain, to aggravate, and to persuade.

Persuasion is common to the rhetorical and Laswell models. Thus, when examining branding, persuasion is a central issue because companies want to encourage people to use products and services. Both the Laswell and Aristotle models view communication as a linear, one-way process in which one entity influences another. The linear nature of the model makes it particularly well suited to the study of mass communication, because mass messages are distributed in one direction, with limited audience feedback. As a result, the Laswell model is frequently used to study political propaganda and advertising messages. Both the Laswell and rhetorical models can help us understand how branded messages communicate information.

Applying these models to an actual advertisement will illustrate how they work. Young & Rubicam Paris created a series of eyewear advertisements for KelOptic, an online eyewear retailer (see Griner, 2014). The print advertisements used classical impressionistic paintings to illustrate the clarity of the glasses. In front of each painting is a pair of glasses. The area within the lens is realistic, while the rest of the painting is impressionistic. For example, a portrait similar to one created by the artist Vincent Van Gogh is shown. The background is in the style of impressionism, while the lens area depicts the image of a man in focus.

The fuzzy paint associated with impressionism is in stark contrast to the in-focus area, which displays the image photographically. The contrast between the areas of the painting illustrates how glasses can make things come into focus for an individual. Moreover, the clarity of the photograph versus the painting demonstrates the sharp vision provided by glasses.

Applying a rhetorical model, the ethos of the company is not well known; indeed, it is unknown to this researcher. Therefore, its credibility is limited for this person. In contrast, the impressionistic paintings are famous, which does lend reliability to the advertisements. The logical argument is communicated through images. The fuzzy painting, in contrast to the photographic image inside the lens, clearly communicates how the glasses improve vision. Moreover, the novel technical aspect of the image is the contrast between painted and photographic surfaces. A viewer does not expect a portion of an impressionist painting to be in focus. Thus the message is clarity of vision presented in an unexpected and upscale context.

The message of the visual is reinforced by the tagline "Turning impressionism into hyperrealism." The pathos or feeling associated with the advertisements is one of amazement. The copy is postmodern because hyperrealism is a postmodern concept. The voice is speaking to an educated audience both through the choice of words and images.

Using this model for branding, a different marketing message can be understood. The company or ethos wants to communicate an image for itself. To understand the branding, the pathos needs to be explored. The feeling of the advertisement is one of amazement or something unexpected. Also, the image speaks to the quality of vision created by the glasses. The choice of using impressionistic paintings also establishes a relationship between the company and a recognized art movement. Thus, the image association creates messages of wonder, value, and elegance. In terms of the company, the branding is telling us that the eyewear manufacturer creates new, unique, and high-quality products that add a touch of class. The consumer may be surprised at the style and quality of glasses provided. Moreover, consumers would expect to find glasses with style and refinement. Thus the branding message is different from the advertising message because it goes beyond the idea of clear sight.

The Laswell model can also be used to examine both the advertising and branded messages. The advertising message is the overt or denotative message, which is easier to identify. In contrast, the branded message is more covert or denotative. Branding is the association we create through the visual and verbal elements in the advertisement and requires a deeper analysis than simply examining the advertising message itself.

When we add the Laswell model to the mix, the "who" is KelOptic. "Says what" is the message that glasses improve vision. "To whom" is an educated audience of people who wear glasses. "In what channel" are magazine advertisements (also duplicated on the Internet). Finally, the desired "effect" is for consumers to visit KelOptic to buy their glasses. Both the rhetorical and Laswell models of communication can be used to help us understand the message of an advertisement. However, the branded message is more complicated because we need to look at the elements individually instead of linearly.

KelOptic is the company. It may be known locally; however, it is also a global company because of its Internet presence. The message is clear vision. However, the context and elements used in the advertisement create a more complex connotative meaning. This meaning is the marketing message. The message as identified in the rhetorical analysis is clarity of vision and is presented in an unexpected, upscale context. In terms of branding, KelOptic is communicating a message that it is a high-class company. This is done through the choice of impressionistic art and the postmodern tagline. Art and hyperrealism are educated ideas. People need to be educated in art history and postmodernism to fully understand the terms. Additionally, the person would wear glasses or sunglasses.

Both the rhetorical and Laswell models can be used to understand branded messages. However, instead of looking at the surface meanings, revealing the branded communication requires a deeper evaluation. Let's see how the models work for another set of advertisements.

Case Study: Keds

When we brand an item with a name, the price of the item will go up as the brand establishes itself within a culture, because brands need to spend millions of dollars to get people to recognize them. As brands rise and fall, so does the value of their products. Despite the rise of sports shoes such as Nike, Converse, and Adidas, Keds has maintained its position in the marketplace.

Keds advertisements dating back to 1917 can be found online (see http://www.vintageadbrowser.com). The canvas shoes, the first of their kind, were introduced in 1916 and are an example of a brand that has been in existence for 100 years and continues to play a role in today's economy. A study of print advertisements for Keds reveals that the company has used a variety of messages to sell its products. Additionally, the company has introduced a number of different products in order to stay competitive in the marketplace. These strategies have kept the company in business for a century.

In 1917 Keds, the first rubber shoe, belonged to the United States Rubber Company. At that time, Keds was advertised as a shoe for everyone, including society folks. Advertisements claimed that Keds would provide foot comfort through the summer. Several styles were offered, from low to high heels. The image was a foot in the foreground with a hiking stick and an image of people and a car in the background having a good time. The ad stated: "You get a better balance of comfort, style and economy in Keds than in any other shoe you can buy."[1] In the past, advertisements had more text or body copy than they do today. As a result, Keds could make a number of different promises about its product, including lifestyle comfort and financial economy.

Moving ahead to 1939, the image becomes very different. Five different styles of shoes are shown, and a number of illustrations depict lifestyle activities. The first is a car with a small child in the front seat; the second is a man with children and a fishing rod; the third is a tennis match; and the final image is of two men in a sailboat. All of the illustrations depict lifestyle activities. A clever headline states: "His feet are as relaxed as his soul." The similarity between the sound of soul and sole makes for a provocative statement. Shoe or human, the headline was designed to capture the audience's attention. Consistent with the previous advertisement, this one stresses comfort. However, instead of promoting style, this advertisement adds suggestions for when a person should wear the shoes. These activities include playing tennis, walking on dirt and grassy ground, and leisure activities. These are situations where people are on the move.

The headline is supported by the body copy, which states: "a day of comfort, happiness and peace. Fabric rubber-soled shoes are in keeping with his mood." The words happiness, peace, and mood relate to soul. In contrast, the term comfort, combined with a description of the shoes, correlates with the other type of sole. The advertisement both shows and tells people specifically how and when Keds can make their lives easier.

Ten years later, a Keds advertisement appeared that was similar to the 1939 one. Many pictures of shoes were displayed along with illustrations of leisure activities. The styles of shoes were generally very different, but one look remained the same. The headline was more direct—more like a command—because after each word was an exclamation point: "Action! Wear! Keds!" In addition, a small illustration of a foot moving with the sole of the shoe was included. The slogan "The Shoe of Champions" had been added. This advertisement was more action oriented and offered more illustrations related to sports and play. The new slogan implied that athletes wear the shoes.

Moving ahead once more, a 1953 advertisement is very different from the previous ones. First, it is in color. Second, instead of many illustrations, there is only one. As in the previous advertisements, a number of different-colored shoes are illustrated. However, only one style of shoe is shown. The illustration is of three running feet, both male and female, with the top of a tennis racket. Again the relationship between Keds and sports is established. A major difference with the 1953 advertisement is that branding is more prominent. Incorporated into the headline is the blue Keds logo that appears on the back of the shoes. It reads, "Summertime U.S.A. begins with Keds [logo]." Thus, the actual shoe logo is visually displayed in the advertisement. The connotative meaning of this advertisement is that Keds are an important part of leisure time during the summer. The message is simpler and changes from an emphasis on sports to one of leisure activity. The action-oriented emphasis is continued from 1949 to 1953.

Keds is an iconic brand and is important in branding history. In the 1960s, Keds first sold "sneakers." The name came from the rubber soles and the fact that people could sneak around silently while wearing Keds. Similar to other brands, such as Xerox, sneakers became a generic name for canvas shoes. A 1972 advertisement represented a departure from previous ads. It pictured four men sitting in chairs wearing Keds canvas shoes. The headline read: "There's nothing worse than wearing 1972 clothes with 1960 shoes." The sub-headline read: "Introducing the 1972 Keds' Knockarounds." Compared to the 1960 shoes, this new brand extension was much more colorful and relaxed, and added a new style to the line of shoes. This 1972 advertisement is similar to the 1917 one because both place an emphasis on style. The men sitting in chairs are in stark contrast to the several previous advertisements that communicated action.

Obviously, by introducing new styles, Keds was trying to retain its position in the marketplace. At this point, Keds was focusing on a male market because, unlike previous advertisements, no women were pictured. As times changed, so did Keds. This holds true today, because now Keds is focusing on the girls market.

In the 1980s and 1990s, a number of different television actresses wore Keds as part of their characters. But then, in the late 1990s, Keds sneakers lost their appeal and the company had to reinvent them. Today, Keds shoes are still in the marketplace, and the company is using newer-branded messages to promote the product.

Beginning in 2013, Keds began to focus again on girls, and Taylor Swift was hired as spokesperson for the new campaign. *The New York Times* stated: "The campaign, scheduled to begin in print, online and in social media on Thursday, appeals to 'brave girls' and 'bravehearts' and offers Ms. Swift as a role model" (Elliot, 2013, p. B4). The article stated that, according to marketing reports, Swift had a strong emotional tie to children ages 6–12. As a result, she was considered an excellent role model for the target audience. One reason why Keds selected a spokesperson is that heroes are important to the brand's target audience.

Swift is considered a brave girl because at age 14 she convinced her family to move to Nashville so she could concentrate on her musical career. The words used to describe her are eternally optimistic and confident. Swift as a spokesperson fit into a larger program called the Million Brave Acts Campaign with the Brave Acts Project.

In contrast to earlier advertisements, Keds is now centering its branding message on a spokesperson. A Keds print advertisement ran in the April 2014 issue of *People Stylewatch*. It featured a large photo of Taylor Swift sitting at the edge of what looks like a pool. She is wearing a polka-dot dress and a pair of white Keds. Her arms and legs are crossed. To the left of the image are two inserts showing different-colored Keds shoes. The headline reads: "Brave lights up a room." Underneath is the Keds logo, and below that is small type that reads: "There are a million ways to be brave. Share some of your own at bravehearts.com." This message attempts to engage consumers by having them share pictures.

Swift was also selected to lead the Keds centennial advertising campaign. Beginning in the fall of 2015, she was featured in advertisements about female empowerment. The campaign's tagline is "Ladies first since 1916." It features other female talent, both on and off camera. In addition to a few other models, "the ads employed notable female artists to make the backdrops—including illustrator Priscilla White, surface artist and pattern designer Kendra Dandy, and street artist Paige Smith" (Nudd, 2015, p. 1). In 1916, Keds offers afford-able and fashionable women's footwear that give women the freedom to walk anywhere.

Returning to the beginning of this chapter and applying a rhetorical model to this advertisement inspires some new ideas. The ethos of advertisements for Keds is based on the company's spokesperson, Taylor Swift, rather than a 100-year-old tradition. This is emphasized by her signature at the corner of the ad. The credibility of the ads is thereby linked to this person. The logical argument is communicated through words. However, the headline does not clearly relate to the product. Instead it implies that Swift is brave and lights up a room. Her face is the focal point of the photo, and her crossed arms and legs help to accent this. However, anyone with knowledge of body language knows that crossing arms and legs is a sign of pulling back. The person does not want to engage in the situation. These gestures could be viewed as being conflicting to the overall message.

In spite of this, one needs to realize that the voice of the advertisement speaks to the target audience. Young people today are very involved with social media and the Internet. They stay connected to each other through smart devices, notebooks, and portable computers. Thus the online aspect speaks to the intended audience. This needs to be considered in a branding analysis.

Unlike the previous print Keds advertisements, this one does not speak specifically about the product. It emphasizes the "brave" concept, which is part of a multimedia campaign. Lauren Johnson (2014) stated that the cam-paign "aggregates video, social media, photos and commerce as a resource to empower women in achieving their personal goals" (p. 1). The point of the campaign is to involve young women with the project by asking them to go to the website. This is an emotional appeal for girls to become involved with the brand, and it is through brand involvement that they will then engage with the shoes. At the website there are contests and a special message from Taylor Swift. Again, the focus of the print advertisement is to engage the target audience rather than stress the features of the product. The logic of the advertisement does not follow a traditional advertising pattern; instead it has been influenced by new media, which is the topic Chapter 10.

Branding is always changing and evolving as new technologies, cultural attitudes, and industry trends evolve. The classic rhetorical model and the Laswell model still work as means of understanding contemporary adver-tising messages. However, current cultural issues also need to be examined. The interest in social media and online interactions has changed the ways in which young people communicate with each other. These factors are now appearing in advertising messages. An overview of the Keds advertisements illustrates how print advertising has changed over the past century.

Following the Laswell method, Keds is telling young girls to be brave. The objective of the message is to create a connection between the idea of being courageous (Taylor Swift) and the product (Keds). Moreover, the desired effect is to convince girls to visit the bravehearts.com web site. In many cases, branding has remained focused on a product message. However, as branding has evolved through the use of technology, a shift has occurred toward creating more emotional connections between the brand and the consumer.

As culture changes, so do advertising messages. When we conduct an overview of the Keds advertisements, we find that in earlier ads the product was described and depicted through illustrations that showed how people would wear the shoes. In the current campaign, the appeal is on an emotional level and is not specifically about the product, but focuses instead on the brand. This radical change in direction is the result of changes in the target market and social trends.

Summary

Communication models can be used to understand branded messages. Traditional models such as the rhetorical and Laswell models can be applied to branded messages. However, to uncover a branded message, people must look deeper into the associations between the images and words to understand the appeal of the brand. Often the appeal is on the emotional level. Marketers deliberately create emotional connections between the product and the consumer, as will be explored in the next chapter.

Exercises

1. Find a print advertisement and conduct a rhetorical analysis. Is the advertising message the same as the branded message? How are they similar or different?
2. Using a magazine advertisement, perform a Laswell investigation on the advertising message of the ad. Is this message the same as the branded message?

3. Find two print advertisements, one that uses websites and one that does not. What are the similarities and differences between the ads? What is the purpose of printing the website in the ad?

4. Go to advertising websites such as AdWeek or Advertising Age and find an article that discusses new trends in advertising. Write about older versus newer directions in the industry.

Note

1. Keds advertisement, *People Everywhere* (1917). http://www.vintageadbrowser.com/search?q=keds&page=2

References

Aristotle. (2013). *Rhetoric* (Rhys Roberts, Trans.). Hazelton, PA: Pennsylvania State University, Electronic Classics Series.

Barry, A.M.S. (1997). *Visual intelligence.* Albany: State University of New York Press.

Edlund, J.R. (2014). *Ethos, logos, pathos: Three ways to persuade.* Pomona, CA: California Polytechnic University, Pomona.

Elliot, S. (2013, January 24). Keds enlists Taylor Swift to transmit girl power. *The New York Times*, p. B4.

Felton, G. (2006). *Advertising concept and copy* (2nd ed.). Englewood Cliffs, NJ: Prentice Hall.

Foss, S.K. (1993). The construction of appeal in visual images. In D. Zarefsky (Ed.), *Rhetorical movement: Essays in honor of Leland M. Griffin* (pp. 210–224). Evanston, IL: Northwestern University Press.

Griner, D. (2014, June 5). Impressionist classics finally come into focus in clever eyewear ads. *AdWeek*. Retrieved June 5, 2014, from http://www.adweek.com/adfreak/impressionist-classics-finally-come-focus-clever-eyewear-ads-158149

Johnson, L. (2014, February 24). Keds kicks content strategy into gear with Million Brave Acts campaign. *Mobile Commerce Daily*. Retrieved April 26, 2014, from http://www.mobilemarketer.com/cms/news/content/17241.html

Levine, M. (2003). *A branded world.* Hoboken, NJ: John Wiley & Sons.

Nudd, T. (2015, July 21). Taylor Swift stars in global rebrand for Keds: "Ladies first since 1916." *AdWeek*. Retrieved July 22, 2015, from http://www.adweek.com/adfreak/taylor-swift-stars-global-rebrand-keds-ladies-first-1916–166018

Ries, A., & Trout, J. (2001). *Positioning: The battle for your mind.* New York: McGraw-Hill.

Tantillo, J. (2010). *People buy brands not companies.* New York: Five Titles Press.

Twitchell, J.B. (2000). *Twenty ads that shook the world.* New York: Three Rivers Press.

Van Praet, D. (2012). *Unconscious branding.* New York: Palgrave Macmillan.

$\cdot\ 4\ \cdot$

CREATING BRAND IMAGES

*Products, like people, have personalities, and they can make or break them in
the market place.*
—David Ogilvy, 1983, p. 14

*Advertising agencies, public relations firms, brand managers, art directors, graphic design-
ers, and copywriters work together to create the personality of a brand. Many people get
paid to construct the thinking behind the brand strategy. A number of these professionals
have described their process for developing a brand message. This chapter provides examples
of the thinking behind the brand. It describes how designers communicate ideas through
branded messages. In addition, the chapter provides information about creativity, the essen-
tials of branding, and examples of the thinking behind the image. It explains what elements
are needed to create a successful brand strategy and brand personality. Finally, it provides
practical information about branding.*

In essence, "branding is about figuring out the core features of a product or service and then using the best way possible to let other people—specifically your
Target Market—learn about and come to depend on these features" (Tantillo,
2010, p. 71). To generate the message, there is often an element of creativity
associated with a brand that is unexpected and innovative. Sometimes advertising people call this the "big idea."

But how do people create this concept? They do not just sit in a room and wait for the "big idea" to reveal itself. Creating brand messages takes work and hard thinking. However, it may come suddenly in a moment of clear awareness. Behind this moment are probably many hours of thinking about the product or service and its characteristics.

Ideas used to communicate the brand message to the target audience are often extremely clever. Advertisers need to break through the clutter of an overpopulated media environment. Ries and Trout (2001) state: "Our extravagant use of communication to solve a host of business and social problems has so jammed our channels that only a tiny fraction of all messages actually get through" (p. 11). As a result, the best way to communicate in an overmediated environment is to create a simplistic message. This is done by being selective and positioning the product or service. "Positioning is what you do to the mind of the prospect" (p. 11). In other words, to brand a product, a simple message about the product needs to be created.

A clear, concise, and memorable image or personality for the brand has to be established in the consumer's mind. One way to make ideas unforgettable is to use the concept of visual appeal described in Chapter 3. The violation of the viewer's expectations causes the person to think more about the message, making it more memorable. Developing visual appeal requires a creative approach to the message-making process. To understand how people create branded messages, the first step is to explore the concept of creativity.

Creativity

Academics contend that "The key idea in the psychologist's conception of creativity has been divergent thinking" (Gardner, 1993, p. 20). This type of original thinking can be ascribed to some of advertising's well-known graphic designers, including Paul Rand, Milton Glaser, and Bob Gill, all of whose work is readily available on the Internet. Rand (1985) is known for his work with IBM, Westinghouse, UPS, Colorforms, and the G.H.P. Cigar Company. He was given the assignment to update the Westinghouse logo and to transform it into something unique. The original logo was a circle with the letter W inside. The unique concept was to suggest a printed circuit to associate the brand with modernization. The final design was made up of a circle, a series of dots, and lines. By modernizing the logo, Rand created a more contemporary look for the company.

Rand is also the designer of the striped IBM logo. The stripes are an attention-getting device that transforms commonplace letters into a memorable design. "Visually, stripes superimposed on a cluster of letters tend to tie them together" (1985, p. 42). The grouping of the letters, which get increasingly wider, creates an open-ended sequence that can be somewhat uncomfortable to look at. In terms of meaning, the lines suggest the ideas of efficiency and speed. These concepts are central to the IBM brand, which moved the brand image into the computer age. Rand's designs, in reflecting the cultural events of their times, update the visual look of companies.

Similarly, Milton Glaser's (1973) graphics reflected the feelings and visuals of the 1960s. His depiction of Bob Dylan as a black-silhouetted face with multicolored wavy hair is one of his classic works. The distinct shape of Dylan's nose makes the portrait immediately identifiable. Glaser's style and use of color is a reminder of the freewheeling attitudes of the 1960s counterculture. In addition to having a keen awareness of his cultural environment, Glaser was also a shrewd marketer. He began his career as a humorous illustrator and later found himself designing supermarkets. In describing his work with the Grand Union supermarket chain, Glaser (1985) stated:

> As a designer you are always concerned with the medium understanding, getting the message across, making a deviation or not, when such an event will take place, how much something will cost, what the benefit and value is if you, the consumer buy such and such. We are always involved with the reality of the need and desire between, usually, a client and its customer. We are the mechanism for transformation—taking an idea, bringing it to the customer and making it effective in terms of being able to produce the effect the client wants. (p. 469)

Unlike painters, who want to share their vision with the world, designers need to consider the many needs of clients, consumers, culture, and production. While Glaser discusses the many facets that are involved in the design process, Bob Gill (1981) simplifies the process by identifying problems and solutions.

Gill states that his graphic design book is based on how graphic problems can lead to unusual design solutions. To move beyond preconceptions, Gill states: "I would have to go *outside of my head* to look for an original idea. I decided that getting involved with the new problem was the most likely way of going outside" (Gill, 1981, p. 7). A unique problem will create a distinctive solution. For example, Gill was given the assignment of designing a title card for a television comedy called *Private Secretary*. He redefined the problem as

"how can an image which says one thing (private secretary) also say something else (that she is stupid) without *actually* saying it?" (p. 8). The solution was to place typing mistakes on the card. For instance, CBS television was spelled "televiisionn," with x's covering the second "i" and "n." These are mistakes from a typewriter rather than a computer. In the computer age, a similar solution would be to misspell a word that would not be caught on a spell checker, such as to, two, or too. The correct word depends on the context of the sentence. Both typewriter and computer mistakes made by a secretary imply that the person is not proficient at his or her work.

Another design solution was to design a counter display for slippers. Gill (1981) asked: "What can hold a slipper and be fun to look at?" (p. 142). The answer is amazingly simple—a dog. Thus, he designed slipper holders that looked like the slippers were in a dog's mouth. Gill's ability to reframe problems helped him to create very clever design solutions. His approach of framing and reframing a problem is a key aspect of his creativity. Dorst and Cross (2001) state:

> Creative design seems more to be a matter of developing and refining together both the formulation of a problem and ideas for a solution, with constant iteration of analysis, synthesis and evaluation processes between the two notional design "spaces"— problem space and solution space. (p. 435)

The problem and the solution evolve together. Building a bridge between the problem and solution does this. Moreover, creativity uses the idea of surprise. "Surprise is what keeps a designer from routine behaviour. The 'surprising' parts of a problem or solution drive the originality streak in a design project" (Dorst & Cross, 2001, p. 437).

These designers illustrate the variety of approaches to creativity. Moreover, cognitive researchers have also described the creative processes.

> [They have studied] the ways in which creative individuals identify problem and solution 'spaces' that appear promising; search within these spaces for approaches appropriate to the problem at hand and for leads that may pay off; evaluate alternative solutions to problems; deploy resources of energy and time to advance their program of investigation in an efficient manner; and determine when to probe further and when to cut losses and move on, and more generally, reflect on their own creating processes. (Gardner, 1993, p. 22)

Creative consultant Edward DeBono, who invented the term *lateral thinking*, has designed a program to help people be creative. Lateral thinking

involves solving problems through an indirect approach; it is a method that uses reasoning that is not always obvious. DeBono (1969) uses lateral thinking "to bring about deliberate arrangements and juxtapositions of information that might never otherwise have occurred" (p. 238). He created the Six Thinking Hat System to help individuals be creative thinkers. However, the different hats do not always follow a linear sequence. DeBono (1999) describes the system as follows:

- White (to get information) …
- Green (for ideas and proposals) …
- Yellow followed by black on each alternative (to evaluate the alternatives) …
- Red (to assess feelings at this point) …
- Followed by blue (to decide what thinking to do next).

On the other hand, in discussing a well known proposal, the sequence might run: red, yellow, black, green (to overcome the negative points), white and then blue. (p. 15)

The White hat examines the information about the product or service and asks questions. It is a fact-finding stage in the process and should not include opinions. It identifies the known facts about the product or service. In contrast, the Red hat focuses on feelings, intuition, and the emotions associated with the subject. In this step, momentary feelings are welcome. Emotions of love, fear, like, and dislikes should be expressed. DeBono (1995) says: "Usually the feeling is genuine but the logic is spurious" (p. 14). The association between emotion and product is key to successful branding.

The Black hat is the point of caution. During this step, a suggestion needs to be evaluated to determine why it may not work with the facts, the lifestyle, or the personality of the brand. This stage utilizes a logical negative thinking approach. It tries to play devil's advocate to understand why something might not work. In contrast, the Yellow hat examines the logical positive benefits of the proposed solution. In this step the benefits of the concept are examined in addition to the positive experiences with the product or service. Understanding the benefits of a product or service along with possible negative connotations is central to identifying a brand strategy.

The Green hat is for creativity. At this point, provocative ideas should be considered along with new and innovative concepts. Strategies that promote creative thinking can be used at this time. DeBono (1995) suggests using a random word to enhance creativity. It can be any word that is used for any

product or service. The purpose of this strategy is to approach the problem from a different entry point.

Finally, the Blue hat is an overview of the entire creative process. Thinking at this stage is to examine the entire solution of benefits and brand strategy. At this point, all the other hats should be reviewed. Just remember that at different points, different types of thinking are applied to discover the solution. Additionally, individuals and groups can focus on one of the hats at different times. Corporations trying to increase their creative potential are using DeBono's approach. His method is one of many that marketers have developed to improve brand strategies.

Creativity and Maslow

Most creative strategies are built around an emotional need that the product or service promises to meet for the customer. (Emotional attachment to brands is described more fully in Chapter 6.) However, understanding what type of need a product or service meets is important in designing a brand strategy. Therefore, brand developers should understand basic human requirements. For instance, it is a basic human need to belong to something bigger than ourselves.

Human needs are part of recognizing human psychology. Based on psychological principles, Abraham Maslow developed a model known as the "hierarchy of human needs." This model is a concept understood by most marketing students because of how needs relate to marketing and branding. "Maslow (1943) stated that people are motivated to achieve certain needs. When one need is fulfilled a person seeks to fulfill the next one, and so on" (McLeod, 2007, p. 1). A person cannot move onto the next level of need until the first one is achieved. For example, brands create products to meet the needs of people in different cultures. Adding vitamins to flour in the Indian culture is an example. Women and children are iron deficient in India, a situation that prompted Unilever to develop a product to meet this need. Similarly, brands will adjust the size of the packaging to make their products more affordable in certain markets. Brands need to be aware of the needs of consumers.

The original Maslow model included five basic levels of motivational needs. These levels were visualized as a pyramid. The first level is biological and physiological needs, which include air, food, warmth, sleep, shelter, drink, and sex. Once people acquire these basic needs, they can move onto the

second level—safety needs. "At once other (and 'higher') needs emerge and these, rather than physiological hungers, dominate the organism. And when these in turn are satisfied, again new (and still 'higher') needs emerge and so on" (McLeod, 2007, p. 2). At the second level, people need to feel as if they are in a safe environment. This point deals with protection from the elements, security, law, and order—in essence, having a stable life. Third is the need for love and belonging. People need to feel as if they are a part of a group or community. This level includes friendship, intimacy, love, romance, and family. The next stage is esteem needs, which include achievement, status, prestige, and independence. Products that cater to luxury needs such as expensive cars, designer clothing, and lavish hotels fit this level. Finally, the highest level is self-actualization. This stage relates to the ideas of personal growth and discovery—that is, finding meaning in life.

Maslow (1943) states: "What a man *can* be, he *must* be. This need we may call self-actualization" (p. 378). People need to try to achieve their potential. However, Maslow contends that people cannot reach this state unless they have met the previous level of needs. For instance, it is difficult to travel when you do not have a home or money. Self-actualization is the highest level in Maslow's model, and all other levels must be achieved before this one can be reached.

The original model of five stages has been expanded to seven- and eight-stage ones. The expanded versions include cognitive, aesthetic, and transcendence needs. Two levels—cognitive needs and aesthetic needs—are added between esteem needs and self-actualization. Cognitive needs include knowledge and meaning. By comparison, aesthetic needs focus on the search for beauty and a desire for form and balance. Finally, an eighth level is added after self-actualization. This is called transcendence needs. Unlike the other levels, transcendence is about helping others to achieve their own self-actualization. Once individuals achieve self-actualization, they then move on to help others reach the same state.

Being aware of Maslow's needs hierarchy can help to locate a target audience. For instance, luxury products appeal to people on the self-esteem level of the model. In contrast, home security systems would interest individuals at the safety point. Knowing your target audience is essential to creating the voice of the branded message. The voice is important in establishing brand identity and the personality for the product or service. For instance, Geico car insurance speaks in a humorous voice, which creates a likable personality for the brand. Needs are an important concept to be dealt with in later chapters

that discuss emotional and relationship branding. Brands can create their own community of users and loyal customers, which is based on the idea of needs. Some of the most successful brands, including Apple, Nike, and Tide, have created loyal customer followings.

Creating the Brand

Designing a brand strategy requires creative thinking. Creativity is a process that can be developed and applied to the branding method. A number of different marketing professions have developed procedures to ensure that branding is successful. For instance, Patrick Hanlon (2006) describes a seven-step plan to design a branded identity for a product or service.

His approach is called primal branding. Hanlon (2006) states: "Primal branding is about delivering the primal code. It is a construct of seven assets that help manage the intangibles of your brand" (p. 6). The seven components are (1) the creation story, (2) the creed, (3) the icons, (4) the rituals, (5) the pagans, (6) the sacred words, and (7) the leader. Underlying this approach is the concept that brands are belief systems: "When you are able to create brands that people believe in, you also create groups of people who feel that they belong" (p. 7).

Before embarking on the seven steps of primal branding, it is important to "determine where your brand exists in the minds of consumers" (Hanlon, 2006, p. 215). To do this, you need to examine a company itself, its personality, its products or services, and its industry. After examining the company's characteristics, ask whether the company has a creation story. Brands that have creation stories are often more established than their competitors. For example, the Ford Motor Company traces back to the inventor Henry Ford. Similarly, most people know that the birth of Apple Computer took place in a garage in California. Additionally, many consumers are familiar with Dave Thomas's founding of the Wendy's restaurant chain. These are three brands that are well established in American culture, along with their creation stories. The creation story can be compared to a family photo album. People want to know about their family backgrounds and heritage.

Creed is the second stage. It is based on the mission statement. Companies need to clearly define their purpose and approach to achieving their goals. Stated another way, what does the company believe in? Is it selling the best coffee in town, providing the best service, or promising lower prices? For

instance, Progressive Insurance, with its Flo personality, promises lower prices than most other insurance companies. Similarly, Geico assures people of a good price. In contrast, State Farm emphasizes its excellent service. The voice of its advertisements implies that the service will be friendly and quick. (Once this type of promise is made, the company needs to fulfill the promise. In this case, State Farm needs to hire people with friendly personalities to support their image.) Other creeds include making the most reliable product, making a safe product, and being an environmentally conscious corporation. In companies such as UPS, the creed is part of their daily activities. The creed needs to be broken down into a brief statement that can be used in the advertising of the product or service. This is essential to a good brand strategy.

The next step is the icon. This can derive from a physical location, a person, a city, an activity, or a concept. An example of a concept icon is the Nike swoosh. Another is the use of an image of a shell to represent the Shell Oil Company. The use of a seashell as a logo is a rebus—that is, the use of an image that sounds like the letter or word. Similarly, Apple Computer uses the image of an apple as its icon. In contrast, the Prudential Life Insurance Company uses an image of the Rock of Gibraltar, which over the years has become an abstract logo. Marlboro cigarettes has an iconic cowboy image, and Camel cigarettes created the character Joe Camel. Moreover, a number of different images have been used to represent Betty Crocker over the years. These iconic images have become synonymous with the names of the companies they represent. When we see the image, we think of the brand.

The fourth step is ritual. It encompasses "actions that involve how the product is used, how the service is engaged, where and how the consumer goes to shop, and how the product is maintained, returned, renewed, downloaded or updated" (Hanlon, 2006, p. 223). Examining how people become involved with a product or service can be key to understanding the ritual—for example, driving in the car, going to the store, seeing a store greeter or salesperson, walking through the store, going to the checkout, or driving home in the car. An example would be driving to work, stopping at Starbucks to get a cup of coffee, and then arriving at the workplace. This activity requires the Starbucks store to be in a convenient location. For packaged goods, looking at how your brand stands out on the shelf would be part of a person's ritual. Considering how difficult or easy it is to acquire the product or service is also important to this process. For a supermarket product, the company would want to understand the ritual of shopping at supermarkets—including, for instance, using a shopping list. The ritual experience should be a positive one for the brand.

Pagans are next. This is the group of nonbelievers or people who do not generally use your product. One way to identify this group is by looking at your competition. For example, have you ever noticed that some restaurants only serve Pepsi or Coke? There are people who only purchase one or the other of these soft drinks. Several television commercials have been made about Coke and Pepsi preferences. Of course, most companies would like to lure customers away from their competition. Being aware of how your branding could sway the pagans is another step in the branding process.

Some advertisements create phrases or words that become part of popular culture. Most people know the phrase "Can you hear me now?" or "Wassup?" These have become phrases that are easy to search on Google and in some cases have been transformed into user-generated content (see Chapter 10). Hanlon (2006) calls these "sacred words." These are words that resonate with consumers. Copywriters, product managers, and scriptwriters try to smash words together to create original, attention-getting phrases. It has been years since Burger King advertisements asked "Where's the beef?" Nonetheless, the phrase is still used by individuals today.

The final stage is the leader. In some television campaigns, the founder, President, CEO, or leader of a company will be featured in the commercial. We know the names of some leaders of companies, such as Steven Jobs, Bill Gates, Martha Stewart, and Richard Branson. Companies should include these leaders—who are sometimes important figures—in creating a brand. Moreover, the unique qualities of the leaders can become the distinctive features of the brand. Leaders can also help to make people feel as if they belong, an idea conducive to brand loyalty.

Hanlon (2006) says: "the failure of brands to gain real emotive power is due to the fact they have relied on only one or two components of the primal code to communicate their brand message" (p. 210). For a brand to be successful, the many facets associated with the product or service need to be considered. No stone should be left unturned.

Creative Documents

In an attempt to understand as many aspects as possible about a product, most major advertising agencies create a document that outlines background information about the product or service. These are often called a *creative strategy*

or *creative brief*. The document is the thinking behind the advertisement. It clearly states the many aspects of the brand mentioned in the previous section.

Felton (2006) contends that a creative brief requires answers to three basic questions:

What benefit are you promising, what's your selling argument?
Who are you making it to?
Why should they believe you? (p. 58)

The answer to these questions should fit into a sentence or two. For example, "The branding should be directed toward Women 25–54 [Who] with sophisticated taste and persuade them to purchase Butterfly perfume because the scent is distinctive and pleasing [What]." Lending support will be the credentials of the perfumer who created the scent, and these credentials will also help to create the brand's personality [Why]. In this case, the leader is the perfume designer, and his or her real or romanticized personality could be used in advertising the product. For instance, many perfumes are named or designed by celebrities, such as Liz Taylor's White Diamonds.

In a creative advertising strategy, the components are the key facts, advertising promise, advertising objective, target consumer, competition, key consumer benefit, and support. All of these concepts relate to the brand identity, because distinguishing the brand needs to be done before an advertisement can be created. All forms of messages relating to the brand need to be consistent with its core message. New to this list is the idea of examining the competition. A prime reason for doing this is to make sure that your branding is not the same as the competition's. It is important for a brand to understand its position in the marketplace as compared to the opposition. This will help to make the branded message unique and distinguish it in the eyes of consumers.

Another approach to creating branded messages is suggested by Mike Moser (2003) in his description of the "brand roadmap." The name was originally created for work with a car company. Another name could be a brand blueprint. Moser (2003) says that "people intuitively understand the concept of what a roadmap does and when to use it" (p. 3). As a result, he coined the term brand roadmap.

A brand roadmap includes five sections: core values, brand message, brand personality, brand icons, and a synopsis. Understanding the core values of a company is essential for branding success. These are values that a company must adhere to no matter what happens. In times of product crisis, these values

are what is going to keep the brand from disappearing. A classic example of how this works is the story of Tylenol, and how Johnson & Johnson, its manufacturer, dealt with a difficult situation.

In 1982, an unknown person contaminated packages of Extra-Strength Tylenol capsules with cyanide (see Levine, 2003). The capsules where placed back in the packages and put on the shelves of a number of stores in Chicago. Unfortunately, seven people purchased the corrupt packages and died. Police began using bullhorns to warn the public of the danger. All of the news networks and local news programs were telling people not to use Tylenol.

Prior to this event, Johnson & Johnson's brand was considered one of the most trusted pain remedies on the market. Now its reputation was tainted. With a core brand under attack, the company had to act fast. "First, the company made sure consumers knew it was more concerned with their safety than its own profits" (Levine, 2003, p. 158). The company recalled approximately 31 million bottles of Tylenol at a value of over $100 million. Production and advertising of the brand stopped until the source of the tampering could be determined. The media immediately announced the recall, and analysts commended the company for doing the right thing.

The only product tampered with was Tylenol capsules, not the tablets. Johnson & Johnson then offered to exchange any capsules for the tablets, which were considered safe. However, the strategy that saved the brand derived from the tampering itself. Tylenol became the first brand to invent tamper-proof packaging. Four months after the murders, the company released its new packaging, which became the industry standard.

Johnson & Johnson was able to turn a potential brand-ruining event into one that kept the brand a major name in the marketplace. By emphasizing the safety of consumers rather than profits, and by introducing the tamper-proof package, the Tylenol brand became a hero in the eyes of its customers. In a very short time the brand was again a trusted medicine in the marketplace.

The public relations messages created by Johnson & Johnson supported the brand message: Tylenol is a reliable headache remedy. The brand message is the central communication that a company will send to all of its audiences. "The more closely your core message reflects the reality of your brand and why it exists, the more effective your brand message will be" (Moser, 2003, p. 37). It is vitally important for the message to reflect the reality of the product or service.

In crafting the brand message, a number of items need to be considered. First, is the message simple and clear? AT&T's slogan "reach out and touch someone" is a perfect example of this idea. The word "touch" is used here as

an emotional feeling rather than a physical stroke. Second, it needs to differentiate the brand in the marketplace. The Kentucky Fried Chicken tag line, "Finger-lickin' good," implies that this fast food is so good that you want to lick your fingers. Generally, people do not think about licking their fingers after eating a hamburger, but they do after eating fried chicken. Third, the statement should be true. A telephone metaphorically enables people to reach out and touch someone. People often eat fried chicken with their hands and lick their fingers afterward. Both of these slogans are based on real actions. Fourth, the message needs to be relevant. AT&T's slogan reminds us that we need to stay in touch with family and friends. The company's products and services can help us to do that. Fifth, the message needs to match the core brand values of the company. AT&T's slogan implies reliability. Whenever individuals have a desire to communicate with others, the service should be available. Consequently, service is a core brand value that AT&T needs to deliver. Finally, be the first to express the message. For example, messages such as "We Try Harder" and "Just Do It" are extremely memorable. Avis and Nike were the first to use them. Later on, they spread into the culture. (More examples of slogans can be found at the Advertising Slogan Hall of Fame [http://www.adslogans.co.uk/hof/].)

These sayings communicate a brand personality (a concept described in Chapter 1). Is the product or service serious or whimsical? Delineating the personality determines the tone and attitude of the brand message. A brand personality should be an accurate depiction of the company—in other words, the personality needs to be a reflection of core ideals. For instance, Tylenol as a brand expresses concern for its customers. Therefore, developing a humorous advertising campaign would seem out of place. Instead, customer testimonials about how the product performs would work better with its personality.

To discover the brand personality, list the traits of the personality and compare them to your core values. Do they match? The Nike personality of "Just Do It" is almost a command. It reflects more aggression, something that is associated with winning, which fits with a sports personality. In contrast, "We Try Harder" is almost an apology. It is a personality that acknowledges that the company is not number one in the marketplace. Therefore, it needs to work harder to move into first place.

Some of the considerations for the brand personality involve comparing the brand to human traits. For instance, does the brand have a gender? How old is the brand? Is it upscale or blue-collar? Is it a local, national, or global brand? Lists of human personality traits should be examined when creating

a brand personality. Further, personalities do not always have to be nice. "If you are a brand that talks to skateboarders, snowboarders, or surfers, traits like *opinionated, antiestablishment, aggressive*, and *loud* could be appropriate for your brand personality" (Moser, 2003, p. 81). Moreover, the personality that is created should forge a connection with its target audience. Remember that the personality traits need to communicate the values of your company to the consumer. For instance, a sales company would want to create an image that is personable rather than one that is tenacious.

Some brand personalities become iconic in their culture. Think about Mr. Clean, the Energizer Bunny, or Tony the Tiger. These personalities have moved beyond the brand to become cultural symbols. (Brand icons will be discussed further in Chapter 9.) Moser (2003) uses the term "icon" in a specific way. He states that a brand icon should be "anything that is unique to your brand and that brings up an image of your brand in the customer's mind" (p. 91). For instance, the graphic of an apple reminds people of Apple Computer.

Many icons are visual. The logos of brands can make associations with the company that produces the product or service. Examples are the logos of fashion designers that are placed on clothing. At times these visual signs become part of the product design. Logos embossed in fabric are a clear fashion statement. People pay extra money to be associated with different fashion designers.

Visual elements such as layout, typeface, and graphics can be used to identify a company. For instance, Target stores have a very distinctive visual look and feel. Generally, you can tell a Target television commercial before the logo is revealed. Moreover, the red Target bullet logo is highly recognizable without the name. Thus, the visual appearance of the creative branding effort is as important as the message that is communicated.

Creative documents help to direct the overall strategy for designing a brand. These documents help to keep the communication message consistent with the values of the product and the company that makes it. All successful branding efforts are based on unique features and characteristics of the product or service. The creative challenge is to uncover the uniqueness.

Summary

A number of different methods for formulating a brand strategy have been discussed in this chapter. However, these are just a few of the many approaches used by companies and advertising agencies. Creativity is a skill that requires

both intuition and logic. By examining a product or service from different perspectives, its unique characteristics can be revealed and a memorable brand created. This process requires both research and creativity.

The creative process has a logical side. When developing a brand identity, the core values of the company need to be considered along with the brand's message and personality. All of these must relate back to the product or service itself and the company. All creative messages need to be grounded in reality and based on the actual product and the company's values.

Exercises

1. Create your own brand roadmap or creative strategy document for designing a brand. Why do you feel these elements are the most important contributions to a brand's identity?
2. Locate a nonprofit agency in your area, such as the Salvation Army or an animal shelter. Design a branding strategy for that organization.
3. Describe the personalities of the following slogans: "The quicker picker-upper," "A little dab'll do ya," and "Have it your way."
4. Pick a brand. Go to its website. Use the website to analyze the brand's core values, brand message, and personality. Finally, answer the question: Is the brand local, national, or international? Why or why not?

References

DeBono, E. (1969). *The mechanism of mind*. New York: Penguin.

DeBono, E. (1995). Serious creativity. *Journal for Quality and Participation, 18*(5), 12–18.

DeBono, E. (1999). *Six thinking hats*. New York: Little, Brown.

Dorset, K., & Cross, N. (2001). Creativity in the design process: Co-evolution of problem–solution. *Design Studies, 22*(5), 425–437.

Felton, G. (2006). *Advertising concept and copy* (2nd ed.). Englewood Cliffs, NJ: Prentice Hall.

Gardner, H. (1993). *Creating minds*. New York: Basic Books.

Gill, B. (1981). *Forget all the rules about graphic design: Including the ones in this book*. New York: Watson-Guptill.

Glaser, M. (1973). *Milton Glaser graphic design*. Woodstock, NY: Overlook Press. Glaser, M. (1985). I listen to the market. In M. Blonsky (Ed.), *On signs*. Baltimore, MD: The Johns Hopkins University Press.

Hanlon, P. (2006). *Primal branding*. New York: Free Press.

Levine, M. (2003). *A branded world*. Hoboken, NJ: John Wiley & Sons.

Maslow, A.H. (1943). A theory of human motivation. *Psychological Review, 50*(4), 370–396.

McLeod, S.A. (2007). *Maslow's hierarchy of needs*. Retrieved April 26, 2015, from http://www. simplypsychology.org/maslow.html

Moser, M. (2003). *United we brand*. Boston, MA: Harvard Business School.

Ogilvy, D. (1983). *Ogilvy on advertising*. New York: Crown.

Rand, P. (1985). *Paul Rand: A designer's art*. New Haven, CT: Yale University Press.

Ries, A., & Trout, J. (2001). *Positioning: The battle for your mind*. New York: McGraw-Hill.

Tantillo, J. (2010). *People buy brands not companies*. New York: Five Titles Press.

· 5 ·

BRANDING AND THE MIND

To be effective, propaganda must constantly short-circuit all thought and decision. It must operate on the individual at the level of the unconscious.
—Jacques Ellul, 1973, p. 27

This chapter takes concepts from cognitive science and describes how marketers apply these ideas to marketing, advertising, and consumers. By examining how the brain works, we can better understand how brands stay in the forefront of the consumer's mind. Are we really in control of the brands we like? This chapter examines the unconscious motivations that cause people to act, noting that the intricate workings of the brain can influence our buying decisions and how we perceive a brand.

The idea of unconscious branding is not new. Many people are familiar with the concept of subliminal advertising, or the distribution of advertising messages below the threshold of consciousness. "Consciousness is the mental activity in our state of being preoccupied with external reality" (Fromm, 1951, p. 29). With subliminal advertising, the technique is to display brand images and messages for a brief moment in a film or television program. The clip is so short that the conscious mind does not detect it. However, the subconscious mind does.

Fromm (1951) defines the unconscious as "the mental experience in a state of existence in which we have shut off communication with the outer

world, are no longer preoccupied with action but with our self experience" (p. 29). Subliminal advertising creates a response in the unconscious mind to suggest an action, such as drinking cola. The person then goes out and buys a soft drink without realizing why. In a conscious state, we are aware of our decisions. Moreover, we can remember these decisions more clearly when they come from the conscious mind, because we are aware of our thoughts. However, we are not attuned to subconscious influences.

The concept of subliminal adverting holds that movie clips saying drink, eat, and showing cola can be spliced into a movie. These are one-second images that are not consciously understood. As a result of these subliminal messages, people will go to the concession stand for more drinks and popcorn. The concept of subliminal advertising originally ignited widespread public outrage and led to a ban on subliminal cuts in the United States. People sought legislation to make sure that this type of corporate mind control could not be used.

The experiment with subliminal advertising was a hoax. However, the legend lives on. Today people are still concerned about hidden messages in advertisements. There are occasionally rumors that the dot patterns in a photograph spell some hidden word. On the contrary, this is also a hoax. Individuals are afraid of mind control by organizations, and this fuels the rumors about subliminal advertising. People like to think that their conscious mind is in control of their actions and decisions. Consequently, purchasing behavior is a conscious preference. In fact, science has shown that the opposite is true.

Many brain processes occur automatically without any conscious awareness. Think about driving a car. Are individuals always thinking about placing their foot on the gas pedal? Do they think that their hands have to be on the steering wheel? Do they stop to think about applying the brake when they see a deer? Or is all of this automatic? In the past 50 years, cognitive researchers have identified different ways in which the mind thinks.

States of Mind

In the past, researchers believed that language was the primary form of thinking. In contrast, Howard Gardner (1983) researched different ways in which the mind works. His finding that there are a number of different ways of thinking prompted him to develop the theory of multiple intelligences. This theory describes a modular view of the human mind wherein it is composed of separate organs or information-processing centers. In his book *The Frames of*

Mind, Gardner argued for the existence of seven separate human intelligences. These include linguistics, logical-mathematical, musical, bodily-kinesthetic, spatial, interpersonal, and intrapersonal. The spatial intelligence is the one that understands visual imagery.

Gardner (1999) defines intelligence as "the ability to solve problems or to create products that are valued within one or more cultural setting" (p. 33). The theory of multiple intelligences is based on accumulating knowledge about the human brain and culture. Its goal is to conceptualize the cognitive aspects of the human mind as numerous distinct semi-independent intelligences. These intelligences work together to allow people to develop their intellectual and social skills. People decide how they are going to use these different intelligences, and individuals use them in different ways.

In addition to intelligence, researchers recognize that brains know more than our minds can report. Unconscious memories that lie deep within our brains can prime our minds to be receptive to brands and their messages. For example, the option of Coke versus Pepsi can stimulate a feeling in the brain. This can happen when a person with a Coke preference is told that the restaurant only serves Pepsi. One might think that Pepsi does not taste as good as Coke. Or a person may have iced tea instead. Our feelings influence our attitudes. Both visual and verbal symbols can create thoughts in an individual.

An important aspect of multiple intelligence theory and branding is the recognition that knowledge acquisition and representation use a variety of intelligences, and that all symbolic forms of representation are equally important. Symbolic forms are systems of knowledge, perception, and experience, including myth, arts, sciences, history, and religion. From the point of view of multiple intelligences, our minds use different symbol systems to make meaning of the world. Different cultures have preferences for different types of symbol systems. For example, American culture has a preference for the visual (television, Internet, films). For this reason, branding has been able to dominate American culture through logos and trademarks.

Visual Intelligence

Visual symbols are embedded in American culture. Billboards, signs, television, and the Internet are all filled with branded images. Van Praet (2012) states: "Great brands are symbols, not signs. They must stand for something

more than the product itself" (p. 159). While our ancestors used symbolic ornamentations—for example, jewelry and tattoos—these artifacts represented affiliations with certain groups and a person's social status. In contemporary culture, brands are new symbols of adornment. For instance, Nike, Apple, Starbucks, and Chanel transcend being simply products to providing emotional feelings for their customers. Similar to our ancestors, brands can also indicate affiliation and social status. Symbols are integral to our cultural awareness and cognitive understanding.

The cognitive revolution began in the 1950s when psychologists, linguists, philosophers, and anthropologists came together to examine symbolic activities and how people make meaning of their world through the use of symbols. It should be noted that this was also the point in American culture when television was entering many homes. Visually, the culture was changing. Building on cognitive science research, neurophysiologist Donald D. Hoffman (1998) argued for the existence of a visual intelligence. He stated: "Just as we enjoy rich literature that stimulates our rational intelligence, or a moving story that engages our emotional intelligence, so also we seek out and enjoy visual media that challenge our visual intelligence" (p. xii). Advertisers know how visual imagery influences people; however, individuals are not always aware of its impact.

Similarly, Ann Marie Seward Barry (1997) argued for the existence of a visual intelligence. She defined it *"as a quality of mind developed to the point of critical perceptual awareness in visual communication. It implies not only the skilled use of visual reasoning to read and to communicate, but also holistic integration of skilled verbal and visual reasoning, from an understanding of how the elements that compose meaning in images can be manipulated to distort reality, to the utilization of the visual in abstract thought"* (p. 6; emphasis in original).

Visual images are understood without filtering through the conscious mind. It is argued that 90% of our brain's activity never reaches consciousness (see Van Praet, 2012). For instance, the brain identifies visual scenes from a movie as though they were real life. However, our conscious mind tells us which is which. In 3-D films, when an object comes out of the screen, people will often move to avoid the thing, which of course is not really there. Using visual images in branding can create a coherent branded message. An example is the shape of the Absolut Vodka bottle (Lewis, 1996). No matter how creatively the advertising incorporated the shape of the bottle, the branding could always be recognized. For instance, Absolut Artists displays the bottle as

artwork created by Warhol, Haring, and Scharf (see Lewis, p. 208). Similarly, the bottle was covered in wildflowers for Absolut Spring (see p. 209), and the shape became a swimming pool in Absolut L.A. A Google search reveals the wide variety of Absolut Vodka images.

Another example is the Coca-Cola bottle, which is now 100 years old. To celebrate the brand's bottle, Coca-Cola has created fifteen new television commercials for broadcast and YouTube (see Beltrone, 2015c). In addition, the High Museum of Art in Atlanta has created an exhibit called "The Coca-Cola Bottle: An American Icon at 100." Branding icons are very much a part of American culture, as illustrated by the bottle exhibit. Bottles, logos, and visual branded information are popular visuals in contemporary society. Moreover, many people prefer visual infographics to reading text.

A recent article in *AdWeek* using research compiled by NeoMam Studios listed a number of reasons why the brain craves infographics or information combined with graphics (Maskeroni, 2015). First, it is argued that 70% of sensory receptors are in our eyes—"or that it takes only 150 milliseconds to process a symbol and 100 milliseconds to attach a meaning to it" (p. 1). The article contends that we are becoming much more of a visual society because people are visually wired. In today's environment of information overload, information needs to be understood quickly. Visual infographics are more accessible to people because color visuals increase the desire to read, and labels with text and pictures are better understood. People follow directions with text and graphics 323% better than with text alone. Audiences are more easily persuaded by presentations that include visuals, and people remember more information when they see it.

An example of a visual brand that has been recognized as a graphic is the Arby's hat logo. During the Grammy Awards, Daft Punk received the Album of the Year award. One member of the group, Pharrell Williams, was wearing a hat that had a similar shape to the one in the Arby's logo. The sandwich chain posted the following message on Twitter: "Hey @Pharrell, can we have our hat back?" Pharrell sent a message back saying, "Y'all tryna start a roast beef?" (see Griner, 2014). This was a responsive marketing tactic that related to a celebrity's antic. Getting a response from the celebrity is a marketer's dream come true, because it brings attention to the brand and associates the celebrity with it. As described, visual branding can capture the consumer's attention. This occurs on both the conscious and subconscious levels.

Two Minds

Goleman (1995) argues that our mental life has two fundamentally different ways of interacting. "One, the rational mind, is the mode of comprehension we are typically conscious of: more prominent in awareness, thoughtful, able to ponder and reflect" (p. 8). Alongside this rational mind is an emotional one. The emotions are sometimes illogical and very impulsive and powerful. The differences between the emotional/rational minds are the distinctions between "heart" and "head." When making decisions, some people will say to follow your "heart" and not your "head." This means that emotional choices can be more positive in one's life than decisions made strictly based on logic.

Van Praet (2012) stated that "Brands are like people. The value you assign to someone is based largely on how the individual makes you feel" (p. 15). Our emotions influence our preferences, satisfaction, and loyalty. This determines which product we pick off the shelf. Brands are learned behaviors established through actual experience. For instance, when Coke tried to change the color of its cola to colorless instead of brown, consumers objected because the clear cola did not seem like Coke. The color of the cola was deeply embedded into the cola drinking experience. This is an example of emotion taking charge over logic. Moreover, it is the emotional and intuitive mind that drives most behavior.

The emotional mind has developed from the primal reptilian mind, the oldest and smallest remnant from our primitive past. As mentioned in the Introduction, this part of our mind creates an associative rather than a logical method of thinking. Our minds were developed to solve the dilemmas of a hunter-gatherer society, not the problems of modern-day consumers. These issues related to evolutionary needs, such as those described by Maslow (1943) in the previous chapter.

Biologically, the emotional centers of our brain emerged from its most primitive parts. In other words, we were emotional before we became logical. "The physical brain is the domain of our natural instincts, our deepest ancestral memories that guide fundamental life functions, including many of our automatic behaviors" (Van Praet, 2012, p. 58). These behaviors include breathing, circulation, digestion, sleeping, eating, foraging, and hoarding food. Because of the need for survival and nourishment, marketing phrases such as "Got Milk?" or "Where's the Beef?" become popular cultural slogans.

The root of our emotional life lies in the sense of smell. Smell helps us to find food and identify mates. In addition, research has shown that signals from the eyes and ears travel first to the thalamus in the brain and then to the amygdala (an unconscious part of the brain). In addition, a second signal is routed from the thalamus to the neocortex—the thinking mind. The amygdala scans every experience for trouble. It is similar to an alarm system because it is ready to send out warning signals to every major part of the brain. The amygdala also helps impulsive feelings override rational thought. Moreover, it can "receive some direct inputs from the senses and start a response *before* they are fully registered by the neocortex" (Goleman, 1995, p. 18).

In other words, information sent to the amygdala can be acted on before it becomes conscious thought. From a marketing perspective, consumers can react to products and services on a subconscious level that is not always fully understood by the rational mind. Stated another way, "our emotions have a mind of their own, one which can hold views quite independent of our rational mind" (Goleman, 1995, p. 20). Thus, "When the mind accepts a brand story as told in advertising and marketing communications, it is both believing the story's rational tenets and bonding to its emotional meaning" (Van Praet, 2012, p. 9). Further, it has been observed that advertising campaigns with primarily emotional content outperform ones that feature rational appeals.

Measuring Unawareness

It is the unconscious part of the brain that drives marketing behavior. Generally, when researchers investigate brand affinity and loyalty, they study the conscious relationship of the consumer to the brand. However, Van Praet (2012) argued that "self-reported data in market research surveys simply can't measure the implicit, nondeclarative memories that unconsciously prime our brain's receptivity to brands and messages" (p. 7). For example, when a person is offered a Snickers bar or Reese's Pieces, personal memories and cultural associations are activated in the brain. The choice between the two candies will be unconsciously influenced.

The new discipline of neuromarketing studies consumer responses to marketing stimuli through, for example, the EEG (electroencephalogram), brain sensors, MRI imaging, and galvanic skin response. The latter measures stress responses through changes in skin moisture. The process is described below:

[Participants]wear an EEG cap and view the commercials on the SensorMotoric Instruments (SMI) eye-tracking system. This allows Sands [Research] to record each viewer's non-verbal brain response on a millisecond by millisecond basis and sync exactly where and at what level their attention is at that millisecond. (Reuters, 2011, p. 1)

The purpose of this research is to narrow the gap between what people "say" and what they "do." It delivers insight into the unconscious mind. For instance, neuromarketing discovered that information is more successfully received from advertisements when images are placed on the left and copy on the right.

An example of neuromarketing occurred with the Silk Cut brand of cigarettes. Prior to the ban on cigarette advertising in the United Kingdom, Silk Cut began to run its logo against a background of purple silk. This image appeared in all of its advertisements. Following the ban on showing cigarette logos in advertising, Silk Cut began running ads with just the purple silk. Consumers had made the association between the logo and fabric and, as a result, people were aware of the brand just by seeing the silk. The logo was unnecessary. This strategy created an awareness of the brand through the association of the silk. The silk metaphor worked as a substitute for the logo.

Metaphors and Research

Metaphors—that is, describing something in terms of something else—are often utilized in advertising and branding. "By identifying the deeper meaning behind brands and ads, by mining for these unconscious metaphors through projective techniques like pictures sorts and storytelling, marketers can consciously create ads directly aimed at these otherwise hidden drivers" (Van Praet, 2012, p. 72). A popular technique for uncovering these metaphors is the Zaltman Metaphor Elicitation Technique. This is a research tool that uses visual and sensory images to help better understand the meaning of brands (Coulter & Zaltman, 1994, p. 501). Coulter and Zaltman (1994) describe it in the following way:

Briefly, the Zaltman Metaphor Elicitation Technique (ZMET) employs qualitative methods to elicit the metaphors, constructs and mental models that drive customers' thinking and behavior, as well as quantitative analyses to provide data for marketing mix decisions and segmentation strategies. The Kelly Repertory grid and laddering techniques are integral components of the technique, as are visual (e.g., photographs) and other sensory images that consumers provide. The constructs elicited during the

interviews are aggregated to produce a consensus map, which represents most of the thinking of most people most of the time. In addition, consumers use digital imaging techniques to produce summary images of their thinking. (p. 501)

ZMET is based on the premise that the larger part of human communication, or 93%, is nonverbal, and only 7% is contained in language (Mehrabian, 1971). Coulter and Zaltman argue that through the use of metaphors, marketers can better understand the thinking and behavior of consumers. The idea of metaphor is illustrated by Shakespeare's analogy that "all the world's a stage." Moreover, brand recognition is often visual, and pictures can be viewed as metaphors. "Pictures typically represent basic concepts, which contain extensive information or defining attributes, and people usually recognize such concepts first. After customers recognize basic concepts, then they can infer or identify associated higher-order concepts" (p. 502). In-depth interviews can reveal these consumer thoughts.

By using the ZMET method in personal, in-depth interviews, researchers are able to uncover both the participants' spoken and allusive thoughts and feelings, making this technique reliable. This is especially so when it comes to interpretation, because it leaves little room for a researcher's subjectivity or false interpretation. Typically, the process involves 20–25 different interviews. With ZMET, the "informants, not researchers, supply the stimuli (i.e., visual images such as pictures or photographs) for the in-depth interview" (Coulter, Zaltman, & Coulter, 2001, p. 4).

Informants are better able to represent their thoughts and feelings because they control the stimuli. The power of this method is that it utilizes visual imagery instead of language to better understand brand awareness. Reasons for this include the fact that nonverbal communication is more prevalent than verbal communication, and visual pictures can be used as an entry point to engage discussion. This research documents the importance of visual communication in marketing. By using metaphor techniques and neuroscience studies, researchers can better understand how messages are communicated by brands.

Participation and Awareness

Neuroscience researchers have discovered that the adult brain is a dynamic organ. New brain cells are constantly created and retained. Participation in activities improves the chances of remembering details. "One key reason is

that the brain creates twice as many new brain cells and connections when interacting with enriched environments as it does when interacting with impoverished surroundings" (Walvis, 2010, p. 144). For this reason, participatory branding activities provide a more robust setting for customers.

The introduction of interactive digital media provides all types of new opportunities for companies to create participatory experiences for their customers. (Digital media's influence will be discussed in Chapter 10.) In terms of cognition, the mind is able to learn more and retain information when it is engaged in an activity. Participation can both personalize and extend brand awareness. For example, Lego developed an experience store in which clients could play with its products. It encouraged people to have fun with the brand, thus giving people the advantage of trying out the product before it was purchased. This provided customers with more control over their experiences with the brand.

People will participate in activities for a number of reasons. First, they engage because they have a desire to do it their way—for example, letting people customize products to their own personal taste. The slogan "Have it your way" illustrates this idea. Letting people decide what condiments they want on their hamburgers involves them in the design of the product.

Second, people participate to gain status and recognition. Brands can provide us with elements that can improve self-esteem. The Keds campaign described in Chapter 3 is an example. Keds asks girls to visit its website and features some of the customers themselves. This strategy creates a connection between the emotion of bravery and Keds shoes; further, it involves individual consumers in the advertising campaign.

Third, people like to have fun. Apple Computer has always branded its computers as more fun. Instead of using computers strictly for office work, Apple has encouraged purchasers to use them creatively. Thus, many artists, designers, and musicians have been attracted to the Apple platform. Moreover, Apple's advertising is often fun and playful, as in the campaign for the iPod with the dancing figures (see https://www.youtube.com/watch?v=mpM5nzSEyXE).

Fourth, people have a desire to connect and interact with others. Discussion lists, Facebook pages, and email lists enable brands to develop a stronger connection with their customers. For instance, Apple Computer's discussion lists have been very popular on the Internet. People use them as a method for sharing ideas and information about the machines. Apple also has its own people visit the lists to provide additional information.

Finally, people have a desire to contribute. Companies have set up Internet forums that encourage customers to contribute feedback about a product or service. Specifically, computer companies have even asked employees to join the group to generate discussions. When a customer participates with a product or service, it means that the product is relevant to the individual. "Customers do not participate just for participation's sake. The interaction itself must be rewarding but the brand has to have value to them as well" (Walvis, 2010, p. 155). For participation to work, it must be relevant to the consumer.

An unusual example of participation occurred in Sweden. When escalators broke down in the Swedish subway, Reebok was there to help give people a lift. The brand made a connection with exercise. "If you're looking for an unconventional workout, Reebok might suggest carrying a stranger up a flight of stairs, just so he or she doesn't have to walk" (Beltrone, 2015b, p. 1). The athletes who participated in this activity wore large Reebok logos on their clothing. People who were carried up the escalator will remember this brand for a long time because of the experience.

Disney Parks has created a live promotion in shopping malls. "A string of shoppers seeming to have a pretty great time when silhouettes of the company's classic cartoon characters start[ed] stalking and mimicking them from behind a backlit set of doors" (Beltrone, 2015a, p. 1). Disney characters are iconic in American culture as a result: they are highly identifiable in a silhouette form. Interacting with them created a fun experience for the shoppers. People can recognize branded icons from their shape. As stated in Chapter 1, Gestalt theory agues that visual perception is the result of organizing visual elements or shapes into groups. People tend to remember the shapes of iconic brands.

Pattern Recognition

Marketers can gain the attention of consumers when they change or interrupt patterns. "If we want to get attention and shift people's behavioral patterns, we need to interrupt their perceptual patterns by doing something interesting and different" (Van Praet, 2012, pp. 89–90). Both of the events described above gained people's attention because they were different and pleasurable. Another pleasurable event is the Super Bowl, with its humorous and interesting commercials.

One Super Bowl ad that gained tremendous emotional appeal was the Volkswagen Darth Vader commercial called "The Force." An adorable child who is attempting to evoke the power of the force plays Darth Vader. As he points toward the car, Dad presses the remote starter from the house. The child is surprised, as the force appears to be working. This commercial breaks with traditional patterns because Darth Vader is an evil villain, but a cute child plays him. When the commercial was analyzed using EEG equipment, there was a "prominent spike in engagement and emotion as dad remotely fires up…not only the car, but also the brains of those watching" (Van Praet, 2012, p. 96). The results were compiled using "a national sample of study participants to measure overall engagement and emotional response to the annual advertising event" (Reuters, 2011, p. 1). The neuro-rankings of the 2012 Super Bowl ads can be found online at http://www.neurosciencemarketing.com/blog/articles/2012-super-bowl-ad-rankings.htm. Positive emotional reactions to a brand support the person's belief system.

Belief Systems

What we believe is often determined by our past experiences. Van Praet (2012) describes three categories in which to place our dimensions of experience or decisions. This is important for marketers, because knowing how people make decisions can help to create advertising that influences decision making. First, people experience their physical bodies. Getting consumers to physically act will help them to relate better to a brand. For this reason, participation marketing makes people more aware of products and their messages.

Second, people's beliefs are influenced by their emotions and feelings of the heart. Damasio (1994) contends that the universal emotions are happiness, sadness, anger, fear, and disgust. "When we have feelings connected with emotions, attention is allocated substantially to body signals, and parts of the body landscape move from the background to the foreground of our attention" (p. 149). For instance, when a couple selects a song as "their song," every time the song is played each person will think of the other. A similar association can be made with a product. For example, aftershaves and perfumes are often associated with specific people who wear the product. If your father wore Old Spice, every time you encounter the smell, you may think of him.

Finally, belief systems are influenced by logical rationalizations that we make in our minds. For instance, an individual can decide that he or she likes the creations of a particular designer. As a result, that person will buy and wear the designer's clothes. It is a smart marketing approach to know how your customer will experience the product or service. How does the product fit into the full range of human existence? Is it a price-conscious item or a status piece?

Primal triggers can drive consumers into action. Our deepest unconscious biological desires are important to survival needs. These drives are called the Six S's: "survival, safety, security, sustenance, sex, and status" (Van Praet, 2012, p. 68). Notice how these desires can be related to Maslow's hierarchy of needs described in the previous chapter. Emotions and desires can be very important in the branding process. "Brands lose relevance when they fail to connect emotionally with people, and without that emotional attachment they can be easily replaced with generic imposters" (Van Praet, 2012, p. 84). The combination of belief system and storytelling, described in the previous chapter, can be powerful branding techniques. These help to place the product in the consumer's conscious mind.

Mental Distractors

Both reinforcing and unsettling techniques can be used to heighten an individual's awareness. Disrupting patterns is one method for gaining a consumer's attention: "confusion not only facilitates behavior change, it is often necessary to the process of learning" (Van Praet, 2012, p. 108). Feeling confused or curious can lead to the understanding of new perspectives. Cognitive research reveals that decision making is influenced by people's feelings. To change brand perceptions, the person often needs to be made to feel perplexed.

However, the new associations need to be positive. Negative impressions can result in the opposite of the desired effect. The experience of Quiznos restaurants provides an example of a negative association. The company created a commercial that featured furry, rat-like characters. The animals sang around a sandwich and praised the food. Unfortunately, people do not like the linking of food and rats. As a result, instead of inspiring people to buy sandwiches, the ad had a negative effect. This is the exact opposite of the consumer response to the Darth Vader advertisement described earlier: people have good feelings about adorable children, but the reverse is true about cute rats.

A cognitive dissonance occurred with the Quiznos commercial. Cognitive dissonance is when people feel discomfort because of two conflicting belief systems. When there is a difference between belief and behavior, something needs to change to eliminate the discord. Rats and food are a perfect example of two ideas that do not go hand in hand. Therefore, the two categories need to be separated.

Another example of a company that created a product that did not cognitively work with the brand's image is Volkswagen. At one point, the company decided to build a top-end limousine called the Phaeton. Conceptually, the chairman of the company wanted to create a car that would rival the prestige of BMW and Mercedes Benz. The Phaeton was designed to compete with flagship models such as the Audi A8 and Jaguar XJ. However, the company that was famous for its slogan "Think Small" could not make the transition to a high-end product. "Psychologists have found that there is a strong tendency in every one of us to seek out stimuli that are in line with our existing beliefs and attitudes" (Walvis, 2010, p. 100). As illustrated by Maslow, economy and prestige are on two different levels of personal need. Volkswagen attempted to move from a low to a high-end level. Because of its divergence from the company's brand, the Phaeton failed. Moreover, an incoherent brand message can harm the brand itself. Volkswagen confused consumers by trying to appeal to two diverse needs—economy and status symbol. Branded messages need to be visually, verbally, and conceptually consistent.

Summary

New research in neuroscience and concepts in visual communication can help marketers to better understand how consumers perceive their brands. Our minds react to feelings in ways that are not always consciously understood. Understanding how the brain works can help marketers from making costly mistakes with their brands. Positive branding requires both the emotional and logical aspects of the mind to work together to understand the branded message. Confusion can be used as a tool to gain the consumer's attention; however, the branded message needs to be clear both emotionally and logically to be a success.

Exercises

1. Take a survey of your home to identify the different brands in your house. List the brands and state a reason why you purchased that particular product.
2. Once you have a list of your branded products, rank them from most important to least important. Is there a brand that you do not want to live without? Write an essay exploring your feelings about your favorite brands.
3. Cognitive dissonance is the concept that two ideas or belief systems are in conflict. Make a list of concepts that do not work together and a list of concepts that do. Can you provide examples of this from recent advertisements you have seen?
4. Try the Zaltman Metaphor Elicitation Technique to conduct in-depth interviews with two people about a visual brand. Compare the answers and summarize the results.

References

Barry, A.M.S. (1997). *Visual intelligence.* Albany: State University of New York Press.

Beltrone, G. (2015a, January 7). Ads make everyone everywhere question everything. *AdWeek.* Retrieved January 8, 2015, from www.adweek.com

Beltrone, G. (2015b, February 24). When the escalators died in Stockholm's subway, Reebok was there to give people a lift: Quite literally. *AdWeek.* Retrieved February 16, 2015, from www.adweek.com

Beltrone, G. (2015c, March 2). Coca-Cola celebrates its iconic bottle's 100th birthday with 15 new ads and a museum exhibit! *AdWeek.* Retrieved March 2, 2015, from www.adweek.com

Coulter, R.H., & Zaltman, G. (1994). Using the Zaltman Metaphor Elicitation Technique to understand brand images. *Advances in Consumer Research, 2,* 501–507.

Coulter, R.H., Zaltman, G., & Coulter, K.S. (2001). Interpreting consumer perceptions of advertising: An application of the Zaltman Metaphor Elicitation Technique. *Journal of Advertising, 30*(4), 1–21.

Damasio, A.R. (1994). *Descartes' error: Emotion, reason and the human brain.* New York: Avon.

Elull, J. (1973). *Propaganda.* New York: Vintage Books.

Fromm, E. (1951). *The forgotten language.* New York: Grove Press.

Gardner, H. (1983). *Frames of mind*. New York: Basic Books.

Gardner, H. (1999). *Intelligence reframed*. New York: Basic Books.

Goleman, D. (1995). *Emotional intelligence*. New York: Bantam.

Griner, D. (2014, January 27). Arby's slayed the Grammys with this tweet about Pharrell Williams' hat. *AdWeek*. Retrieved January 29, 2014, from www.adweek.com

Hoffman, D.D. (1998). *Visual intelligence*. New York: W.W. Norton.

Lewis, R.W. (1996). *Absolut book*. Boston, MA: Journey Editions.

Maskeroni, A. (2015, February 19). Infographic: 13 reasons why your brain craves infographics. *AdWeek*. Retrieved April 26, 2015, from www.adweek.com

Maslow, A.H. (1943). A theory of human motivation. *Psychological Review*, 50(4), 370–396.

Mehrabian, A. (1971). *Silent messages*. Belmont, CA: Wadsworth.

Reuters. (2011, February 16). VW Darth Vader achieves highest score to date on Sands Research annual super bowl ad neuro ranking. *Reuters.com*. Retrieved February 20, 2015, from http://www.reuters.com/article/2011/02/16/idUS171484+16-Feb-2011+BW20110216

Van Praet, D. (2012). *Unconscious branding*. New York: Palgrave Macmillan.

Walvis, T. (2010). *Branding with brains*. New York: Prentice Hall.

· 6 ·

EMOTIONAL AND RELATIONSHIP BRANDING

While propaganda substitutes opinion for facts, pseudo-events are synthetic facts which move people indirectly, by providing the "factual" basis on which they are supposed to make up their minds. Propaganda moves them directly by explicitly making judgments for them.
—Daniel J. Boorstin, 1987, p. 34

Consumers become emotionally attached to different brands. This attachment can be described as a consumer-brand bond. One cannot discuss the emotional impact of branding without talking about relationships. One of the extreme cases of emotional branding is Apple Computer. Through advertising, the company positioned its product as countercultural. As business people gravitated to Microsoft versions of the personal computer, Apple went against the mainstream. People became so attached to Apple's products that they formed conferences, discussion lists, and organizations to discuss the products. The idea of Mac users versus Microsoft users has distinguished people and created a sense of personal identity. Apple is an extreme case of relationship branding.

People become emotionally attached to brands. This attachment can occur on a conscious or unconscious level. "When a brand consistently repeats a coherent and compelling message over a period of time, the net result is actually a physical change in the brain's circuitry on a cellular level" (Van Praet, 2012, p. 212). This rewiring of learned associations predisposes individuals to

think and behave in certain ways toward the brand. For instance, if you hear part of a slogan, your mind will fill in the rest. Can you fill in these blanks?

"You're in good hands with ______________."
"______________ melt in your mouth, not in your hand."

These slogans have become so common in popular culture that board games have been developed to test one's brand knowledge. Marketers do an exceptional job of bringing brands to the consumer's attention.

Relationship Marketing

The concept of marketing can be traced back to ancient times. In the twentieth century, marketing focused on transactions and exchanges. However, at the end of the century, marketing began to undergo a reconceptualization in its focus from transactions to relationships. First developed through direct marketing, this new advertising and marketing is communicated directly to the consumer. Direct marketing includes mail, phone marketing, text messaging, email, catalog distribution, and targeted television commercials. Direct marketing is also known as direct response, because an individual customer immediately responds to the message. Popular items are cat toys, makeup, home tools, and kitchen aids. Direct marketing was the first form of relationship marketing. Some stores, such as Walmart, now have sections called "Seen on Television" that sell direct-marketing items on a retail level.

When producers and consumers interact directly, there is a greater potential for emotional bonding. People can develop such close relationships with brands that they feel almost like friends. Chapter 2 discussed how manufactured products altered economic transactions from individual buyers and sellers to mass-marketed items. When a buyer knows the seller personally, a friendship can form. Today's technological changes once again place merchants in a position where they can sell directly to consumers. As a result, producers now interact directly with clients and can engender a feeling akin to friendship.

"The concept of relationship and relational behavior is universal. It is in physical, animal, plant and human sciences" (Sheth & Parvatiyar, 2002, p. 9). In essence, relational behavior applies to almost everything. However, relationship marketing requires a focus on understanding and managing customers and their buying, paying, and consuming habits. Definitions of

relationship marketing emphasize a long-term relationship with customers. From a business perspective, "relationship marketing attempts to involve and integrate customers, suppliers, and other infrastructural partners into a firm's developmental and marketing activities" (Sheth & Parvatiyar, 1995, p. 399). This includes relationship branding.

Building relationships and preserving long-term relationships is an idea that dates to the 1980s. Prior to that time the focus of marketing was on attracting new customers to products. Ideas that support the notion of relationship marketing are service strategies, relationship customization, service augmentation, relationship pricing, and internal marketing. To build strong consumer relationships, a company must design and market its core services. A key point to communicate is how your product or service is different from other companies. For example, the Enterprise car company is unique among other rental companies in that it will pick people up from different locations, such as car dealers or hotels. People who need to have their cars repaired can call Enterprise to rent a car during the repair process, and Enterprise will drive them to the rental office.

Customizing a relationship for clients' different needs can influence a person's choice of one product over another. For example, would you select a service that has actual people answering the telephones over a recording or an automated system? American Express ran print advertisements telling people that real people answered its customer service phone calls. The emotional appeal the company used involved "human understanding." Berry (2002) states:

> If the customer receives custom service from company A but not from company B—and if receiving custom service is valued by the customer—then the customer is less likely to leave company A for B than would otherwise be the case. (p. 65)

Another approach to building customer rapport is service augmentation. This concept involves adding "extras" to a service. Computer professionals call this "value added." Value is the worth that consumers perceive when they purchase a product. "By adding more value to the core product (the product quality is improved, supporting services are included into the offering, etc.) companies try to improve customer satisfaction so that the bonds are strengthened and customer loyalty thereby achieved" (Ravald & Grönroos, 1996, p. 19). The customer's perceived value of a product is expressed by the following formula:

Customer-perceived value = $\dfrac{\text{Perceived benefits}}{\text{Perceived sacrifice}}$

The value is what customers receive when they purchase a product. Customer-perceived value is the ratio of benefits to sacrifice. Perceived value is the consumer's overall assessment of a product. The perceived sacrifice is the cost of the product, including transportation, installation, shipping, maintenance, and risk of poor performance. It should be noted that a person might value a product differently at different times. For example, "the price may be the most important criterion at the time of purchase; a clear and easily comprehensible manual may be of importance at installation and assembly" (Ravald & Grönroos, 1996, p. 22).

Consumers need to believe that a company's offerings are a better value than those of the competition. Superior product quality, brand/image, adapting, supporting services, and customer support are areas to consider when calculating value. In a long-term customer relationship, safety, credibility, security, and reputation become important. By offering customers additional meaningful services, companies can encourage customer loyalty. An example of an "extra" is providing breakfast for customers at hotels. When traveling, what type of extras do you look for? Is free Internet service important? Are pancakes at breakfast? Different hotels offer benefits to inspire loyalty on the part of different people. For instance, consumers who would want a mint or cognac are different from someone who would want a laundry room.

Relationship pricing is another strategy for promoting customer loyalty. It is "an old marketing idea…. [A] better price for better customers…forms the basis of relationship pricing" (Berry, 2002, p. 66). Chico's clothing stores do this. Customers with a Chico's card receive a discount on everything they purchase. Additionally, these customers receive special coupons for clothing discounts, so that faithful customers rarely pay full price for merchandise. In addition, giving customers special reward cards places them in a group of loyal customers. Some retailers are better at building loyalty communities than others. For instance, when customers produce loyalty cards and are told the program no longer exists, they can become disappointed with the retailer. Once customer loyalty is established, it is a good idea to maintain it.

Internal marketing perceives the customer as an employee or someone working inside the company. In this case, the job itself becomes the product. The purpose is to attract qualified personnel and keep them. Quality personnel provide better customer services. "Offering services that consistently meet the

quality requirements of target markets is clearly an important factor in building strong customer relationships in many service industries" (Berry, 2002, p. 68). Attracting and maintaining customer relationships requires support from all levels of an organization. Therefore, viewing the job itself as a product that attracts customers (employees) can help a company to attract and maintain qualified people. This can improve overall customer relationships.

Economics

Relationship marketing gave rise to a selling approach in which marketers realized that they needed to supplement transaction-oriented sales with an orientation that showed more concern for the customer. The shift occurred along with economic alterations. Gummesson (2002) contends that relationship marketing is part of changing economic times. This new economy emphasizes "the network society, a focus on services, new customer roles, information technology (IT), globalization, deregulation of financial systems, and mega-alliances between countries (such as the European Union, EU, and the North American Free Trade Agreement, NAFTA)" (p. 38). In an era of networking, organizations have become more inclusive. The relationship between customers and products is altered as communication channels between different groups become available.

Consider how companies use email to gain customer information and how they use twitter to distribute information. "Many authors have attributed the development of relationship marketing to the ease with which technology can now allow large organizations to communicate with thousands, or even millions of individual consumers of their products" (Palmer, 2002, p. 83). One technological change is the use of database information. Before network databases existed, consumer information was collected by evaluating small groups of customers. Now, data warehouses enable organizations to "mine" useful information from entire customer databases. Along with new understandings about the emotional behavior of consumers, technology has also influenced the development of relationship marketing.

Another contributing factor is the growth of the service economy. "As more and more organizations depend upon revenues from the services sector, relationship marketing becomes prevalent" (Sheth & Parvatiyar, 1995, p. 410). Competition in the marketplace also makes it more important to build a strong connection with customers.

Relationships

Core relationship dimensions support the emotional relationship between customer and product. "Socioemotional provisions include psychosocial identity functions (e.g., reassurance of self-worth, announcement of image, and social integration) as well as the rewards of stimulation, security, guidance, nurturance, assistance, and social support; instrumental provisions are functionally tied to the attainment of objective, short-term goals" (Fournier, 1998, p. 364).

Further, the bonds between a customer and product need to be considered. These can be grounded bonds, such as investment needs, task-oriented necessities and obligations, or emotional ones. Emotion-based bonds can be as simple as liking the product or as complex as being addicted to it. Cigarettes are physically addictive, while ice cream may be emotionally addictive. Another factor is whether or not a product is friendly or hostile. The popularity of icon-based computer interfaces called user-friendly over text command designs illustrates this point.

The one-time purchase of a product does not make for a relationship. Relationships are a series of repeated exchanges. People buy products because there are "no streaks" (Windex), "no tub ring" (Zest soap), and "no residue" (Spic 'n Span). Moreover, individuals believe in brands that have superior performance records, such as Frigidaire, Maytag, and General Electric. Women may also develop close relationships with perfumes, makeup, and lingerie, because these support a woman's sense of identity. "Themes that people use to define themselves can be played out in the cultivation of brand relationships and how those relationships, in turn, can affect the cultivation of one's concept of self" (Fournier, 1998, p. 359).

Behavioral patterns contribute to the formation of relationships. Making purchases as part of a routine results in habitual actions and loyalty in purchasing decisions. Shopping in the supermarket is often when people tend to experience repeat buying habits. People will buy the same brand of their favorite ice cream or preferred brand of cookie. Risk is also a reason for a repeat purchase. When people are familiar with a particular product or service, they may not want to risk trying something new. Another reason is remuneration. After consumers are promised benefits from purchasing or using a product, a relationship can be formed—for example, using one credit card exclusively because purchases on the card result in added frequent-flyer miles. The goal of being awarded a free airline ticket is motivation for loyalty.

Brand Loyalty

The repeated purchase of products by the customer is essential for successful branding. Thus, the idea of brand loyalty was developed. "Strong, enduring brands are built with the concept of brand loyalty in mind—the idea that consumers will develop a bond with the brand that will strengthen over time and will make changing to another brand feel like a betrayal of trust" (Levine, 2003, p. 194). An example of brand loyalty is Dyson vacuum cleaners. The words "reliable," "innovative," "leader," and "cutting-edge" come to mind when one thinks of the product. This creates an emotional anchor for the merchandise. "A great brand is not a mark burned into a product—it's something we want to belong to" (Jiwa, 2014, p. 5)

However, loyalty needs to be reinforced. Even products that people use every day, such as salt and soap, need to be advertised. Public relations efforts communicate information about the brand to the public. This is a method for creating the brand's personality. For instance, advertising can make a connection between Nike and its visual swoosh logo. Public relations messages tell the story of Nike's relationship to sports figures. Together, the two make the brand the epitome of sports. Loyalty to the Nike brand is also loyalty to one's favorite sport.

Brand loyalty begins with a promise made by the company. Once the consumer feels that the promise has been met, brand loyalty can begin. Customer satisfaction is central to loyalty. For example, Starbucks provides more than coffee. It creates an environment in which people can enjoy drinking their coffee. Think about brands such as Dunkin' Donuts or McDonald's. Are their environments friendly and welcoming to coffee drinkers? Or are these two brands designed to have high turnover with fast food? As a result of brand loyalty, people will drive miles out of their way to patronize a Starbucks.

Among the factors that discourage customer loyalty are poor customer service and situations in which individuals are made to feel that they don't matter. For example, a company wanted to handle more calls, so it told employees to keep the customer service calls short. As a result, people had to call several times to get their complaints answered. Smart businesses know that customer service is as important as getting your brand's name publically recognized. Sprint "extended loyalty to its customers in a number of ways throughout its operations, from simplified billing to better call center experiences" (Malone & Fiske, 2013, p. 46). Two other companies recognized for

good customer service are the online shoe store Zappos and Mercedes Benz. Success depends upon how customers feel about your brand.

An interesting aspect of product loyalty is the idea that people who complain can be turned into devoted customers. Malone and Fiske (2013) argue that clients who complain and then experience swift and respectful service from the company often become faithful customers. Once a trusted connection is made between a consumer and a company, loyalty can be established.

Young people tend to be loyal to brands. They adopt brands more readily and develop friendships with them. Young people are also more aware of the role that brands play in their lives. "Young people have an innate understanding of marketing and of their value as consumers. And they're significantly more likely than older generations to believe they have the capacity to help a brand succeed or fail" (Hoffmann, 2014, pp. 1–2). With the increase of branding in today's culture, younger individuals are more savvy about marketing issues.

Lovemarks

Lovemarks constitute a newer marketing concept that goes beyond branding. The idea is that people need to love brands. Brand loyalty needs to go beyond reason. Love is the key ingredient to making brands transform into lovemarks, which were originally publicized by Kevin Roberts, CEO of the advertising agency Saatchi & Saatchi, in his book *Lovemarks* (2005).

For a brand to become a lovemark, it must be high in love and respect and create a level of extreme loyalty in customers. Brands included in this category are Nike and Coca-Cola. These brands communicate emotional messages to people. Although it is not directly a lovemark concept, trust is another characteristic that is important for transforming a brand into a lovemark.

Trust

When customers are truly loyal to a brand, changing brands will feel like an act of betrayal, a violation of a relationship between themselves and the brand. An important emotional aspect of relationship marketing is trust. Trust encompasses the concept that people will fulfill their commitments to other people. The cognitive state of trust is a combination of benevolence and credibility. Benevolence is the belief in the good will of another person, and credibility is

the belief in the character of a person and his or her commitment to doing no harm. How individuals perform and meet their commitments, along with the reputation of the individual, contribute to building trust. Performance histories, including past experiences with a person or company, will establish trust. In addition, third-party endorsements, such as the recommendation of a friend, will develop a reputation for trust.

In business, trust occurs when the consumer builds a relationship with the supplier. "The customer knows that this company is able to fulfill his [or her] needs and wants and is assured that the company will take care of the commitments it has made" (Ravald & Grönroos, 1996, p. 24). For many people, the idea of trust is developed over time and through experience. In business it involves establishing and maintaining collaborative relationships.

However, it needs to be stated that trust is more difficult to establish in electronic environments (see Ferraro, 1998). People need to make sure that identification, authorization, and authentication are all accurate. These are issues of concern because people do not physically see those they are interacting with on the Internet. The building of trust and loyalty are essential for successful branding.

Influencers

Influencers are the people who have a strong impact on other consumers. Hearing word-of-mouth recommendations about brands from friends, celebrities, and people in power can make the information seem more real and credible. Influencers are believed to make up 1–15% of the population (see Moffitt & Dover, 2011). Digital technologies have made it easier for this group to spread the word.

According to Moffitt & Dover (2011), "harnessing Influencers' feedback, involvement and evangelism for organizations has never been more critical" (p. 52). The Internet has created new forms of connection that help people to identify influential voices. "Twenty-seven percent of Influencers' discussions are about brands" (p. 52). Companies can help to develop their own group of influential people. For instance, Lego discovered a group of adult fans that had developed their own enthusiast community, and the company's web producer began spending several hours a week promoting the group. Eventually, this Lego community became an army of influencers. Many decisions to purchase are made as a result of an influential message from another person.

Influencers have larger circles of friends, associates, and colleagues. They tend to adopt products earlier, pay attention to new trends, and pass along more recommendations. Additionally, they are perceived as being better informed, more authoritative, and honest. As individuals, influencers are strong communicators with a passion for the subject. In general, they are the people others listen to. When brands can harness the passion of influencers to work for them, these people can be their best allies.

Communicating Emotion

Communicating emotional messages from the brand to consumers is an important aspect of building any relationship. Marketers know that brands must communicate human characteristics to their target audience. Two emotions that researchers have been able to study are warmth and competence. Warmth is an emotion that can be communicated through the expression on someone's face. "People with slightly surprised, happy faces and baby-faced people tend to gain our trust almost immediately" (Malone & Fiske, 2013, p. 23). Research by Malone and Fiske has confirmed that "customers reward perceptions of warmth and competence with feelings of admiration, purchases, and customer loyalty" (p. 31). Through worthy intentions and communicating the emotions of warmth and competence, brands can win our loyalty and support.

Brands that are involved with philanthropic work are perceived by consumers to be more compassionate and competent. A study conducted by Malone and Fiske on Hershey, the chocolate manufacturer, demonstrates this point. Hershey donates money to the Milton Hershey School in Pennsylvania, a boarding school for underprivileged children. Most consumers are not aware of this charitable work. However, when consumers were told about Hershey's relationship with the school, their perceptions of the Hershey Company became more favorable.

In another study for Coca-Cola, Malone and Fiske determined that the stronger the relationship between the company and the consumer, "the more closely that relationship resembles a one-on-one human relationship in terms of warmth and competence" (p. 35). By examining the warmth and competence dimensions of a brand's perception, companies can gain better insight into a consumer's feelings about the brand.

An example of emotional branding is the association with the blue Tiffany box which, for the recipient of a gift, demonstrates special appreciation on the part of the giver. The symbol is so strong that seeing an empty box still evokes good feelings. In another example, the feelings for the Rolex brand are totally different than the ones for Timex. Having a product designed by Giorgio Armani or Prada instills a different feeling than one purchased at Walmart. Prada additionally enhances the shopping experience by providing customers with its own shopping bags.

Brand Experience

Companies that create a brand experience include Apple, Lexus, Starbucks, Target, and JetBlue. It is difficult to define brand experience. Consumers experience it, but marketers have found it difficult to research. Vincent (2012) states:

> Brand experience lives entirely in the mind of your audience. That's why it's so hard to define and discuss. A brand experience is not a package, it is not a retail environment, and it is not an advertisement. All of those elements contribute to brand experience, but none of them *are* the brand experience. A brand experience isn't tangible. It's the by-product of our thoughts, our feelings, and our behavior. (p. 189)

Target has created a brand experience through the design of its stores, its advertising, and the products it sells. All of the stores have a specific look and feel. Entering a target store creates a specific shopping experience that exists across most stores in the United States. Moreover, there is an aesthetic used in Target advertising that distinguishes its commercials from all others. All of these elements contribute to the Target branding encounter.

A number of factors contribute to the creation of a brand experience, including sensory, affective, intellectual, and behavioral ones (see Vincent, 2012). Sensory is when a product appeals to one of our five senses. For example, Pepsi appeals to taste, and Chanel grabs our sense of smell. Affective marketing occurs when a brand invokes strong feelings or sentiments—say, feeling warm and happy when you eat a Hershey's Kiss because your grandmother used to give them to you. These feelings can be associated with significant life events. Intellectually they make us think in a certain way. Brands influence the ways in which we think, feel, and act. For example, the Disney brand generally evokes happy feelings. Going to a Disney park with your

family is an event that many people never forget. Finally, behavioral encounters inspire people to do something or change their actions. Many times when people go to a Disney park, they feel like children again. The atmosphere can change behavior. People do not always realize how much a brand experience can influence them.

Emotional Design

The design of a product also influences its experience and brand image. Norman (2004) argued that there are three aspects to emotional design: visceral, behavioral, and reflective. He contends that visceral design is related to nature. Visceral design is how we experience our environment. Certain visuals can trigger emotions in our brains. Human reactions to everyday items are complex. Nature co-evolves along with humans. "The human love of sweet tastes and smells and of bright highly saturated colors probably derives from this co-evolution of mutual dependence between people and plants" (Norman, 2004, p. 66).

Behavioral design is about the use of the product. This focuses on the performance and usability of the item. What matters in the behavioral design is the function, understandability, usability, and physical feel of the product. Have you ever encountered an object that you cannot figure out how to use? Technical items such as smart phones may require assistance in their use. However, knowing how to use a corkscrew should be intuitive. If it isn't easily understandable, people can get frustrated.

Another example is buying a car. Are there certain features that you look for in an automobile? Are cup holders important? Or maybe a navigation system is crucial? In some decisions a rear camera or alert system is essential. How we interact with a product is also important in behavioral design.

Reflective design is about the meaning of a product. The meaning covers its message, cultural connotations, the intention for its use, and personal remembrances. What does it mean to wear a Swatch versus a Timex? One is known for style and the other for keeping time, and the one you choose is therefore a reflection of your personality. This is especially true for designer-label clothes and high-end products. This level of design often influences a person's overall concept of a product and affects the relationship between the person and the brand as well.

Sensory Experiences and Branding

People's experiences with brands are emotional. Engaging customers through their senses is also an important part of the branding process. As discussed above, how people feel, behave, and interact with a brand is central to the branding method. A fact not always taken into consideration is how the brand appeals to the five senses. For example, Abercrombie & Fitch stores engineered their own unique scent that sales associates spritz every hour. As a result, people can identify the store by its smell.

To create positive feelings about a product or service, marketers can use the senses. Norman (2004) argued that people are genetically programmed to feel positive about situations that offer food, warmth, and protection. Again, Maslow's needs come into play. Some of these conditions include the following:

> warm, comfortably lit places,
> temperate climate,
> sweet tastes and smells,
> bright, highly saturated hues,
> "soothing" sounds and simple melodies and rhythms,
> harmonious music and sounds,
> caresses,
> smiling faces. (Maslow, 1943, p. 29)

Senses can be used in branding strategies. Moreover, using the senses can distinguish one brand from another. For instance, some people prefer the specific smell of a laundry detergent. Without this smell, the clothes may not seem clean. What types of nonverbal cues can be associated with a product?

One occasion on which sensory elements can be used to stimulate a branding experience is during shopping. Shopping creates a fertile ground for imaginative sensory cues. For example, what music is played in your favorite store? What do the colors of the store tell you about the brand? In a Target store, one would expect to see the red that is used in the company's logo. Companies such as Mobil have created custom colors that their printed materials use. Consistency in corporate identity is important for many companies, and corporate identity programs attempt to control the image of a company through the media. These programs specify how logos will be displayed, how colors are to be used, and requirements for signage. From uniforms to advertisements, the logo will always be displayed in the same way.

Corporations insist on a consistent application of their visual guidelines to convey a strong and cohesive presence. This policy appeals to the sense of sight. Every time a consumer sees the corporate logo, it will be presented in the same way. Graphic designers need to follow these rules when working for a corporation. Often these guidelines are made available to designers, printers, web artists, and others working with corporate visual imagery.

Imagery is an important factor in branding. However, the sense of sound can also make a powerful association with a product. "Sound has an immediate and, to a large extent, cognitively unmediated effect on recall and emotions" (Gobé, 2009, p. 73).

When a car backfires, people pay attention because it can sound like a gunshot. Think about how you react to a sudden sound. The instinctual part of the brain takes over to protect us from harm. Stores such as Abercrombie & Fitch play music that appeals to their target audience. Sound identification can be so strong that certain music can bring a product to mind. However, this can also work in reverse. Recently a shoe store used the same music as the television program CSI. When the commercial was played, people became confused because they would think of the program rather than the shoes. Sounds must be unique to the brand.

The Discovery Channel identifies sections of its stores by sound rather than sight. In wandering through the store, customers encounter different sound zones. This encourages people to explore the store and experience the sounds. Sounds do create different types of feelings. Slow sounds can make us sad and bored; by contrast, fast sounds are often pleasant and happy. Think about how the sound of circus music makes you feel. The use of sounds and color in branding can have a powerful effect on people.

Color

What brand do the words "Golden Arches" bring to mind? What color do you associate with Target stores? Brand strategies need to consider the color they associate with the brand itself. Colors can convey critical information to a customer. Moreover, they can trigger reactions in the brain that stir up memories, thoughts, associations, and perceptions. As stated above, the feelings of arousal help people to process information. Gobé (2009) states: "The effect of colors arises both from acculturation and physiology, and these influences are enforced by one another" (p. 80).

The color red is used in stop signs because it is a color that physiologically stimulates the brain. Similarly, the color blue lowers blood pressure. Colors can influence us physically. With animals, colors that blend into environmental backgrounds protect them from predators. Colorful male animals, such as the peacock, use their color to attract mates. Color has a functional effect, biologically speaking. For instance, black print on a white page is easier to read than colored text.

In contrast, color can be culturally defined. White is a color that is culturally associated with Western weddings. In China, that color is red. Colors associated with death are also different across cultures. In many ways, our response to color is culturally learned just by being in the social environment. The African color wheel is completely different from the Western one. As a result, color meanings are culturally learned. For this reason, branding strategists know that they can create an association between their brand and a color that will stimulate the consumer's mind. Once the association is made, people will think of the brand when they see the color. Color associations include green for John Deere (because the color implies nature), yellow for Hertz, and red for Avis. The FedEx colors are orange and purple.

Taste

Taste is also a sense that marketers should consider. Be aware that color can also be associated with taste. Red, for example, generally has a cherry, raspberry, or strawberry taste because the color resembles the fruit. In the same way, the color orange is associated with the fruit of the same name. Green is lime, and yellow is lemon.

In recognition of the relationship between coffee and reading, the Barnes & Noble bookstore chain installed coffee shops in its stores that allowed people to sit and read books before purchasing them. Likewise, department stores have added restaurants to make the shopping experience more appealing. And hotel chains offer cookies to arriving guests. The availability of food can influence people's decisions. Do you prefer to stay at a motel that does or does not serve breakfast? How many times have you walked through a supermarket when food was being offered? "Food is a form of social exchange and is imbued with special meanings in many cultures" (Gobé, 2009, p. 92). Offering a cup of coffee can influence a customer's purchasing decisions. For this reason, people manning booths at conferences often offer sweets to passersbys.

Scents

Smell and taste are two senses that are related. Scents are not filtered by the brain, which enables them to evoke emotional feelings. In fact, smell is the strongest of all the senses. When people want to sell their homes, they bake cookies to make the house smell good. Conversely, a strange odor in a house will turn people away. However, people are not always aware of their reactions to smell.

Marketers have discovered that people prefer scented over non-scented products. An example of this is the rapid expansion of the scented candle business. "Organizations interested in sharpening their brand identity or simply improving their stores or showrooms should capitalize on the advantages provided by smells" (Gobé, 2009, p. 103). Today, retailers create scents for their stores. Additionally, perfume manufacturers create a business from our sense of smell. For instance, when we say Old Spice, people generally think of a specific smell. The type of cologne or perfume people wear can sometimes identify different men and women. People can self-identify with these scents.

Stimulating Senses Through Experience

As discussed previously in brand experience, the sensory, affective, intellectual, and behavioral factors can be combined with sensory elements to create a stimulating brand experience. By engaging consumers through action and scents, brands can become part of a consumer's lifestyle. Music, color, and scents stimulate people's emotional centers to create stronger brand recognition.

Branding a product is much more than creating a logo or slogan. Everything about the brand needs to be considered, from its color to how it relates to a person's senses. Savvy marketers known how to excite our emotions. Today, brands have become an integral part of our culture and our lives.

Summary

Emotional bonds are formed between customers and brands. The concept of relationship marketing has been developed to focus on the creation of relationships between consumers and products. Customer service and value-added service are central reasons for establishing a long-term relationship.

These changes in marketing correspond to economic and technical alterations that have led to the creation of a network society. Brand loyalty and trust are part of these new social changes. Moreover, the emotional impact of branded messages supports these ideas. By creating brand experiences through the senses, our emotions shape what and how we feel about a product and can assist in brand-to-consumer bonding.

Exercises

1. What type of extra services would you offer if your business were a hotel? Sports Club? Bank? Who would you market these services to? Who makes up the target market? Write a proposal arguing for these improvements.
2. Observe someone using a product—for example, eating a candy bar, doing the laundry, drying their hair, etc. Write down what you observe. What do your observations tell you about the product?
3. Select a product that you often use. Write an essay describing how the product makes you feel, behave, and think about its use. What emotional attachments do you have to the product?
4. Survey the different products in your home and record the senses that they stimulate. State how arousing the senses makes you feel.

References

Berry, L.L. (2002). Relationship marketing of services: Perspectives from 1983 and 2000. *Journal of Relationship Marketing, 1*(1), 59–77.

Boorstin, D.J. (1987). *The image.* New York: Atheneum.

Ferraro, A. (1998). Electronic commerce: The issues and challenges to creating trust and a positive image in consumer sales on the world wide web. *First Monday, 3*(6). Retrieved March 5, 2015, from www.firstmonday.org

Gobé, M. (2009). *Emotional branding.* New York: Allworth Press.

Gummesson, E. (2002). Relationship marketing in the new economy. *Journal of Relationship Marketing, 1*(1), 37–57.

Fournier, S. (1998). Consumers and their brands: Developing relationship theory consumer research. *Journal of Consumer Research, 2*(24), 343–373.

Hoffmann, M. (2014, October 6). Attention brands: This is how you get millennials to like you. *AdWeek*. Retrieved October 15, 2014, from http://www.adweek.com/news/advertis ing-branding/attention-brands-how-you-get-millennials-you-160575

Jiwa, B. (2014). *Marketing a love story*. Australia: The Story of Telling Press.

Levine, M. (2003). *A branded world*. Hoboken, NJ: John Wiley & Sons.

Malone, C., & Fiske, S.T. (2013). *The human brand*. San Francisco, CA: Jossey-Bass.

Maslow, A.H. (1943). A theory of human motivation. *Psychological Review, 50*(4), 370–396.

Moffitt, S., & Dover, M. (2011). *Wiki brands*. New York: McGraw-Hill.

Norman, D.A. (2004). *Emotional design*. New York: Perseus Books.

Palmer, A. (2002). The evolution of an idea: An environmental explanation of relationship marketing. *Journal of Relationship Marketing, 1*(1), 79–94.

Ravald, A., & Grönroos, C. (1996). The value concept and relationship marketing. *European Journal of Marketing, 30*(2), 19–30.

Roberts, K. (2005). *Lovemarks: The future beyond brands* (2nd ed.). New York: PowerHouse Books.

Sheth, J.N., & Parvatiyar, A. (1995). The evolution of relationship marketing. *International Business Review, 4*(4), 397–418.

Sheth, J.N., & Parvatiyar, A. (2002). Evolving relationship marketing into a discipline. *Journal of Relationship Marketing, 1*(1), 3–16.

Van Praet, D. (2012). *Unconscious branding*. New York: Palgrave Macmillan.

Vincent, L. (2012). *Brand real*. New York: American Management Association.

· 7 ·

BRAND PERSONALITY

You have to decide what "image" you want for your brand. Image means personality. Products, like people, have personalities, and they can make or break them in the market place.
—David Ogilvy, 1984, p. 14

Advertising veteran David Ogilvy discusses brands in terms of personality. The personality of the brand helps to create a unique image in the consumer's mind. Describing the personality of a brand also involves the concept of developing brand names, telling the brand's story, developing logos and tag lines. This chapter will describe techniques for developing brand personality and distinguishing brand images from the competition.

Brand loyalty, discussed in the previous chapter, is a relationship that is established between a person and a brand. For example, a man who wears only one type of designer suit has a relationship with the designer's label. A brand's behavior should be guided by a reliable promise that is consistently reinforced throughout the branding process. In fashion, the quality of the material and style of the clothing would support the guarantee. Branding behavior is determined by the personality of the product. Serious products need to be described in an earnest tone. In contrast, humorous products need whimsy. Trendy items need to speak to their target audience in a tone the listeners can understand.

The personality of the product is developed through a number of different elements. These include the brand's name, the story behind the brand, its logo, and its tag line. All of these factors contribute to the formation of a personality that is recognizable to consumers.

Personality

The concept of brand personality was first introduced in Chapter 1. People can anthropomorphize most brands. Consumers tend to think of products and services in terms of human traits. This is another reason why people build emotional attachments to brands. "Words like 'honest,' 'inspiring,' 'sympathetic,' 'reassuring,' 'fun,' 'intelligent,' and 'supportive' often crop up when passionate customers describe their favorite brands" (Healey, 2008, p. 82). In order for people to recognize a brand as a personality, its visual image and voice must be consistent. Moreover, at the center of the branding must be a worthwhile, quality product. It is vitally important that the promise, which is integral to the product or service's personality, is met. Inferior products cannot support strong promises.

A quick method for attaching a personality to a brand is to use a celebrity endorsement. Think of the movie stars who have attached their names to perfumes and fashion lines. Elizabeth Taylor for "White Diamonds" perfume and Jaclyn Smith for Kmart are examples. However, brands can run into trouble when their celebrity endorser has problems, such as drug use, arrest, or scandal. For example, Jared—the spokesperson for Subway—was caught with child pornography, and the company had to sever its association with him. Anything negative about a brand, including its endorser, can tarnish its image in the eyes of consumers.

"Positive" and "confident" are necessary characteristics in establishing a brand's personality. Sometimes choosing a celebrity endorser can be risky. For instance, Justin Beiber modeled in advertisements for Calvin Klein. As a result, Beiber became a topic of discussion, including jokes on late-night television. "Surprise, bargaining, regret—are apparently the relevant considerations when weighing the cultural significance of Justin Bieber wearing C.K. jeans and underwear" (Beltrone, 2015, p. 1). Bieber, rather than the product, became the major topic of discussion. Similarly, the choice of Matthew McConaughey as a spokesperson for Lincoln cars became material for *Saturday Night Live* when Jim Carrey convincingly spoofed the commercials.

In the spots, McConaughey portrayed characters that were similar to roles he has played in movies. "It seems as though McConaughey is inadvertently channeling his mysterious island drifter character from the acclaimed 2013 indie *Mud*" (Zakarin, 2014, p. 1). *AdWeek* referred to his performance as baffling and perplexing. This is another example of a personality overshadowing the product. The depiction of the product should always be more important than the celebrity.

Snapple, the maker of fruit-flavored teas, conveys the idea of cheerful confidence through the use of playful colors. Similarly, Google, the search engine, expresses its bold confidence through its uncluttered web design. Moreover, its whimsical alteration of its logo to salute holidays further demonstrates the company's self-assurance.

Every brand, like every person, has a personality. Even a "zero" personality communicates an impression. However, if the brand personality is not clearly defined, every piece of communication can take on a slightly different image. As a result, a brand can become a mish-mash of a variety of traits with no clear focus. An ill-defined personality makes your product or service vulnerable to competitive brands. David Ogilvy (1984) states: "The manufacturer who dedicates his advertising to building the most sharply defined *personality* for his brand will get the largest share of the market and the highest profit" (p. 102). The brand identity fulfills a function similar to that of a person's name. "Your brand identity reflects your brand's true character because of who you are and what you do, not because of its design" (Vincent, 2012, p. 169).

Identities can be emotionally charged. Consider the associations with Target stores versus Walmart, or Apple versus Compaq. Target and Apple have more of an emotional connection with people. A successful brand personality will also have an emotional appeal with its consumers. Individuals identify with brand personalities.

Issues with Personality Development

According to Moser (2003), there are several common issues associated with the development of brand personality. These include outside companies developing the personality, changing personalities, misjudging how messages are communicated, creating an unrealistic personality, and creating a provocative personality without any substance. It is important that the people creating the brand image thoroughly understand the product or service.

Who should be responsible for creating your brand's personality? Often the responsibility is given to marketing people, advertising agencies, speechwriters, design firms, public relations companies, brand consultants, or web designers. When delegating the job to an outside firm, a company needs to make sure that an accurate personality is being created. There should be someone from the company who oversees the work to make sure that everyone is on the same page. A slightly different perspective can confuse the consistency of the identity. The personality needs to reflect the company itself, not the consultant.

Another mistake can be made when companies place too much emphasis on their target markets. Political advertising is a perfect example of this. Politicians rely on polls that instruct them on who they are, and how to communicate with people. Turning your personality into what you think the audience wants can turn your message into personality chameleons. This occurs when the voice used in the marketing message is different for various groups. For example, the voice may be trendy for young people and more traditional for older adults. The same brand personality needs to be consistent across all marketing efforts and public relations campaigns.

In the United States, people tend to like the newest and most innovative products and services. Moser (2003) argues, however: "I have learned that most product differences aren't remarkable enough to base a brand upon" (p. 71). Moreover, when one company introduces something new, the competition is generally not far behind. Set aside the rational reasons for purchasing your product and focus on the emotional appeals. By tapping into the emotional realm, a personality can emerge. In addition, in order to develop brand loyalty, an emotional bond needs to be developed between product and consumer.

An unrealistic type of personality can be created when too many personality traits are incorporated into one image. A method for creating a realistic personality is to model it on a real person. In some cases, the founder of the company becomes the personality. Examples are Dave Thomas, the head of Wendy's, and Steve Jobs, the founder of Apple Computer. Another is Michael Dell of Dell, the computer company. If no founders or CEOs are available, companies can create personalities around cultural icons. An example is the Marlboro cowboy.

Personalities can also be created around mythological characters. For instance, an American myth is the story of the successful immigrant, which was applied to Kia Motors America. Other traits associated with America are

humility, hard work, honesty, humanity, and a sense of humor. However, a different solution is to combine four or five traits to create a unique personality.

The personality of a company's product cannot be more outrageous than the company itself. An example of an extreme personality is Crazy Eddie, the spokesperson for a chain of electronics stores. Jerry Carroll, the actor who played Eddie, developed his frenetic character from watching used car salesmen. Trying to garner attention by planning an event or marketing program that does not fit with your personality can be problematic. On the other hand, if you have an outrageous product or service, a provocative personality can be appropriate. The Eddie character contributed to the success of the electronics chain that had 43 stores in the Tri-State Area of New York. The personality needs to match the product or service.

The voice used in marketing campaigns should resemble people talking to each other. Making a company into a person requires a voice that speaks like a human and eschews corporate-speak. Remember that it is by stirring the emotions that brands become successful. Advertising and marketing are essential for promoting the personality of a brand. Martin (1989) states: "Great brands are built over a long period of time with advertising that is faithful to product personality" (p. 89). The personality of the product is repeated and magnified through the advertising, which is designed to promote the name and logo association.

What's in a Name?

A name brings to mind all of the emotional and rational associations of a brand. Creating the name for a brand is exciting and challenging. Finding the right name could be the most significant aspect of the branding process. For instance, in 1879 one of the founders of Procter & Gamble heard the word "ivory," and it stuck with him. Later it became the name of the company's soap. Ivory is white like the soap and has a positive association. The name works because "the brand promise of Ivory hasn't changed in 118 years" (Travis, 2000, p. 152). The soap floats and is 99 44/100 percent pure. Finding the right name can enable the product to last a lifetime or more.

Names that command attention, such as Red Hat, Amazon.com, and Excite, are also easy to remember. Some general rules about names are: be careful of monograms; remember that generic names support nonspecific businesses; do the unexpected; and sound distinctive. Monograms look great on shirts, but they don't always work for companies. Often people do not remember what the initials stand for. Can you provide the full names for these companies: IBM, BMW, or ABC?

Generic names are plain. Names such as Financial Services Corporation, Auto Sales Company, and Twin Cities Incorporated are so broad that it is difficult to distinguish the name from other businesses. In contrast, the name Yahoo! stands out. Further, names should not be expected. Quality Cleaners, Artistic Designers, and Expert Repairs are generic because these terms are what consumers expect. People anticipate good quality cleaning, design that is artistic, and repairs done with expertise. In contrast, names should be distinctive—examples are Federal Express, Apple Computer, and Target.

Some successful product names have visual associations. A grocer is called Peapod. A car is named Beetle or Jaguar. The name Amazon suggests that something is big like a jungle. Names can be made up or taken from family names. Coined names are made-up names for a particular product or service. An example is the name Kodak, created by George Eastman. It has no meaning and was used because it was short and easy to say. "George Eastman's trade name was so successful that it was soon in danger of becoming a generic name" (Sacharow, 1982, p. 104). To solve this problem, the company adopted the following tag lines: "Only Eastman makes the Kodak" and "If it isn't an Eastman, it isn't a Kodak." Other made-up names include Häagen-Dazs and Exxon, which also say and mean nothing other than the brand itself.

There are numerous examples of brand names that have been based on family names. One of the most well-known of such names is Procter & Gamble. William Procter made candles, and James Gamble boiled soap. They perfected a formula for creating hard soap. Hallmark is also based on a family name. The company was founded by Joyce Hall, a Kansas City stationery dealer. The company was originally called Hall Brothers Greeting Cards, and in the 1920s it was changed to Hallmark.

Reynolds aluminum foil began as Reynolds Metals and was named after Richard Samuel Reynolds, Sr. His interest in developing foil came from wanting to provide such packaging for cigarettes and tobacco. In 1940, the company changed its focus to aluminum products. Another international company based on a real name is McDonald's. Ray Kroc named his restaurant chain after a drive-in restaurant operated by the McDonald brothers. "Recognizing that the McDonald brothers had 'something good,' he persuaded them to allow him to franchise similar restaurants nationwide in exchange for 0.5 percent of the sales of the franchised restaurants" (Sacharow, 1982, p. 122). The rest is history. Most major cities in the world are home to McDonald's restaurants.

Logos

Names provide verbal branding, and logos create a visual one. "A logo is the visual symbol a brand or company uses to identify itself to consumers" (Drewniany & Jewler, 2008, p. 38). Target's red bull's-eye logo is an example. In some cases, the name of the brand also becomes its logo—for example, IBM, Ford, and Coca-Cola. A new brand may want to use its name as a logo to reinforce it in the minds of consumers.

In addition to names, Coca-Cola is associated with the color red and IBM with a distinctive blue. "*A logo by itself is not necessarily a communication tool, but it can most definitely act as a symbol of what a company represents (or hopes to represent) and the consumer perceptions*" (Gobé, 2009, p. 126; emphasis in original). According to Gobé, logos need to be humanized, which means they need to have an emotional connection. The reason for this is that we now live in a people-driven economy, thanks to the rise of interactive technologies. This shift reflects the concept that corporations need to have contact and dialog with consumers, which can occur through the Internet.

In designing logos, companies need to be aware of whether or not their symbol is "dictated" or personal. Dictated logos are based purely on the concepts of visibility and impact. Abstracted images tend to be more dictated— for example, the AT&T logo. In today's people-driven economy, logos need to have more emotional contact with consumers, as does the MTV logo. Designs based on emotion are more personal and may be interpreted differently from one consumer to the next. An example is the Apple Computer logo. The apple can be interpreted in many different ways—as a favorite fruit of the founder or a company that humanizes computers.

Gobé (2009) describes three different eras of logo development: the Pragmatist Age (1940–1967); the Evangelist Age (1968–1989); and the Sensualist Age (1990–present). The Pragmatist Age was contemporaneous with a period of unprecedented economic boom, at which time American industry began distributing products and services on a global level. Business was fueled by a post-war economy, and production was on the rise. In keeping with the American Dream, people believed that anyone could be successful. Corporate design began to be recognized as an important marketing tool. Corporate identity programs worked to create a unified visual look and a cohesive visual identity. Logos were developed to be simple, powerful, and easy to remember.

Designers such as Paul Rand and advertising agencies such as Young & Rubicam and McCann Erickson developed the visual and verbal messages of the corporate world. The brand identities they created became cultural symbols. Successful brand icons included Coca-Cola, IBM, the Ford Motor Company, TWA, Marlboro, and Levi's. This was the era of corporate identity programs and omnipresent advertising.

During the Evangelist Age, baby boomers continued to enjoy a high level of economic freedom and prosperity. The United States became the most active consumer market in the entire world. However, baby boomers did not share their parents' faith in the American Dream. As Gobé (2009) describes:

> The Vietnam War, the growing negative perception of the influence of international big business in local and foreign politics, and the realization that the same socioeconomic opportunities were not available to everyone led business entrepreneurs for the first time in history to speak about righting political and social wrongs through business practices—to literally evangelize about the values they believed in. (p. 129)

Corporations needed to appeal to the average man and woman. Business practices combined with idealistic philosophies in order to mitigate the sometimes negative impact of business on society. For example, the Benetton clothing company initiated a series of corporate messages that visualized injustice in the world and forced issues such as violence, racism, and the AIDs epidemic onto social consciousness. Jobling and Crowley (1996) described their designs as follows:

> The "United Colors of Benetton" have been widely exposed throughout the world on billboards and the pages of glossy magazines. Much of this controversy centers on the fact that these images seem troubling "out of place", thereby confusing the kind of compartmentalized and specialised organisation of graphic communications. One editor of a British fashion magazine refused to accept Benetton's depiction of David Kirby, a young American dying of AIDS, precisely because it was not in the "right context". These representations, making no claims about the merits of Benetton's products, seem to reflect on the condition of the world—or more accurately, they make space for the viewer to speculate on the knowledge that they contain. Benetton's advertisements are spectacularly "open" texts. That is, they encourage the spectator "to produce a signification which should be neither univocal nor stable". In this sense, Toscani's [the photographer] images for Benetton seem to celebrate the fundamental instability of all texts that Deconstruction takes as a matter of fact. (p. 285)

During this era, the concept of deconstructive graphic design was cre-ated. Design professor Katherine McCoy (1998) stated the following about this topic:

> The deconstruction of meaning holds important lessons about our audiences for visual communicators, but poses some problems as well. While these theories applaud the existence of unstable meaning because of audiences' varying cultural contexts and personal experiences, this can be at odds with the client's need for a single, clear interpretation of the message. (p. 10)

Branding began to communicate countercultural messages. "Just Do It" with Nike and the "Good Life" as defined by Ralph Lauren influenced the lives of numerous consumers. Lifestyle-oriented brands had business success and influenced people's lives. Humanistic vision and corporate social respon-sibility became important during these years.

In the Sensualist Age, values changed to become more hedonistic, glam-orous, celebrity-oriented, and individually expressionistic. Emphasis shifted to the individual's drive to garner immediate rewards, combined with a need for constant change. The Internet speeded up many transactions. A new gen-eration of digital millionaires emerged as innovation turned young people into huge financial successes. A new corporate vocabulary emerged through the pages of *Wired* magazine. Branding strategies now needed to be success-ful within six months, as the digital world changes on an almost daily basis. Two-dimensional print logos were now being replaced by websites. The online world created instant buzz and viral YouTube videos. As new technologies were developed, new methods of branding became available. Brands associ-ated with this age are Red Hat, Herring, Fast Company, and *Star Wars*. (The Internet and branding will be presented in Chapter 10.)

In the past, logos had to look good on everything from a building to a uniform. Today, logos are more active. An example of this trend is the MTV logo. When it first appeared, it changed and danced to the music played on the station. "*An identity program in the twenty-first century is a multidimensional expression of a brand vision brought to life in the most imaginative way*" (Gobé, 2009, p. 133; emphasis in original). Another example of this is the creative use of the Target logo in the company's television commercials and print advertising. These logos are not only visual markers; they are also cultural connections for people.

Tag Lines

In addition to the logo, brand personalities are also established through the use of tag lines. A tag line (also called a slogan) it is a short phrase that is used with the brand name or logo. Examples are "Got milk?", "Can you hear me now?", and "Like a good neighbor." Tag lines are updated and changed over time, and people associate the tag line with the brand. Winters and Goodman (1986) describe a slogan as follows:

> Slogans are repeated selling points or appeals which are of prime importance to a product, brand, or institution. The slogan should sound as good to the ear as it reads to the eye and mind. It must be memorable and bear repetition in all of the firm's advertising. (p. 224)

In addition to being memorable, tag lines must also communicate the core brand values. In essence, the product itself must reflect the values being stated. For instance, a defective product, poor distribution, or weak service can undo all the promises made through advertising and promotion. The first step is to be honest about the product and its value in the marketplace. Once key features of the product or service are identified, the creative team can come up with the "big idea." The big idea is the timeless message describing the product. Moreover, it is a unique way to present the idea to the consumer. Tag lines based on core messages will also create an emotional feeling on the part of the consumer. Examples are "Be all you can be," to communicate individual betterment, or "The Citi never sleeps," to illustrate perseverance.

When developing a tag line or slogan, many different perspectives need to be considered. In addition, one needs to be aware of whether or not the competition can say the same thing. "The concern should not be with what your competition can theoretically say, but which message you can actually own" (Moser, 2003, p. 46). An example is the tag line of American Express. When the company coined the slogan "When it absolutely, positively has to be there overnight," the competition could say the same thing. Emery Express, Airborne Express, and the U.S. Postal Service could also deliver packages overnight. However, Federal Express focused its brand on this one message. Federal Express made people believe the message, and now the company owns it.

Another factor to consider is whether or not the target audience is receiving the message you want to communicate. For instance, a number of years ago Tab soda created the message "Let's Taste Tab." However, when the slogan was stated on the radio, people heard "Less Taste Tab." When the company became aware of the misunderstanding, it pulled the slogan. On a more formal level, tag lines should be tested in focus groups to study people's interpretation of them.

Moser (2003) offers a number of reasons why a slogan will not work for a company. These include: (1) a more popular brand already owns the message; (2) the message is not believable; (3) the message is not easily understood; (4) the message is too new; and (5) a previous message affects your new message. Messages from the competition need to be understood to make sure that yours does not say the same thing. The message also needs to be believable for your product or service. It should be simple enough for most people to understand. Another issue is whether or not the message is culturally progressive. This can be the case with new products and services that need to be established in the marketplace—in other words, the product category may need to be recognized prior to the brand, as occurred when personal computers were first introduced. This challenge continues with new high-tech products and services, because people may need to be taught what the product is (and does) before the branding is identified. Finally, the experience of other brands can influence your message. For instance, Kia was the second Korean car company to enter the U.S. market. Hyundai was the first. As a result, Hyundai clouded the perception of buying a Korean car because it was the first Korean car in the market. This undermined people's concept of Kia. Kia's marketing needed to deal with the Hyundai perceptions of Korean cars.

Slogans are catchy and easy to remember. Many become part of popular culture. Over time, if the tag line becomes less a brand and more a punch line in a joke, it indicates that a new slogan is needed. A slogan needs to remain strongly connected to the product or service. It should also support the story being told about the product.

Telling the Story

Although visual styles may change, an aspect of branding that remains the same is telling the story of the product, company, and service. It is the story that helps to connect people to brands and helps to establish a personality. Communication about the brand takes place through advertising and public relations. A distinction between the two is that adverting is paid for and totally under the control of a company. Public relations, on the other hand, is not paid for and is under the control of the publication sharing the story.

The two can work together. For instance, a company will pay for a Super Bowl advertisement, but it will not pay for all of the publicity generated about the ad it runs during the Super Bowl game. Today, the narrative about the Super Bowl is both one of football and advertising; both of these are topics for news stories.

Super Bowl ads have included Procter & Gamble, Snickers, Fiat Chrysler, Nationwide, Budweiser, and BMW. The 2015 Super Bowl commercials were funny, sentimental, socially conscious, popular, though some were duds. According to *AdWeek*, the five best advertisements were from Procter & Gamble (Always), Snickers, Loctite, Kia, and Clash of Clans. "Procter & Gamble's Always brand, though, reminded us yet again that you can make a brilliant ad with a social message as long as you have a clever creative concept" (Nudd, 2015, p. 2). The spot was titled "Like a Girl" and asked young people what it is like to run, hit, and throw like a girl. It challenged the notion that being like a girl can be insulting to females. It placed stereotypical actions against real ones.

In contrast, one of the funniest Super Bowl spots was Snickers's Brady Bunch commercial. It used the theme "You're not you when you're hungry" and had Danny Trejo from *Sons of Anarchy* playing Marcia Brady. "The BBDO commercial shows Marcia Brady brushing her hair and being so grumpy that she turns into villain Trejo" (O'Leary, 2015, p. 2). Once she eats a Snickers bar, she turns back into herself, and Jan Brady turns into Steve Buscemi. Other notable advertisements were Kia's "The Perfect Getaway," featuring Pierce Brosnan imagining action films instead of a quiet weekend getaway, and Loctite Glue's "Positive Feelings," which shows people dancing around and gluing odd things.

Not all the stories conveyed in the Super Bowl commercials were successful, however. According to *AdWeek*, the worst advertisements included Nationwide Insurance, Jublia (toenail fungus), Game of War, WeatherTech, and Nissan. The Nationwide spot tried to communicate a serious message about accidents involving children but had disastrous results. The narrative pictured a young boy showing all of the things that he would never be able to do because he died. The spot showed a bathtub at the end, suggesting that the boy drowned in the tub. The negativity of the ad made it difficult to watch. The audience did not receive the social message. A number of viewers sent Twitter messages making fun of the commercial.

Similarly, the social message of the Nissan commercial was unclear. It showed a child growing up while his father is away racing cars. In the images, it is obvious that Dad is missing his son's childhood. Finally, when the boy is college age, Dad is there to pick him up in a car. In emotional terms, the happy ending does not make up for the lost childhood. The negative reaction to these spots reflects poorly on the brand personality.

People are narrative thinkers, and stories are important. "The experience of enjoying a good story is a powerful one that pulls in all of our senses and immerses us so that we feel as if we ourselves are actually living the story" (Healy, 2008, p. 28). In fact, storytelling may be part of human genetics. "We crave a story so much that we will piece together unrelated information to rationalize what was actually random and unpredictable" (Vincent, 2012, p. 147). Brands can hint at a story and let the mind of the consumer fill in the rest of the information. Thus, communicating a story about your product is going to make it more memorable in the consumer's mind, because the mind has to work harder to understand the message. A logical story has a beginning, a middle, and an end, a structure that works with the idea of cause-and-effect relationships. For instance, there is a problem and the product solves it. This is a popular format for many television commercials, especially for cleaning products.

The message itself needs to make an emotional connection without using emotion. Successful slogans that evoke emotion include:

The softer side of Sears
Like a rock
We bring good things to life.
When you care enough to send the very best
It's the real thing.
When it absolutely positively has to get there
We try harder.
Wait until we get our Hanes on you.

The purpose of developing a good story about the brand is to create relationships with the consumer that encourage emotional preferences for the brand. "Brand storytelling should primarily be the driver of participation, not sales" (Jiwa, 2014, p. 62). Storytelling allows consumers to ascribe meaning to a product or service. Jiwa (2014) describes six strategies for becoming part of the customer's story. Turning a brand's story into an integral part of a consumer's story begins by understanding the rituals of a customer's day—for example, wake up and make a cup of coffee, get the children ready for school, dress for work, drive to work, and so on. Additionally, creating a story that helps to bring joy or happiness to the consumer's life is a great way to appeal to your target audience. Some helpful hints include:

1. Create a service or product that people enjoy and want to come back for; examples: Instagram and Amazon.
2. Change the way the people feel; example: Starbucks.
3. Have the product or service solve a problem; example: cleaning products.
4. Create a story that people can tell themselves; example: "Got milk?"
5. Figure out ways to become part of the consumer's rituals; examples: Zappos and YouTube.
6. Make things easy for people to come back or make a repeat purchase; example: Netflix.

Solving a problem is a popular method for showing how a product can be incorporated into an individual's personal ritual. Procter & Gamble tends to design commercials that are based on the "slice-of-life" formula. This style generally shows a household situation in which the product is the hero of the ad. For example, there is dirt on the floor and the product cleans it up. Or there is a stain on a laundry item, and the soap makes it disappear. This strategy attempts to convince consumers that using the product will help them solve their cleaning and laundry problems. In addition to demonstrating the product, the scenario could be a conversation between two women in a suburban kitchen who discuss the benefits of the product or service.

Sometimes a single piece of communication can act as such a powerful motivator that it remains unchanged for many years. An example is the Arm & Hammer logo. Other companies have updated their look, but the Arm & Hammer logo remains the same graphic of a literal arm and hammer. Another highly successful idea is the "uncola," which positions itself as the opposite of a cola drink. The ideas depicted in commercials are often stories that people can relate to their own individual lives. Beer commercials, for instance, tend to show people in a bar or having fun. Most individuals can identify with this.

Self-Identity

Self-identification helps people to relate to the personality of a brand. For a brand to be successful, consumers need to relate its personality to their own lives. "Contemporary consumers are inclined to express identity via consumption, so we tend to choose those consumption objects that help us to express our sense of identity" (Richardson, 2013, p. 16). Increasingly, our relationship with brands enables individuals to express their own sense of self. Brand attachment is how much people consider the brand to be an extension of themselves. Brand attitude measures how much people like a brand. In contrast, brand attachment measures how much a brand is identified with people's values and how they see themselves.

Attachment to a brand can be measured by asking questions such as "To what extent is [brand X] like you and who you are?" and "How does [brand X] make a statement about you?" Consider the hard-core owners of Harley-Davidson motorcycles. Would they be caught dead on another brand of motorcycle? Similarly, some businessmen don't feel successful until they own an Armani suit. In the same way, loyal Macintosh owners would have trouble buying a personal computer running Microsoft Windows. We create emotional attachments to brands. For instance, do you feel different wearing designer clothes? How do you feel when your wardrobe is from Walmart? Do clothes from Target feel different from clothes purchased at Kmart, Macy's, or JC Penney?

"It might seem a little self-delusional to assume that buying a mass produced commodity says something unique about you as an individual" (Richardson, 2013, p. 17). However, buying an item such as a car or computer can be a meaningful experience. Think about the status that accompanies a BMW or Rolls-Royce for the owner. Moreover, when the brand becomes accessible to you, you know it is yours, and you can identify with it.

Brand Expansion & Extension

Promoting the continued personality and promise of the brand is an important aspect of branding. "The strongest brands occupy a clearly defined and well-focused position in consumers' minds" (Healy, 2008, p. 38). These are brands that dominate their categories. One way to increase a brand's shelf space is to add line extensions. When trying to expand a brand, companies should never lose sight of their brand identity. For instance, Cherry Coke and Vanilla Coke are natural extensions of the Coca-Cola brand. New Coke was not. New Coke was developed to replace the core product, and consumers revolted. Brand extensions need to work with the core product, not against it.

Concerns with brand expansion include: the original brand product can become muddled with the expansions; brand loyalty can be compromised; brand expansion can be very costly. As a result, the perceived benefits may not be as profitable as imagined. One of the central issues with brand extensions is that they never expand category demands and can take business away from the original product.

However, brand expansion may be necessary when the competition introduces a new product to the market. An example is toothpaste. Crest and Colgate needed to address the threat of Arm & Hammer's baking-soda toothpaste (a line expansion). A successful expansion was Nabisco's introduction of fat-free fruit bars and SnackWell's products. Consumers liked these new cookies so much that competitors' profits withered. Another example is Sanka, the caffeine-free coffee. It became so popular with consumers that other brands began introducing caffeine-free extensions. The Harvard Business Review (1999) states:

> Diversifying the product line, creating new products, and splitting large stock keeping units into smaller ones both ensure that the parent brand will evolve to meet the demands of consumers and make it much tougher for the retailer to supplant the species with a store label. (p. 135)

The line extension needs to match the promises of the core product. The brand identity is associated with the promises a company makes. If you make a promise to have clean restaurants, the rest rooms had better be clean. If you promise fast service, all of your stores need to deliver on that promise. Add a brand extension and it runs the risk of tarnishing the brand itself.

Brand expansion is never a hasty decision. It should not be confused with brand extension. Brand extension is the addition of a product that will place the brand in a new product category. Kellogg's has been doing this with the extension of its Special K cereal into the markets of chips and breakfast bars. In contrast, a brand expansion would be Doritos Cool Ranch Flavored chips or a low-fat version of Doritos. These new products would expand the brand, not extend it.

A business needs to pay careful attention to how a decision to expand will impact the long-term value of its brand. Successful expansions include Chevrolet's Corvette, *Time* magazine's *People* magazine, and Frito-Lay's Doritos. "Think of the brand in terms of three components: maker image, product image, and user image" (Harvard Business Review, 1999, p. 138). Sometimes it's better to create a separate brand than to cloud an existing one. For instance, when Gallo wine decided to market wine coolers, it created a new brand called Bartles & Jaymes. The wine brand was not confused with the wine coolers.

Both brand expansion and brand extension require careful planning and research. Once a brand personality is established and successful, a company wants to maintain its image and not detract from it.

Summary

Brands create personalities that resonate on an emotional level with consumers. These personalities dictate how people differentiate one brand from another and thus should be realistic and based on a product attribute. The personality is also reflected in the name of the product or service. Names can be made up or based on a family name. Names and tag lines or slogans are the verbal aspects of brand personality. Tag lines should be unique yet simple enough for people to remember.

The visual personality of the brand is expressed through logos. Today, logos have become more personal and less abstract. In addition to names, tag lines, and logos, recounting stories develops personality. By telling a story with emotional appeal, people can self-identify with a brand. Once its brand personality is established in the marketplace, a company can then expand or extend its product line.

Exercises

1. Storytelling is important to commercials. Watch the commercials shown during the airing of a popular program and write down the different stories being told. Which ones resonate with you and why?
2. Use the brand attachment question to explore self-representation and brands. Pick several brands (fashion, soft drinks, and computers, for example) and ask three people these questions: "To what extent is [brand X] like you and who you are?" and "How does [brand X] make a statement about you?" Compare and contrast the answers.
3. Select a product that you use frequently. Can you write a story about it that could be turned into a YouTube video?
4. Self-identity: Do products from different brands make you feel different? Which ones do you identify with? Please explain.

References

Beltrone, G. (2015, January 7). Justin Bieber's Calvin Klein ads make everyone everywhere question everything. *AdWeek*. Retrieved January 8, 2015, from http://www.adweek.com/adfreak/justin-biebers-calvin-klein-ads-make-everyone-everywhere-question-everything-162197

Drewniany, B.L., & Jewler, A.J. (2008). *Creative strategy in advertising* (9th ed.). Boston, MA: Thomson/Wadsworth.

Gobé, M. (2009). *Emotional branding*. New York: Allworth Press.

Harvard Business Review. (1999). *Harvard Business Review on brand management*. Boston, MA: Harvard Business School Press.

Healy, M. (2008). *What is branding?* Mies, Switzerland: RotoVision.

Jiwa, B. (2014). *Marketing a love story*. Australia: The Story of Telling Press.

Jobling, P., & Crowley, D. (1996). *Graphic design: Reproduction and representation since 1800*. Manchester, UK: Manchester University Press.

Martin, D.N. (1989). *Romancing the brand*. New York: American Management Association.

McCoy, K. (1998). Education in an adolescent profession. In S. Heller (Ed.), *The education of a graphic designer* (pp. 3–12). New York: Allworth Press.

Moser, M. (2003). *United we brand*. Boston, MA: Harvard Business School.

Nudd, T. (2015, February 2). The 5 best ads of Super Bowl XLIX. *AdWeek*. Retrieved February 3, 2015, from http://www.adweek.com/news-gallery/advertising-branding/5-best-ads-super-bowl-xlix-162716

Ogilvy, D. (1984). *Confessions of an advertising man*. New York: Atheneum.

O'Leary, N. (2015, February 2). Snickers' Brady Bunch ad wins first Super Clio for best in the big game. *AdWeek*. Retrieved February 26, 2015, from http://www.adweek.com/news/advertising-branding/snickers-brady-bunch-ad-wins-first-super-clio-best-spot-big-game-162736

Richardson, B. (2013). *Tribal marketing, tribal branding*. New York: Palgrave Macmillan.

Sacharow, S. (1982). *Symbols of trade*. New York: Art Direction Book Company.

Travis, D. (2000). *Emotional branding*. Roseville, CA: Prima Venture.

Vincent, L. (2012). *Brand real*. New York: American Management Association.

Winters, A.A., & Goodman, S. (1986). *Fashion advertising and promotion*. New York: Fairchild Publications.

Zakarin, J. (2014, December 30). The new Matthew McConaughey Lincoln ads will leave you dazed and bemused. *AdWeek*. Retrieved December, 30, 2014, from https://www.yahoo.com/movies/matthew-mcconaughey-new-lincoln-ads-106619743477.html

· 8 ·

BRANDS, PERSONAL BRANDING, AND COMMUNITY

With personalization, however, the customer becomes a co-creator of the content of the experience. More and more customers want to play this role.
—Daryl Travis, 2000, p. 127

From personal marks in ancient times to today's personal branding, symbols have been used to identify people. Personal branding and brand communities will be addressed in this chapter. With the creation of the term "selfies" comes the idea of personal branding. New media, the Internet, smartphones, and tablets now enable people to individually brand themselves. People identify with different brands because people wear them as a sign of personal branding. For example, Jimmy Choo shoes are extremely expensive, and the design of the shoes lets people know who is wearing them. The branded logo can appear on the front and back of the shoe. Moreover, the name is embossed on the soles. When walking in sand, snow, or any soft surface, the name leaves an impression. There is no doubt that Jimmy Choo's design is letting individuals know that the wearer has paid $600 for a pair of shoes (unless you can find them on sale for $400). People wearing these shoes will identify with each other, because only a person with money and taste can buy these products. At times individuals with similar brand interests form a community.

What personal branding and brand communities have in common is using the brand on a personal level. Personal branding is taking the concept of branding and applying it to oneself. Brand communities use a specific brand to personalize it for the group. Individual members create the norms and behavior of a brand community, not the brand itself. In many cases, brand managers need to learn the nuances of the community and its relationship to the brand. Personalization of branded concepts is what unites the two concepts of personal branding and branding communities, because individuals use the brand as a form of personal expression.

Personalization

Personalization is the customizing of a feature of a product or service so that the customer benefits from more convenience, lower cost, or some other advantage. In the past, personalization was printing the consumer's name on a piece of direct mail, such as the Publishers Clearing House Sweepstakes. Today, personalization is the involvement of the consumer with the brand. Richardson (2013) argues that the postmodern consumer has a desire to express and complete the self through individualized consumer identity.

Customers expect relevant content from the brand; thus, marketing needs to be made personal. One way to do this is through personalized digital marketing. Technology now makes it possible to reach customers on a one-to-one basis, and interactive marketing can be used for personalization. This can be achieved through the display of personalized banners and web content. Marketers want to turn data into action. Actions can range from signing up for an e-newsletter or promotion, clicking on a web link, or moving from being a visitor to a paying customer (see Neustar, 2014). Another example of this is sending personal messages to consumers' mobile phones and devices.

Personalization can also be achieved by placing customers in different groups, depending on the TV shows they watch, the stores they shop, and the media they read. Using these audience profiles, different banners can be displayed on a website. An excellent example of personalization is collaborative filtering. According to Montgomery and Smith (2008):

> Collaborative filtering was one of the first examples of personalization technologies widely available on the web. Search engines will keep track of a user's searches and will automatically repeat the search options as a form of personalization. For

example, collaborative filtering systems have been employed by Amazon, Barnes & Noble, LibraryThing, and Storycode to recommend books; Blockbuster, Eachmovie, Hollywood Video, Movielens, and Netflix to recommend movies. (p. 134)

By adapting a product or service to the needs of the consumer, personalization can increase earnings. "The practical advantages of personalization lie in greater customer satisfaction and higher profits" (Arora et al., 2008, p. 307). New technological developments have contributed to the increased use of personalized marketing. Similarly, programs such as Twitter, Facebook, LinkedIn, and YouTube have contributed to the concept of personal branding, because brands are often cited in consumer-created messages.

Personal Branding

In addition to the increased use of personalized marketing, individuals are now using marketing strategies to brand themselves. Personal branding is the use of marketing to create a brand for oneself. It is a person's image and reputation. Gehl (2011) states that "it is the metaphorical expansion of the practices of marketing of branded goods and services into the realm of individual workers, freelancers, and entrepreneurs" (p. 2). The explosion of social media, combined with a difficult job market, has made personal branding a necessity for many people. For professionals, strong personal branding is the key to achievement. "Consumers were increasingly aware of the need to build an online construction of themselves that enhanced or mirrored their physical presence" (Barnes & Hair, 2009, p. 233). In today's economy, personal branding translates into social capital and utilizes social media as a primary means of communication.

Personal branding "means that you create the right kind of emotional response you want people to have when they hear your name, see you online, or meet you in real life" (Deckers & Lacy, 2013, p. 7). The concept derives from twentieth-century self-help literature. Tom Peters's 1997 article in *Fast Company* first used the term "personal branding." The increased use of branding in our daily lives, on our clothing, and in the media landscape makes a logical leap to place branding on the atomic level—the idea of branding you. Since the late 1990s, a number of different authors have become personal branding advocates, including Karen Kang, Erik Deckers, and Kyle Lacy. Using self-help concepts, the road to individual success can be found in self-packaging, that is, the organization of personal skills and expertise into a package that is marketed like goods and services. With increased use of self-expression on the Internet, personal branding became a new tool for the twenty-first century.

Personal branding is a form of self-promotion that does not employ boasting or bragging. It involves an intense monitor of one's sense of self and how the self is represented through written words and images that are circulated through the Internet. Experts view it as a carefully groomed image on the web. But instead of having others post information about you on the web, personal branding involves individuals' control of their own images.

People can promote themselves and their skills just as a small business does. Instead of thinking about personal branding as boasting, think of it as educating potential employers and colleagues about yourself. In today's world, in which people will generally have more than one job, personal branding becomes a necessity for success. Like traditional branding, personal branding is based on the reality of a person and his or her work. People who are passionate about their work tend to be more successful in their careers.

Personal branding is developing a strategy and action plan to guide the promotion of your brand. Karen Kang (2013) has developed a five-step plan for creating a personal brand. Prior to beginning the steps, you need to establish your goal. The goal may be to let people know about your current job, to find new employment, to change careers, or to get funding to start a new business.

Step 1 is to position yourself. Your goal will influence how you place yourself. Knowing your goal should help to shape the way in which you present yourself. For instance, if you were interested in a sales position, emphasizing people skills would be helpful. Similarly, a management job requires leadership skills, which would mean demonstrating that you are good at working with people. Other factors to consider are your target audience or what type of company would be interested in hiring you. Approaching a trendy new company would require a different type of message than communicating with standard corporations. Competition that you are aware of in the marketplace is another factor to consider. Finally, understanding your strengths and values is essential. Here is an example: Valarie wants a new leadership position. Her business experience, combined with her volunteer work, makes her a good candidate for a leadership job. Few of her competitors share her passion and values as a concerned citizen. Her target audience is corporate America, and her personal brand has been accordingly designed.

Another method for achieving your goals is to understand the problems that you could solve. How can you provide a solution to an employer's problem? By understanding the challenges facing your target audience, you can show directly how you could solve that issue. Your experience may be a valuable contribution to the company. Or, you may bring a unique point of view to your work. Like the design solutions discussed in Chapter 4, problem-solutions work well in personal branding. Problem: the company needs managers. Solution: you have managerial skills. Positioning identifies your individual strong points and helps to differentiate you from others.

Step 2 is messaging. When the positioning category is clearly understood, it is easier to create a message about yourself. The words you choose and descriptions you state are important. What do you tell people when they ask: "What do you do?" It is important to establish your name and your occupation when meeting people, especially if you are engaged in a networking situation. Key messages about you need to be a component of all written and spoken conversations. If you are a person who does many different things, you may need to focus on just one or two. In some cases you may need another business card for different target audiences. For example, a graphic designer may create websites and printed brochures. Her website clients may not perceive her as doing the print work, and vice versa. People tend to identify you with one thing and may not be aware of all your talents. When engaging in personal branding, you want to control the one thing they associate with you.

In addition to making claims about yourself, the claims need to be backed up. Back-up information may consist of college degrees, work experience, awards, or publications. Think about the core message and then what facts you want to use to support the message. The more clarity you have in your communication, the easier it will be for people to understand the information.

Step 3 is developing a brand strategy. The strategy helps to achieve the goal. "The brand strategy platform provides the vehicle to help you to put into words the essence and value of your brand" (Kang, 2013, p. 78). The brand strategy begins by examining a person's core values, which include one's personal ethics, passions, and dreams. Next is an assessment of a person's strengths. Strengths are your hard and soft skills combined with your areas of expertise. Remember that volunteer work should also be included in the skill set. Another factor is an individual's personality. Personality attributes also need to be considered when developing a brand strategy. Consider all of these elements and articulate your brand image along with the promise of your brand. What are the key words that describe your brand?

Step 4 is to identify the ecosystem or the spheres of influence that can create perceptions about your brand. An example of a simple ecosystem would start with you and then move to your inner circle. The department you work in, your company, and external perceptions move outward, making larger circles around yourself. The ecosystem is built on relationships, and communicating your brand message should move from those closest to you to the wider public. People close to you should understand your message, because as the information spreads, people will reference each other. Networking is also part of an ecosystem. When networking with new people, try to be liked and remembered. If you communicate your brand message clearly, people will remember you for your brand image.

Step 5 is the action plan. In this step, the focus is on brand communication and developing actions that will communicate your message. For example, one approach would be to communicate with a handful of influential people rather than undertaking a large media campaign. Consider what actions you can take to communicate your message to your target audience.

This five-step plan is one method of personal branding. Gehl (2011) describes a four-step procedure:

1. Self–examination resulting in differentiating oneself via textual and hypertextual representations.
2. Adopting the language of transparency and authenticity.
3. Making connections with others by offering quantifiable affective exchanges.
4. Most importantly, engaging in autosurveillance. (p. 7)

Self-examination is a necessary step in self-positioning. Understand your personal strengths and be able to communicate them. Articulating your individual qualities in text is a form of self-scrutiny that is helpful in the first step of personal branding development. Instead of cataloging work experience, education, and skills on a resume, personal branding begins with self-evaluation. Quantifiable items become emotional characteristics.

A tool that can be used for achieving an employment goal is to reverse-engineer your desired job. Write down all of the skills needed for the career situation you want. Then figure out how your skills can be customized to meet the needs of the job. Writing these down will clarify qualities of self and help you to identify your message.

The branded message is transformed into context for the World Wide Web. Sites such as Facebook, LinkedIn, and Twitter all provide places for personal data. Some of these even provide fields to be filled in. Once the information is circulated on the Internet, it becomes hypertext links that can be spread across the web. In contrast to mass media, which spreads the same message to large audiences, the Internet is the medium for sharing individual messages like personal branding.

The purpose of personal branding is to design a marketable image that sets you apart from your competition. However, this image must be based on authentic personal traits. The language of authenticity requires self-branders to be honest about their strengths and weaknesses. Personal branding does not trick people into buying your services or create a false persona. It is about establishing who you are and what you are good at, in order to place you above the competition.

The emotional nature of personal branding requires connections through reciprocity. To form friendships and develop relationships, people need to be reciprocal with each other. Do not expect to receive help without giving back. It is through exchanges that relationships are formed. "In the cross-pollination of Web 2.0 practices and personal branding, the object is to provide an easily measured quantity of emotional content to others in order to receive emotional content in return" (Gehl, 2011, p. 11). Blog comments, "like this" features, and connections illustrate how the web can be reciprocal.

Autosurveillance is required in the personal branding process. Once personal material is presented on the web, people need to check to make sure the information is correct—for example, using Google to check your name to see what is being said about you online. Individuals must maintain a watchful eye over how their brand is being presented. One method for doing this is to use Google Alert on your name to monitor your online persona.

Further, the Internet creates a space for sharing emotional content and personal information, including self-published blogs. Blogs enable people to publically express intimate feelings and confessional content. Thus, the process of branding oneself is extremely personal. By carefully evaluating yourself and understanding your strengths and weaknesses, you can develop a personal brand message that will shape how people perceive you. It is argued that personal branding can be leveraged into personal and financial success.

Personal Branding Paradox

The concept of personal branding is important in today's economy. However, it does create a social paradox. If everyone is unique, then no one is unique. Personal branding advocates argue that anyone who uses this practice can (to use a common phrase in the literature) "stand out from the crowd" (Gehl,

2011, p. 5). Personal branding advocates contend that it places responsibility on the individual. Branding is no longer in the domain of corporations. People maintain individuality in a world of rampant layoffs. Everyone has a chance to stand out. Take control of your own image before someone creates it for you. We have a responsibility to cultivate our brands, and a new phenomenon that encourages the promotion of one is the selfie.

Selfies

A selfie is a self-portrait created with a cell phone or digital device that can be immediately shared over a network. It has become a popular new genre in American culture. These pictures are often silly and boring and include a body part. Many images are taken at arm's length, with part of the arm in the photo. Saltz (2014) says: "Selfies are usually casual, improvised, fast; their primary purpose is to be seen here, now, by other people, most of them unknown, in social networks" (p. 2). They are instant and spontaneous, not meticulously framed or shot images.

Wide-eye grins, ice cream cones, bizarre poses, shirtless men, pig masks, and whatever else you can think of have probably been shown in selfies. "It features the corporeal self, understood in relation to the surrounding physical space, filtered through the digital device, and destined for social networks" (Hess, 2015, p. 1629). Selfies portray the individual in contexts that occur in everyday life. Hess (2015) states:

> They afford for users the means to materialize the self via their immediate photographic composition in everyday existence, giving credence to our emplacement in the here and now. Contained in pockets and purses as users travel, and held at arm's length as selfies are composed, smartphones document the spatial and temporal coordinates of a life that is simultaneously extraordinary and mundane. (p. 1629)

There are four distinct elements of a selfie: the self, physical space, the device, and the network. Individuals decide to capture a moment in time with a photograph of themselves, and moments in time occur within physical spaces. The physical place relates to the individual in the photo. Is the place unique or ordinary? The device is often indicated by the frame and angle of the photo. For instance, often an arm or body part can be seen in the image, and the hand holding the device influences the angle. The selfie is not complete until it is circulated through the network. Others need to see the picture.

Unlike vacation photographs, selfies are media events. Their relationship to media can turn selfies into self-advertising.

Commercial brands have embraced selfies. In 2013, brands such as Target, Samsung, and Aflac created selfies or selfie contests (see Griner, 2014). Samsung ran a campaign called #TogetherWeRise that featured a mosaic of LeBron James pictures from selfies created by fans. Samsung offered free phones to individuals who would jump into a lake and take a selfie. The point was to prove the phone could withstand being submerged in water. Selfie contests involve people in the branding process. Another way consumers become involved is through branding communities.

Brand Community

A brand community is a specialized, non geographically bound community based on a structured set of social relationships among admirers of a brand. It is specialized because at its center is a branded good or service. Like other communities, a shared consciousness, rituals and traditions, and a sense of moral responsibility mark it. "The social contact experienced through shared devotion to an activity or brand becomes an important means whereby their need for community is fulfilled" (Richardson, 2013, p. 4). Car enthusiasts, fan clubs, and quilting bees are early examples of consumer communities. "Consumers also endlessly discuss and debate the meaning of brands and products, offering up a wealth of information about their perceptions and accrued meanings" (Kozinets, 2006, p. 287). Consumers will discuss and debate the meanings of brands with each other, thereby creating a social context in which the brand is central.

In the late 1880s, Ferdinand Tonnies observed that the nature of community was changing from a familial, emotional rural community to a mechanical, contractual, and urban one. Depersonalized, mass-produced communities were displacing "real" ones. These changes were brought about by the transformation of the Industrial Revolution and the rise of communication technologies. A central difference brought about by this change was a shift from geographic communities to communities of interest. Topics, instead of location, became the focus of the groups. At the same time, branded products replaced unmarked goods, and mass advertising replaced personal selling. With these alterations, the concept of branding should have a central place in the discourse of modernity and society.

Brand communities are liberated from geography and informed by mass media. These are imagined communities, and members believe that they are similar to each other. Moreover, these communities are explicitly commercial. Members of these groups do meet face to face and in communal gathering sites. For instance, beer communities meet at bars and share a drink of the brand. Brand communities can be company-driven communities or "joint ventures" between companies and customers. An example of a company-driven community is the Salomon sports company, a maker of winter sports equipment. The company was excluded from some of the ski distribution channels and decided to focus on the snowboarding community.

> In 1995, Salomon decided to set up a marketing unit made up of snowboarders. It designed a specific "logo" for its snowboard activities and supported a team of good snowboarders fitted out with non-Salomon boards (Salomon boards did not yet exist!). Some of the tribe members were invited to join the design of Salomon projects. (Cova & Cova, 2001, p. 18)

In 1996, the company was ready to launch its snowboarding products. Instead of advertising, Salomon appeared at snowboarding camps with boards for pro shops. The company respected the special nature of the tribe and launched an untraditional marketing campaign that focused on the snowboarders themselves. Three years later, it became established in the French snowboarding market.

People become involved with brand communities for a number of different reasons. Wang, Meng, and Dong (2012) explain why:

> Some see them as an efficient way to obtain information about certain organizations or their products and services, some simply enjoy interacting with people of shared interests, and still others want to take advantage of the opportunity to vent their negative feelings and to express personal concerns. (p. 3)

Companies cannot control brand communities. Examples of two groups that formed without company support are the Saab car and Macintosh communities. Muniz and O'Guinn (2001) researched these group. The Midwest Saab Club was a central group for the car fans, and Macintosh user groups and clubs attracted the Macintosh users. Both groups used the Internet to share information. To be a member of these groups, participants must be true believers in the brand. "Differentiating between those who are true believers in the brand, and those who are merely opportunistic is a common concern voiced by brand community members" (Muniz & O'Guinn, 2001, p. 16).

Members of a brand community may compare themselves to brands for other products. For example, Macintosh users compare themselves to IBM PC users. PC users are considered more business oriented and politically conservative, while Macintosh users are considered more creative and liberal. Saab communities will compare their brand to Volvo. Volvo owners are considered dull compared to Saab owners. Saab cars are perceived to be more fun.

Brand communities also have rituals and traditions. For instance, Saab owners will beep their horns or flash their lights when they see another Saab driver. Waving, honking, and asking about the other car is another form of acknowledgment. "Every time such a greeting ritual is initiated or returned, members are validated in their understanding of the community" (Muniz & O'Guinn, 2001, p. 23). Some car companies have car rallies and events where owners can meet up. For instance, Saturn turned a brand community meeting into a television commercial.

Communities are also aware of the history of the brand. The story of Steve Jobs and Steven Wozniak creating a computer in a garage is the classic Macintosh tale. The launching of the Macintosh began with their famous Super Bowl commercial stating that "1984 won't be like *1984*," a reference to the book of that name. For the Saab community, it is the distinctiveness of the brand over time and its technological innovation. Saab's story goes back to World War II, when the company was trying to find a non-war product to build. After trying to manufacture boats unsuccessfully, the company turned to cars. The unwanted boats were sunk in Lake Vanern. A similar story is told about Apple's unsuccessful Lisa computers, which were buried in the desert in the United States. Myths like these become part of the community culture and are told over and over.

Pictures of older models of cars and computers can be found on the web pages of brand community members. These historical models can become the subject of brand stories. Brand stories are generated from commercial texts, the significance of the brand image, and the product itself. Images from the past and present become part of the communal tale. Community members will recognize the year of older logos and their meaning. For instance, "an old Saab logo with airplane-like fins on it makes the connection between Saab cars and airplanes and also reveals that the logo came from the 1960s" (Muniz & O'Guinn, 2001, p. 27).

Advertising is an important part of the brand community. For example, the phrase "For the Rest of Us," used in the introductory Apple Macintosh campaign, is a central concept for the Macintosh brand community. When a new advertisement is created, the ad must speak to the brand community and those outside it. For example, the Macintosh community embraces its anti-establishment roots. These commercials help to define the group.

Group membership is greatly enhanced through the sharing of experiences with the brand in computer-mediated environments. Stories about the joy of driving the car or the ease of use of the computer build communal relationships. Similarly, sharing horror stories about competitive brands is a popular practice. The superiority of the brand reinforces the idea of loyalty to the product. It also elevates the brand in the eyes of members. A part of this membership is also helping others with the use of the brand. This is especially true for computers. Community members can turn to each other for information about the product.

Companies in the Community

Brand communities recognize that companies manufacture brands. Saab owners understand that General Motors (GM) took over a small Swedish company to make the cars. GM is a large American corporation, and some community members believe that GM basically leaves the Saab division alone. Rather than acknowledge that GM makes the cars, the notion that the Saab division is separate distances the brand from GM itself. This is important for some community members.

Awareness of the corporation as a social actor in the world is also important. Community actions and volunteerism can gain recognition for a brand. For instance, the Panera Bread Company was the first national restaurant chain to create a policy of taking end-of-the-day baked goods to food banks and homeless shelters. "These measures taken with its customers' interests in mind have helped to make Panera the most successful restaurant chain in the first decade of the new millennium" (Malone & Fiske, 2013, p. 21).

Being a good corporate citizen is a brand image that appeals to many customers. For example, soul branding is the procedure of placing corporate behaviors with higher social values, such as environmental concerns. "There is a growing contingency of consumers who see their purchase decisions as equivalent to a voting record, and they are sometimes willing to change their buying habits or pay a bit more for a product if they believe they are helping a worthy cause" (Levine, 2003, p. 106). For example, in 2002 Anheuser-Busch distributed canned drinking water to flood victims in Kentucky. This type of activity creates a positive image for a brand. Another way in which brands develop affirmative perceptions is through the loyalty of brand communities that are sometimes called tribes.

Tribal Marketing

Tribal marketing is a term used to refer to branding communities. Cova and Cova (2001) describe a tribe: "A tribe is defined as a network of heterogeneous persons—in terms of age, sex, income, etc.—who are linked by a shared passion or emotion; a tribe is capable of collective action, its members are not simple consumers, they are also advocates" (p. 10). People are essentially social and need social relationships. "Individual consumers discover that they have something important in common with each other, the social contact experienced through shared devotion to an activity or brand becomes an important means whereby their need for community is fulfilled" (Richardson, 2013, p. 4).

Consumers, not companies, create tribal marketing. It is a form of social connection, and members have a shared sense of values and emotions. Members demonstrate their tribal credentials through shared identity and activities. For example, *Star Trek* fans wear sci-fi regalia, and sports fans wear the color of their team. Moreover, tribes tend to have a linking value that bonds them together. Harley-Davidson owners have a sense of patriotism, personal freedom, and rebelliousness. The group wears biker gear, Harley-Davidson logos, and tattoos, and participates in biker rallies. Beamish beer drinkers have a sense of tradition and playfulness but want to be distinguished from boring beer drinkers. Their practices include Beamish tours and brand-related events.

Tribal marketers realize that they must support the tribe's agenda. Company programs cannot be imposed on the tribe itself. By backing the tribe, the company can become part of the tribal group. Brand tribes benefit the makers, because members are advocates for the brand and thus spread the word about the brand. Also, tribe recommendations are considered to be independent from commercial interests and are therefore more objective. Tribal behavior can be studied by conducting ethnographic research.

Ethnographic Research

Brands are an integral part of contemporary social life. Understanding the impact of brands on people and culture requires in-depth studies of groups and individuals. Brand groups have been researched by a number of scholars through ethnographic studies. A number of different ethnographic studies have been conducted to illustrate how brand communities may be investigated. These include Cova and Cova (2001), Muniz and O'Guinn (2001), and Richardson (2013). These detailed examinations provide valuable information about branding and branded communities that would be difficult to produce through quantitative methods.

Ethnography utilizes the concept of participant observer. "By actively participating, rather than observing, the marketer undergoes the experience of a novice or apprentice member of the culture, and consequently much deeper insight can be obtained" (Richardson, 2013, p. 59). Knowledge that might not be revealed to an outsider is available to a participant observer. Thus, ethnographic research uncovers concepts and behavior about groups that would not be revealed through other research methods.

Summary

Consumers have become more involved in the branding process. They identify with products and want personalized items. Companies understand the importance of consumer participation in the branding method. The popularity of branding has been transformed on a personal level. People now brand themselves. A number of authors have developed methods for self-branding. Another means of personalization is through brand communities or tribes.

Exercises

1. Find examples of personalized marketing and describe them. A good place to start would be by examining Amazon.com or Netflix.
2. What brands do you identify with? Look for logos on your clothing and make notes on what food brands you eat.

3. Follow the five-step plan to create a personal brand.
4. Observe selfies on the network. What type of settings are the images taken in? What does the selfie context tell you about the person?

References

Arora, N., Dreze, X., Ghose, A., Hess, J.D., Iyengar, R., Jing, B., et al. (2008). Putting one-to-one marketing to work: Personalization, customization, and choice. *Market Lett*, 19, 305–321.

Barnes, S.B., & Hair, N.F. (2009). *From banners to YouTube: Using the rear-view mirror to look at the future of advertising* (with Neil Hair). *International Journal of Internet Marketing and Advertising*, 5(3), 223–239.

Cova, B., & Cova, V. (2001). Tribal marketing: The tribalisation of society and its impact on the conduct of marketing. *European Journal of Marketing*, special issue: *Societal marketing in 2002 and beyond*, 1–26.

Deckers, E., & Lacy, K. (2013). *Branding yourself: How to use social media to reinvent yourself.* Indianapolis, IN: Que Publishing.

Gehl, R.W. (2011). Ladders, samurai, and blue collars: Personal branding in Web 2.0. *First Monday*, 16(9). Retrieved September 6, 2016, from http://firstmonday.org/ojs/index.php/fm/article/view/3579/3041

Griner, D. (2014, February 11). Infographic: How brands became selfie obsessed; Charting the birth of a photo frenzy. *AdWeek*. Retrieved June 3, 2015 from http://www.adweek.com/adfreak/infographic-how-brands-became-selfie-obsessed-155651

Hess, A. (2015). The selfie assemblage. *International Journal of Communication*, 9, 1629–1646.

Kang, K. (2013). *Branding pays: The five-step system to reinvent your personal brand.* Palo Alto, CA: Branding Pays Media.

Kozinets, R.V. (2006, September). Click to connect: Netnography and tribal advertising. *Journal of Advertising Research*, pp. 279–288.

Levine, M. (2003). *A branded world.* Hoboken, NJ: John Wiley & Sons.

Malone, C., & Fiske, S.T. (2013). *The human brand.* San Francisco, CA: Jossey-Bass.

Montgomery, A., & Smith, M.D. (2008). Prospects for personalization on the Internet. *Journal of Interactive Marketing*, 23(2), 130–137.

Muniz, A.M., & O'Guinn, T.C. (2001). Brand community. *Journal of Consumer Research*, 27(4), 1–51 [Online].

Neustar. (2014). *An A–Z glossary of personalized marketing* (white paper). Retrieved August 26, 2014, from www.neustar.biz.

Peters, T. (1997). The brand called you. *Fast Company*. Retrieved August 22, 2016, from http://www.fastcompany.com/28905/brand-called-you

Richardson, B. (2013). *Tribal marketing, tribal branding*. New York: Palgrave Macmillan.

Saltz, J. (2014, February 3). Art at arm's length: A history of the selfie. *New York Magazine*. Retrieved June 2, 2015, from http://www.vulture.com/2014/01/history9of9the9selfie.html

Travis, D. (2000). *Emotional branding*. Roseville, CA: Prima Venture.

Wang, H., Meng, J., & Dong, F. (2012). Sharing as "frands": Personified branding strategies on social network sites in China. *First Monday, 17*, 5–7. Retrieved April 15, 2015, from http://firstmonday.org/ojs/index.php/fm/article/view/3718/3201

· 9 ·

BRANDS BECOME ICONS

An "icon" as I use the word here is a thematized commodity: an object, person, or experience that has acquired added value through the commercial heightening of meaning.
—Ernest Sternberg, 1999, p. 4

Iconic brands are brands that have become cultural icons. These brands are so common that children learn the brand image. In fact, "The Logo Board Game" is based on our knowledge of brands, which is now so common that it can be used in a game. Some people identify themselves by the branded clothes they wear. Is the dress you're wearing from Walmart or Neiman Marcus? It is the rare person who wears a dress from Walmart and a pair of designer shoes. Advertising agencies work their magic when they create a branded image and personality. As these brands are spread around the world, they can become iconic. However, not all brands become icons.

Iconography is the study of symbols, and iconology is the study of symbols in relationship to a specific historical time period. Iconography is a discipline that examines images in order to understand their direct or indirect meaning. Gombrich (1972) states: "Images apparently occupy a curious position somewhere between the statements of language, which are intended to convey a meaning, and the things of nature, to which we can only give a meaning" (p. 2). Illustrated texts tend to be part of iconography. For example, iconographers will try to match a complex illustration with a text that accounts for all of its principle features. These are images and texts that have existed for long periods of time.

Icons

Iconic images and texts were originally considered to be religious artifacts. The term "icon" was applied to Orthodox Christian religious pictures. This included images of Christ and depictions of his life. Often these images were portrayed through highly restrictive conventions of representation. As a result, Christian icons share a similar appearance, because the visual elements have tended to remain the same over time. In addition, images portraying the same story would have similar elements.

Cultural icons have existed since ancient times. In pre-modern times, icons were depicted in paintings and sculpture, then communicated through oral storytelling. With the development of mass communication, iconic images are now distributed through books, magazines, newspapers, film, television and the Internet. "Today, the culture industries—such as film, music, television, journalism, magazines, sports, books, advertising, and public relations—are bent on cultivating and monetizing these icons" (Holt, 2004, p. 2). As a result, icons are pervasive in contemporary culture.

Today's icons do not have to refer to a text. The term icon comes from the Greek word meaning image or portrait. Icons are people or things considered to be representative symbols. These are used as shorthand to represent concepts. For instance, James Dean was the symbol of American rebellion in the 1950s. Contemporary icons are part of everyday life. "Icons serve as society's foundational compass points—anchors of meaning continually referenced in entertainment, journalism, politics, and advertising" (Holt, 2004, p. 1)

An icon that developed in the twentieth century was the Berlin Wall. The wall divided the city of Berlin into two different zones. It became a metonym—a figure of speech in which one thing stands for another—for the division of Germany into two countries. Many connotations became associated with the Berlin Wall image, including the difference between ideological beliefs, political systems, and the Cold War. When the wall came down, it represented a global symbolic act—the removal of the division between East and West, or communism and capitalism. Walls are generally symbols that represent division or defense. For instance, the metaphor of a brick wall is used to describe an impasse or unyielding position. Over time, the Berlin Wall became an icon of conflict, and its removal was a representation of peace.

This type of icon is interwoven with everyday experience in complex ways that embody powerful images and evoke personal emotions. Moreover, icons express an idea that is immediately obvious to us. "The promises made by icons go to the heart of the Western experience of life in the current era in a way that is not superficial" (Fridell & Konings, 2013, p. 12). They are universal social signs.

Rushkoff (1999) argued that young people were attracted to iconic representation. He states: "Icons have become the new unit of communication in the mediaspace characterized by deconstruction" (p. 186). Icons are more specific symbols than pictures. A photograph can be deconstructed, but an icon has a specific idea associated with it. For instance, there is no mistaking what the Nike swoosh means. Iconic symbols are more universal. As a result, young people place iconic stickers on computers, backpacks, and skateboards. "By adopting the postlinguistic currency of an iconic culture, marketers can reposition themselves and their brands in a manner consistent with the operating system of today's point-and-click marketplace" (p. 186). Our consumer culture has been influenced by digital technologies.

Icons frequently occur in mass media to communicate visual messages. For example, flags are often used to identify a particular country. Combined with other visual elements, flags can quickly convey a message. For instance, every time an American sees the U.S. flag, he or she thinks of the country. Icons are also associated with geographic locations. Liberty Mutual insurance films its television commercials with the Statue of Liberty in the background. The statue is a visual icon that reminds the viewer of the name of the company. Other popular geographic icons are the Eiffel Tower and the Golden Gate Bridge.

Sternberg (1999) contends that today we live in a culture with an economy of images. The driving force in our economy is the image. He states:

> To begin understanding the new economy, we must absolve ourselves from the prejudice that images are merely attached to goods after production, through some variety of hucksterism, as if commercial images were parasites. The making of icons now has to be understood in itself as a kind of production, one that fulfills consumer longings. (p. 5)

Additionally, contemporary icons are objects that can be bought and sold on the market, and they have cultural meaning in the transaction. Some of the icons are personalities and celebrities, such as Oprah Winfrey, Michael Jackson, Bill Gates, and Brad Pitt. These icons influence debates in the public sphere. Consider the humanitarian work done by Bono and Angelina Jolie. These icons encourage people to act. For example, actor John Travolta used one of his airplanes to bring food and medical supplies to earthquake victims in Haiti. The act was viewed as one of kindness and generosity.

Fridell & Konings (2013) argue that iconic personas are woven into the everyday experience of capitalist life. News stories about celebrities and their actions appear each day on the evening news. They describe icons as expressing "something in a way that is immediately obvious to us; they are intuitively representative of the time and place that people live in" (p. 11). Icons represent something larger and complex. Iconic brands fit the description because the meaning associated with the brand goes beyond the product or service.

Brands can also act as social activists. An example is the Benetton Group's advertising campaign using images of social controversy. Images expressed such concepts as racism, war, AIDS, and overpopulation. The jarring pictures the company used in its campaign evoked a tremendous amount of social commentary. The pictures appeared throughout the world on billboards and in glossy magazines. No products were depicted in the campaign. Instead, the brand focused exclusively on social issues. In this way, Benetton promoted its role as a socially concerned corporate citizen. The advertiser was more interested in promoting a positive institutional image through social concerns than selling specific products. Cultural branding aligns with cultural topics.

Cultural Brands

Holt (2004) developed a set of principles to describe cultural branding. Based on a systematic analysis of six American icons, he created a series of axioms to explain how icons evolve and are sustained over time. The first axiom is that iconic brands speak to strong contradictions in society. They address the anxieties and desires of a society, feelings that are generally widely shared by a large portion of the nation's citizens. For example, in the 1980s, Budweiser became one of the most popular beers in the country because it appealed to working-class men. The economic and political meltdown in the United States in the 1970s, combined with the increasing independence of women, left men feeling emasculated. President Ronald Regan invoked the myth of the American frontier to restore the country's economy. This myth resonated with masculine ideals. Budweiser took advantage of this acute tension to create a new masculine identity based on the vocations of skilled manual laborers. The title "This Bud's for You" connected with working men. "The campaign firmly established Budweiser as an icon, one of the most persuasive and cherished cultural leaders of America's working men" (Holt, 2004, p. 102). By making the connection between male identity and the product, Budweiser became iconic.

The second axiom states that iconic brands create identity myths to address the desires and anxieties of society. Iconic brands communicate through the mass media, most commonly by way of television commercials. Advertising often uses status appeals to reach consumers; however, iconic brands do not. They feature a more attention-getting approach, using things like mechanical lizards and celebrities doing crazy stunts. Iconic brands capture our attention by creating simple fictions that relate to identity myths. It is the mythic quality of these brands that makes them iconic.

By identifying cultural contradictions that have created social anxieties, iconic brands create myth markets around these tensions. For example, in the 1960s, American life was becoming suburbanized. The norms of suburban life had an emasculating effect. To counter this, Mountain Dew created a hillbilly myth based on moonshine with a caffeine and sugar rush. The hillbilly image was a populist weapon to be used in the fight against the emerging ideology of the suburbs. The television programs *The Beverly Hillbillies* and *Hee Haw* illustrate this trend. By touching on the anxieties of suburban life, Mountain Dew was able to gain market recognition.

Third, within the brand are identity myths that consumers share and experience. Over time, the brand becomes a symbol for the myth it embodies. When people drink, drive, or wear the brand, it is like experiencing part of the myth. In modern societies, the most influential myths are ones that address an individual's identity. Drinking Mountain Dew enables people to imagine themselves as hillbillies who don't fit suburban norms.

Fourth, the identity myths are located in a populist world. These are places that are separated from everyday life and the domain of commerce. These worlds exist at the edges of society, and people behave in a populist world the way they want to. Marlboro cigarettes utilized the populist world of the cowboy, Harley-Davidson featured outlaw bikers, and Nike made use of the African American ghetto. Populist worlds are believable because they are grounded in real groups of people with particular beliefs.

Fifth, iconic brands lead the culture and work as activists. Iconic brands encourage people to think in different ways because they are always on the cutting edge of cultural change. They create myths that resonate with cultural issues. For instance, the Marlboro man provided men with a strong masculine image at a time when women were becoming more liberated. As women challenged the role of men in society, branding created an image to restore men's masculinity. The emotional identification with the brand was one of masculine distinctiveness.

Sixth, iconic brands rely on innovative communication rather than consistent performances. Provocative and attention-getting performances make the commercials and messages from iconic brands stand out. As an iconic brand, Snickers candies' recent advertising gimmick of substituting different characters for the original ones hits a home run with viewers. To illustrate how grumpy people can be when they are hungry, villain Danny Trejo, carrying a hatchet, stands in for Marcia Brady, a character from the television series *The Brady Bunch*. The spoken lines are Marcia's, and the visual is jarring, especially when Danny drives a hatchet into a coffee table. The camera then moves to Marcia's parents, who say, "Marsha, eat a Snickers…. You get a little hostile when you're hungry." These Snickers commercials use Foss's concept of visual appeal (described in Chapter 3) to attract the viewer's attention. The disruptive image of Danny in the Brady home jolts our senses and engages our minds.

Finally, iconic brands have a halo effect. A halo effect is when a person's overall impressions of an individual, company, brand, or product influences their feelings and thoughts about the entity. People who are attractive usually generate more positive feelings. The concept is used in the discipline of brand marketing to describe when the positive features of a product extend to the larger brand. For example, Apple's iPod generated interest in other products, and the perception of Subway as a "healthy" restaurant caused people to underestimate the calories in their sandwiches. When people like the brand, they may think the product is better.

A number of different advertisements have become iconic symbols representing cultural attitudes. These include: "Uncle Sam," "We Can Do It!," the "Marlboro Man," "Think Small," and "*1984*." These images have all become a part of American culture and have inspired near-universal recognition. The "Uncle Sam" posters, of which the James Montgomery Flagg image published in 1916 was the most well known, motivated people to become involved in

World War I. The bearded, white-haired, finger-pointing patriot has been reprinted in many different ways for different political and cultural agendas.

"We Can Do It!" was created by the Westinghouse Electric Company, and it featured a strong, muscular woman taking her place in the workforce. The image was originally used to boost the confidence of female workers who had replaced men during World War II. The poster became associated with Rosie the Riveter, a fictitious female factory worker created to inspire women to join the war effort. Later it was used as a symbol for women's rights.

In 1954, the already-discussed Marlboro Man appeared. The masculine image was used by Phillip Morris & Company to sell filtered cigarettes to men. "Now insecure men could feel tough smoking a Marlboro, because hey, it was the smoke of choice for a weathered, cleft-chinned cowboy" (Baer, Taube, & Feloni, 2014, p. 6). The change was necessitated by the fact that Marlboro was originally marketed as a women's cigarette. With this new image, sales increased, especially with men.

The 1959 "Think Small" campaign gave voice to the public's dissatisfaction with mass consumerism. While car manufacturers boasted of their automobiles' luxury features and spoiler fins, Volkswagen, in contrast, focused on utility. The campaign developed by Doyle Dane Bernbach was in such stark contrast to other car advertisements that it struck a chord with down-to-earth consumers. Volkswagen's voice was personal and self-deprecating. It even called attention to potential blemishes in the car.

The "1984" Apple Super Bowl commercial ran once on television and has since played thousands of times. To introduce its new Macintosh computer, Apple decided to use the science fiction theme of the book *1984*, a dystopian view of the future. Directed by Ridley Scott, the commercial focused on a woman in a tank top and running shorts carrying a sledgehammer through a grey room full of of skinheads. She tosses the hammer through a big screen of "Big Brother" (IBM) to inspire a generation of people to envision the computer as a creative force. The Macintosh thus freed computers from the tyranny of business.

To celebrate the 30th anniversary of Macintosh and the Super Bowl advertisement, Apple threw a birthday party. It created a 3-minute video and online timeline to show its impact on human creativity. The video highlighted the creators of the Macintosh, who told the story in their own words. Apple's timeline featured vintage photos, quotes, and stories about the machine that changed the world. "There's also a section where you're encouraged to share the story of your first Mac" (Nudd, 2014a, p. 2). Apple has such a strong public following that people are interested in its history.

Apple's *1984* advertisement also inspired copycat ads and parodies. For example, Ben & Jerry's ice cream created a parody to promote its Brrr-ito ice cream sandwiches. The commercial's first showing was scheduled for April 20th, unofficial "marijuana appreciation day." It featured a young woman running down a hallway into a grey room where men stare at a screen with the picture of an ice cream sandwich. The woman throws a Brrr-ito into the screen, and the announcer tells us that after Ben & Jerry's introduces the Brrr-ito, 4/20 will be exactly like 4/20 (see Griner, 2015). Brands will make fun of another brand's iconic image.

Cultural Blunders

When advertisers use cultural iconic images in advertisements, the result is not always iconic branding. For example, using a picture of Jacqueline Kennedy to sell Tide by saying it "removes the toughest stains" did not work. Similarly, placing an image of women burning bras to sell Cheer laundry detergent also missed the mark. The body copy stated: "You'll have time to clean the house, make dinner and marvel at your clean new bras before the hubby gets home." The message supported the suburban myth that women were rejecting. Finally, Netflix failed with the image of the Lincoln assassination and the headline "Why go out…when you can stay in?" Using iconic symbols can be tricky, because these images are filled with so much meaning that adding a commercial message can communicate the wrong message. (For more examples, see http://www.cracked.com/photoplasty_839_29-iconic-images-from-history-shamelessly-turned-into-ads/.)

Though Apple hit a home run with the "*1984*" commercial, its attempt to use Moses to sell digital computer tablets in a print ad was not as successful. Other blunders include Match.com exploiting the images of Nazi Germany to attract singles and bringing Martin Luther King into play to sell Calvin Klein underwear. Probably the ad displaying the worst sense of taste was a Viagra print advertisement that used the iconic World War II image of the raising of the U.S. flag on Iwo Jima to sell its product. The copy read "Raise your flag with Viagra." Linking sex with war did not work.

Although these advertisers identified myths occurring in popular culture, their combining of the product with the myth was unsuccessful. In many of these cases, the visual applied to the copy may have had such a strong cultural meaning that the original image overpowered the product. In some cases, the images selected may be considered to be in poor taste. Finding the right myth that resonates with consumers is not always easy. When the combination works, an iconic brand can be created.

Products as Icons

Advertisements are not the only iconic symbols associated with brands. As previously discussed, in 2015 Coca-Cola celebrated the 100th anniversary of its iconic glass bottle. The company even fabricated a story about the creation of the bottle itself, called "A Tale of Contour." The animation has a lump of glass transformed through its travels around the world into its present form.

Another iconic bottle (as discussed in Chapter 5) belongs to Absolut. A simple outline of the shape brings the brand to mind. Moreover, Absolut collaborates with people in the art world to promote its product and to make a social statement. Working with creative visionaries implies that the vodka is visionary and iconic.

McDonald's created visual icons of its products. The images stood by themselves with no branding identification. These simple graphics were recognizable as McDonald's food. It was a minimalist campaign. Nudd (2014b) stated: "Instead of the actual products, now we get clean, simple drawings of the products—turning them into actual icons" (p. 2). To add to the message, some advertisements also featured iconic tiny golden arches next to the illustrations of the menu items. These strong graphics were used as outdoor signage and on billboards. It is sometimes amazing how a simple iconic graphic can communicate a wealth of information.

Cultural Myths

Icons and myths are part of our cultural awareness. For this reason, fairy tales, dreams, and myths use the same symbolic language. Fromm (1951) states:

> symbolic language is the one foreign language that each of us must learn…. [I]t it
> helps us to understand a level of experience that is specifically human because it is
> that level which is common to all humanity, in content as well as style. (p. 10)

It is a language that icons use to communicate human emotions and experience. This is the language of myth. A myth is a story that attracts consciousness by communicating human emotions or cultural ideals. For example, a common American myth is the myth of progress. It believes in perpetual economic expansion and material compensation. The myth of progress is also an idea that accepts technological development and innovation. These types of myths are a key ingredient of iconic brands.

Knowledge of mythic structure can help an individual to decode a number of different types of visual messages. For instance, films such as *Star Wars* or *Indiana Jones* follow the storyline of the mythic hero. "Myth transforms the temporal common sense of ideology into the sacred realm of cultural prehistory and thus of eternal truth. Myth thereby serves an important political or organizational foundation" (Himmelstein, 1984, p. 4). As an example, American Western films use essentially the same sequence of events over and over again:

> A strange man appears seeking someone (the hero).
> Bad men who wear black endanger the man.
> A woman pleads with the man to give up his pursuit.
> The hero refuses and continues his quest.
> The bad men are killed through skill and courage.

This narrative pattern is based on a mythic structure, and the figure of the hero is an archetype. The hero can be from any type of cultural background, and he can be outlandish or inspirational. He progresses along the same path or journey. In short, the mythic tale is one of a hero who is lured, taken, or voluntarily embarks on the threshold of adventure. He encounters a shadow or figure that blocks his journey. At that point the hero must defend himself or pacify the negative force to obtain its power. Afterward he moves into the kingdom of darkness, such as a brother-battle, dragon-battle, or charm. Or he is slain by the opponent and he descends into death.

Outside the threshold of adventure, the hero must travel to an unknown world that contains strange forces—forces that will test and threaten him. However, he will be given magical help. When the hero arrives at the highest point of his mythological recoil, he faces extreme peril in his quest to gain his rewards. The hero finally returns under protection or flees back to his home. Campbell (1949) describes the climax as follows:

> At the return of the threshold the transcendental powers must remain behind; the hero re-emerges from the kingdom of dread (return, resurrection). The boon that he brings restores the world (elixir). (p. 246)

Mythic tales follow similar elements of the full cycle. However, a single element can be changed and may reappear many different times. Often the tales are revised to fit cultural motifs. This is especially true when brands use the mythic structure to tell their story.

Myth Making

Screenwriters working on film and television scripts use a mythical archetypal journey of the hero as a structure to organize the storyline. (See Chapter 1 for a discussion of the concept of archetypes.) Jung and fellow researchers (1964) used the concept of archetypes to describe the basic building blocks of the human psyche. These reside in the collective unconscious of our cultural memories. They emerge from universal human experience and are often found in folklore, myths, and art. Symbols can be connected to themes of human experience, including birth, death, marriage, fear, and hope. Humans universally convey the same emotions, and these can be expressed through universal symbols. These universal images are archetypes that are embedded into human consciousness and are used to express feelings.

For example, animals are an important symbol in dreams and myths. Individual animals often represent an aspect of the individual and signify instinctual parts of human nature. In an image of a mounted horseman, the horse represents the human will or consciousness. In contemporary culture, the car driver can replace the horse's rider, and these two images can be related to one another.

These are "representations that can vary a great deal in detail without losing their basic patterns" (Jung et al, 1964, p. 67). Although the patterns remain the same, archetypes are culture-specific. As an example, in Western culture angels are celestial beings that exist somewhere between humans and higher spiritual powers. However, in another culture, symbols of angels may be unknown.

Archetypes are found in our art, our dreams, our films, and our advertising. "The archetypes are there to challenge us, to stretch us, to take us out of our normal everyday life and throw us back into the mysterious world of myths and magic" (O'Connell, Airey, & Craze, 2011, p. 264). Myth can take us out of everyday life and make us more aware of social issues.

Myth Markets

When designing a marketing strategy to create a product's myth, the first step is to map out different myths occurring in a particular culture. The marketer needs to be aware of the cultural dynamic of a society. For instance, public perception of the Confederate flag changed after the 2015 shootings in a Charleston, South Carolina, church. Using the Confederate flag as a personal statement of rebellion was turned into a statement about race relations. Advertisers need to be sensitive to changing social trends. As a result of this controversy, a number of companies stopped manufacturing Confederate flags, and retailers stopped selling them.

According to Holt (2004), there are three aspects of myth markets: national ideology, cultural contradictions, and populist worlds. He states: "Contradictions in the national ideology create myth markets" (p. 59). Every nation has its own story that enables citizens to identify with it. In America, a mythic story is that anyone, no matter how poor, can become a success. This ideology corresponds to the notion that people have equal opportunities for advancement. All people are created equal. This is the myth of individual success. It is also the myth that enables immigrants to integrate into American society.

America as the melting pot is in conformity with the immigrant experience. We can say that at one point we all came from different countries. National ideology is "a system of ideas that forges links between everyday life—the aspirations of individuals, families, and communities—and those of the nation" (Holt, 2004, p. 57). These ideologies are not directly stated; rather, they are communicated through myths and cultural attitudes. These myths enable individuals to identify with a nation's economic and political power.

People aspire to the nation's ideals. However, life's circumstances can make it difficult to achieve these goals. For example, American business has witnessed many layoffs, and large numbers of people have been out of work. This creates a tension between ideology and a person's individual experience.

Further, these tensions can occur at times when a nation's ideology shifts. Symbolic resolutions can help to smooth over these tensions.

Myths depend upon elements from populist worlds. Holt (2004) stated: "Populist worlds are perceived as 'folk cultures'—their ethos is the collective and voluntary product of their participants. The ethos has not been imposed on them" (p. 58). When people engage in these activities, they are valuable to them. The motivations are not from political or commercial interests. "Populist worlds are places where the public assumes that people's actions are motivated by belief instead of interest" (p. 59). Iconic brands use elements from populist culture to create their myths. An example of this is the Mountain Dew hillbilly myth described earlier. As culture changed, the myth morphed into the redneck myth and finally into the slacker myth.

The myths of iconic brands are not totally original. Brands borrow and add to myths that already exist in other media, such as films, television, and comic strips. For instance, the hillbilly myth borrowed from the comic strip *Li'l Abner*, and the redneck myth borrowed from the television program *The Dukes of Hazzard*. However, a difference between branding myths is their association with a product. Products are something that can be used every day, making them a part of an individual's lifestyle. When cultural disruption disturbs the myth, iconic brands need to abandon or revise their mythic structure.

Summary

Not all brands become iconic. Originally, icons referred to paintings and sculptures. Moreover, religious icons had similar elements, especially when they depicted the same story. In today's highly visual world, the term is also used in marketing to refer to iconic brands. Iconic brands develop a marketing myth around themselves. Myths rely on elements from popular culture to symbolize different ideologies. There is a strong relationship between cultural and marketing myths and ideas.

Exercises

1. Identify your favorite iconic brands. How do these brands use mythic ideas to sell their products?
2. Examine American culture. What myths can you identify in current society?

3. Identify a television commercial that attracts your attention. What is the message of the commercial and how does it relate to your identity?
4. Pick a historical period (1950, 1960s, 1970s, etc.). Identify the iconic brands of that period. Can you identify cultural myths associated with the brands?

References

Baer, D., Taube, A., & Feloni, R. (2014, August 20). 14 ads that changed the world. *Yahoo Finance*. Retrieved September 7, 2016, from http://finance.yahoo.com/news/ads-that-changed-the-world-180746057.html

Campbell, J. (1949). *The hero with a thousand faces.* Princeton, NJ: Princeton University Press.

Fridell, G., & Konings, M. (2013). *Age of icons.* Toronto, Ont., Canada: University of Toronto Press.

Fromm, E. (1951). *The forgotten language.* New York: Grove Press.

Gombrich, E.H. (1972). *Symbolic images.* Chicago: University of Chicago Press.

Griner, D. (2015, April 17). Ben & Jerry's has brought back Apple "1984" as a burrito anthem for stoners. *AdWeek.* Retrieved April 18, 2015, from http://www.adweek.com/adfreak/ben-jerrys-has-brought-back-apples-1984-burrito-anthem-stoners-164165

Himmelstein, H. (1984). *Television myth and the American mind.* New York: Praeger.

Holt, D.B. (2004). *How brands become icons.* Boston, MA: Harvard Business School Press.

Jung, C.G. (1956). *Symbols of transformation* (R.F.C. Hull, Trans.), Princeton, NJ: Princeton University Press.

Jung, C.G., von Franz, M.-L., Henderson, J.L., Jacobi, J., & Jaffé, A. (1964). *Man and his symbols.* Garden City, NY: Doubleday.

Nudd, T. (2014a, January 24). Ad of the day: Apple lavishly celebrates Macintosh's 30th birthday. *AdWeek.* Retrieved January 24, 2014, from http://www.adweek.com/news/advertising-branding/ad-day-apple-lavishly-celebrates-macintoshs-30th-birthday-155188

Nudd, T. (2014b, May 22). McDonald's unveils the simplest ads it's ever made. *AdWeek.* Retrieved May 23, 2014, from http://www.adweek.com/adfreak/mcdonalds-unveils-simplest-ads-its-ever-made-157906

O'Connell, M., Airey, R., & Craze, R. (2011). *The illustrated encyclopedia of symbols, signs, and dream interpretation.* New York: Metro Books.

Rushkoff, D. (1999). *Coercion: Why we listen to what they say.* New York: Riverhead Books.

Sternberg, E. (1999). *The economy of icons.* Westport, CT: Praeger.

· 1 0 ·

BRANDING IN A DIGITAL WORLD

Good public-relations specialists have voluntarily abandoned their most coercive styles in this environment, opting to work as best they can with the truth as it exists or can be altered. Advertising agencies, on the other hand, whose work hasn't had anything to do with real-world facts for half a century, have proved much more eager to retool their techniques for the interactive age and its interactive audience.
—Douglas Rushkoff, 1999, p. 161

The introduction of the Internet as a global communication medium has helped to foster the recognition of global brands, especially computer-oriented brands such as Apple, Google, and Dell. Digital technology has become fully integrated into our movement from one place to another, in our interactions from work to downtime. There is no line, no starting point or ending, between our digital selves and the rest of our lives. This total immersion of our lives into digital technologies creates the perfect outlet for brands to spread their identities. The computer's interface, along with digital devices, is truly a new digital marketplace.

Digital technologies enable marketers to spread the images of branding and turn networking technologies into marketplaces. Media ecologists contend that technologies influence the messages distributed through a medium. For example, Postman argued in *Amusing Ourselves to Death* (1985) that the commercial nature of television turns the content into entertainment. The World Wide Web transforms the Internet into a shopping mall. The ease of buying and selling online, combined with search engines, enables people to locate any kind of product or service. "The platforms and tactics we use to reach our customers in a digital world keep changing, but the strategy for touching human beings who make decisions with their hearts and not their heads remains the same" (Jiwa, 2014, p. 32). Interactivity online enables advertisers to find new and unique strategies for engaging customers emotionally to interact with their brand.

While technologies change, humans tend not to. The key reason for the difference between the Internet and television is interactivity. Wright (2006) refers to this as engaging versus transmitting. In the past, corporate communication was a one-way message from the company to the consumer. Today, networks enable corporations to have a two-way dialog with customers. Activities such as blogging support strong consumer engagement with companies and brands.

"The new interactive technologies collapse the space between the consumer and the producer" (Travis, 2000, p. 66). As a result, it is now much easier for companies to communicate directly with their customers. Additionally, it raises consumer expectations because when one company uses these new tools, it expects other companies to use them as well. The space between customer and producer is now direct; the need for a middleman has been eliminated. This is called disintermediation. "Disintermediation assumes there is nothing between the merchandiser and a customer, except a direct and personal connection from one computer to another, from one browser to another" (Ferraro, 1998, p. 4). In other words, communication is from the producer to the final client.

As a result, Internet branding is about creating a dialogue with the customer and allowing the conversation to be ongoing and always improving. "Good e-marketers are like brilliant conversationalists. They listen as well as they talk" (Zyman, 2000, p. 160). In this new branding environment, participation is important, and a new conversation economy is emerging.

E-Commerce

A major reason why the Internet has now become the marketplace of choice for many people is the development of e-commerce. E-commerce is the performing of business transactions and the sustaining of business relationships through computer networks. "E-commerce is fundamentally World Wide Web-based buying and selling of goods and services" (Ferraro, 1998, p. 1). It provides opportunities for buyers and sellers to connect. Kalakota and Whinston (1996) describe e-commerce as "a modern business methodology that addresses the needs of organizations, merchants, and consumers to cut costs while improving the quality of goods and services and increasing the speed of service and delivery" (p. 1).

The web also enables companies to sell directly to consumers without an intermediary. For instance, Dell and Gateway sell their products directly to consumers through the Internet. There are advantages to using the Web for branding. "It allows you to be taken straight from an online ad to the advertiser's 'virtual' retail outlet with a click of the mouse" (Travis, 2000, p. 139). Moreover, payment can be collected at the time of purchase. Thus, companies can conduct a complete transaction online, from advertising to sale.

Branding Online

In 1994, the web began to be utilized as an advertising and branding medium. Websites were used to reinforce brand identity. They also provided additional information to the consumer. The Internet became a direct method of communication with consumers. "You [could] talk to the consumer you most want to reach—and who most wants to hear about your product or service—without any interference or editing from news media, reporters, editors, producers, or networks" (Levine, 2003, p. 166). Brands were no longer an abstract concept: now they were engaging the consumer in a two-way conversation.

Because the web was constantly changing, people often returned to the same websites. Companies needed to give the consumer reasons to come back to their sites. Product updates, coupons, press releases, and sale notices all created a motivation to return. Moreover, it was important to have your web address on all your advertising, including print, television, and billboards. The website itself needed to include contact information, corporate material, customer service, product information, press contacts, and links to relevant sites. In addition to providing information, brands might also acquire data by asking questions of consumers. The answers could be used in market research.

Branding online required a new business model that tapped into four new principles—being open, peering, sharing, and acting globally (see Moffitt &

Dover, 2011). By being open, customers had more access to a company's intellectual capital or business knowledge. This enabled brands to collaborate with consumers to create new and improved products.

Peering—as in person-to-person relationships—is the second principle. People form communities in which they interact with each other. Often they prefer personal recommendations to messages from corporations or hierarchies of control. Simply stated, individuals prefer acquiring information from other people rather than mass-advertising messages.

As an advertising medium, the Internet supports the sharing of interactive messages. Moreover, it is easy to copy and paste information to share with others. Information is easily shared through digital media. Often this information concerns personal experiences with the brand or product. As a communication medium, the Internet supports the wide distribution of information and ideas. Disclosing personal knowledge with products and services is developing brand awareness.

Brand awareness is the degree to which a brand is familiar to potential customers. It is how well a person recognizes the brand under different circumstances. The Internet can act on a global level to spread brand awareness and develop customers. The network can be used to enlarge a company's customer base, because direct communication with individuals is feasible. Long-distance collaboration is possible over the network. Brands can reach a larger number of people and potential clients. Online geographic boundaries no longer exist. Thus, global information technologies can be utilized to develop brand identity and awareness and to capture new customers.

The future of branding online requires brands to be malleable. In other words, they need to be open to new forms of communication and customer engagement. Companies should always be looking for new types of brand experience. Five key elements anchor the brand in this ever-changing environment: the logo, name, core idea, belief system, and community. Outside of these elements, the brand needs to focus on customer relevance, filling customer needs, and delivering promised product benefits (see Moffitt & Dover, 2011).

One benefit of digital branding is the ability to communicate directly with customers. Some companies can bypass mass-media filters to connect directly with their intended audiences. Microsoft seeks three benefits from online media: (1) product feedback; (2) brand advocacy; and (3) customer service support. These benefits are achieved through the development of corporate blogs, sponsored forums, and video uploads. All of these applications communicate directly with customers.

In a similar way, Dell Computer is an example of an extremely engaged online brand. It has a range of blogs, hundreds of its employees use Twitter accounts, and it has more than 100 Facebook pages. In addition, Dell has YouTube and Flickr channels. To support online interaction, the company also recognizes community ambassadors. As a result of these efforts, Dell interacts with millions of people across its online communities.

Companies such as Dell seek out methods of engagement for consumers. Sheehan and Morrison (2009) describe this:

> Engagement is a consumer relationship that recognizes that people are inherently social and look to create and maintain relations not only with other people, but also with brands. An engagement perspective changes the view of a brand from a transactional perspective of a brand addressing a transient need to an interactional perspective where the brand story becomes part of a person's own story about him or herself. (pp. 4–5)

New media can work with old to communicate the brand story. The goal is to get consumers involved with the story and share it with others. The story should entertain and inform customers to help them form a relationship with the brand. One method for communicating the brand story online is through the use of a website.

Websites

In the early days of the World Wide Web, companies created their own corporate websites to promote their brand. These sites were originally modeled after printed corporate materials. Corporate websites were part of the online advertising evolution. In 2006, they pulled in more viewers than prime-time TV shows and print magazines (Neff, 2006b, p. 1). Although corporate websites initially represented a throwback to print-based advertising, the addition of interactivity brought a new dimension of direct engagement with consumers. As a result, corporate websites have evolved over the years.

Websites are a popular place to find brand information, because corporate websites are easy to locate with a search engine. Thus, websites are an integral part of a brand's advertising efforts, and they have been researched in similar ways as traditional advertising. One method that has been used in the analysis of advertising is called "attitudes toward advertising." This method examines consumers' overall perception of advertising's impact and its effectiveness. Several studies have examined attitudes toward advertising on the Internet, including Chen and Wells (1999); Lee and Choi (2005); Schlosser, Shavitt, and Kanfer (1999); and Wolin and Korgaonkar (2003). Lee, Hong, and Lee (2004) examine how attitudes toward a website influenced brand choice. They state: "This study found that attitude toward the Web site appears to be a good predictor of consumer brand choice and confidence in that choice. In other words, the extent to which a Web site is able to help form and sustain positive attitudes toward the site has a distinct impact on purchase decisions regarding the brand" (p. 12). The website characteristics that the participants found most appealing were entertainment, information, and organization. Brands need to create appealing websites that support the brand's image. Moreover, they need to be engaging for the customer. One way to engage consumers is to place a blog on your website.

Blogs

Wright (2006) defines a blog as "a website comprising *blog* posts, or content written by the blogger, which are typically organized into categories and sorted in reverse chronological order" (p. 7). In addition, many blogs enable people to comment on their messages. Blogs help companies obtain feedback from consumers by interacting with them directly. As a result, blogging enables brands to create positive experiences with their customers.

Companies should develop an open and honest public blog that is written by an authoritative voice. Tell the customers what you are doing, build a solid base of positive experiences in the relationship, and share company knowledge. In 2004, Nike began using blogs as a marketing tool to promote its indie-film series "The Art of Speed" (Oser, 2004a). These short films, which use well-known actors, have been very popular on YouTube. Peter Blackshaw, chief marketing officer at Intelliseek, stated: "Consumer adoption of blogs has been on a steady rise for two years or so and marketers have realized that you can't ignore them, because they tend to disseminate information so fast" (cited in Oser, 2004b, p. 3) Advertisers understood that bloggers' influence on public opinion was something they could not ignore. However, blogs could be a tricky business. For instance, Audi, as the sole sponsor of a blog, ran the risk of having its products criticized. Upon entering the world of networking, a company needs to have a plan of attack for negative reviews, because both positive and negative information can be spread around the network. How a company handles negative comments is important for maintaining its brand image.

When receiving negative feedback, the best online policy is to be honest and to address the issue. Online communication can establish trust and build relationships with customers. Trust is built because people are communicating with a real person and not a marketing brochure. Moreover, it can create user experiences with a brand. The brand becomes the impression left on people, and personal online messages leave a lasting impression. Wright (2006) states: "Your brand lies in the minds of your customers, and like a wildfire, each of your customers can spread your brand message (the way they perceive it) to others—and they often will" (p. 42). Information spreads through the use of blogs.

As an example, Microsoft understands the power of blogs. Thousands of its product managers, developers, testers, and executives utilize blogging to communicate directly with clients. They listen to customer complaints, suggest ideas, and keep track of what customers are saying. Development teams use blog feedback before they make significant changes to a product. Microsoft employees are reading and talking on blogs on a daily basis, and these activities improve Microsoft products. Blogs are generally organized by an individual blogger. However, blogs with similar topics can band together to form a community.

Online Communities

Online communities offer another opportunity for brands to communicate with their customers. This is done is by developing a brand audience and building a community around the group. To build a community, "you need to have a well-articulated point of view and a promise that will engage and excite people" (Moffitt & Dover, 2011, p. 94). Understand what people like and which subjects they share. Communities are built around a shared topic of discussion. Additionally, "members of brand communities want to connect, play, react, reach out, create, and collaborate" (Moffitt & Dover, 2011, p. 182). Moffitt and Dover (2011) claim that a study revealed that one-third of e-retailing users generate two-thirds of sales.

For the community to grow, three ingredients are essential. First, the members need to be very motivated and committed. Second, the community needs to be filled with rich content and outreach. Finally, it needs to provide and support a number of different member induction activities. Members need to be committed and motivated to share and participate in online events. Communities need people to actively contribute to make an online community successful.

Today, brands are creating online forums that support participation and engagement. These forums tap into people's shared interests and socialization needs. For example, the Lego community would meet at offline sites to share their Lego creations. The Lego company tapped into this community involvement and created a Customer Innovator and Ambassador program. The program led to the formation of podcasts, blogs, fan clubs, and auction sites. All of these various activities, which use interactivity on the Internet, provided community participation and company feedback.

Interactive Branding

The unique characteristic of interactivity enables brands to create commercial messages that engage consumers in different ways. For instance, Burger King's created the landmark interactive "Subservient Chicken" campaign, which won the Gold Medal at the Viral Awards (Anderson, 2005). Anderson (2005) stated: "Within a day after being released, the site had a million hits. Within a week, it had received 20 million hits" (para. 2). The technology utilized on the site enabled users to type in a command that the chicken would perform. On the tenth anniversary of the campaign, the chicken went missing. Burger King took out a series of advertisements asking if anyone had seen the chicken, thereby revisiting its original success with the chicken website.

Interactivity can be used as a method to create innovative branding campaigns. Once a campaign is on the Internet, word of mouth can cause it to be seen by millions of people. Websites provide spaces for people to interact with information. In contrast, social networks are places for people to interact with each other.

Social Networks

In 2006, social networking changed the landscape of the Internet, and advertisers were extremely aware of this change. Social networks enabled brands to combine their messages with the daily communication of users. Social networks form a blend of social interaction, relationships, and self-expression using features that include updates, walls, applications, messages, chats, and games. "Social networks' key strengths for brands are the abilities to scale conversations through a user's social graph, establish rich media impact across a range of activities, and provide a more casual face to a corporate brand" (Moffitt & Dover, 2011, p. 188). Companies such as Procter & Gamble are forming new connections with consumers through word-of-mouth forums on Facebook. Smart companies use active online participation to get their brands noticed.

Moffitt and Dover (2011) report that 85% of people surveyed "want a stronger connection with brands" (p. 32). Moreover, 56% felt a stronger association with companies they interact with online. Online users interact with brands through social media more pervasively than does the average population. Many companies are now using Twitter, Facebook, YouTube, and blogs for brand awareness.

A popular trend is to create live Facebook chats. Brands including VH1, the Discovery Channel, and Sony have used video in their virtual meet and greets. "It's all part of Facebook's plan to turn the site into a video platform for brands, publishers and creators" (Johnson, 2015, p. 2). Consumers can also become involved with branding efforts through social networks. For example, Mike Melgaard posed as a Target customer service representative to counter negative posts about Target's gender-neutral product labeling. Target stated publicly that Mike was not speaking for the brand. "But behind the scenes, the brand was apparently loving it—at least judging by this Facebook photo that Target posted on Thursday evening" (Nudd, 2015b, p. 2). Target uploaded a picture of a couple of troll dolls with the caption: "Remember when Trolls were the kings of the world? Woo hoo! They're back and only at Target stores."

Social networks can build strong relationships between brands and consumers. In addition to Facebook and Twitter, other social media sites support the sharing of information between brands and people. Brands are now also sending messages to smartphones. Mobile messaging provides a new method to communicate branded messages. These new platforms are engaging for youth and become another channel for brands to engage with consumers. As improved methods of delivering branded messages emerge, the marketing industry needs to find new ways to measure brand awareness.

Brand Metrics

Brand metrics are characteristics about a brand that are measured to determine the strength of the brand. Categories that are measured include brand promise, brand attributes, brand equity, and brand management. Academics also research consumers by examining Brand Relationship Quality (BRQ) and relational norms (Thorbjørnsen, Supphellen, Nysveen, & Pedersen, 2002; Matwick, 2002). This is what consumers think, feel, and relate to a brand. The Internet can be used as a research tool to examine these characteristics. Surveys can be posted online for consumers to complete. As marketers have become more consumer-research oriented, creative directors have become more daring in their use of Internet advertising because of the personal reach of the medium and the feedback it provides.

For example, to directly attract consumers through the Internet, BMW released a series of online films using well-known actors, and Frito-Lay took its TV advertising online to offer teens the chance to view its commercials. The streaming of media has become a popular new force in Internet advertising. Popular television commercials can be found online, and YouTube is another digital application that is filled with branded images. Further, the counter on YouTube provides marketers with information on how many people are viewing the videos.

YouTube

Since 2006, advertisers have been developing video advertisements that can easily be forwarded through email exchanges. In addition, commercials can be placed on YouTube for easy access. One of the most popular ads in 2006 was Dove's "Evolution," a 75- second viral spot. The campaign centered around the question of whether or not real beauty was skin deep. The seed idea for the commercial "came from a global research group that evaluated women's mind-sets about beauty issues in ten different countries" (Moffitt & Dover, 2011, p. 60).

Another brand viral video from 2006 was the "Mentos-Coke fountain geyser." Mixing the Coke and Mentos together resulted in an explosion of soda that spread around the network. Sales for mint Mentos increased 20% after news of the phenomenon broke. Today, brands are working with You-Tube talent to produce engaging advertisements.

Advertisers are also using the site to promote their Super Bowl commercials. Brands have traditionally wanted to keep the spots a surprise until game day. However, the number of YouTube views prior to the game can be an indicator of a successful Super Bowl ad. For instance, Budweiser's "Puppy Love" commercial generated 17 million views before game night. After the game it received 43 million views (see Shields, 2014). Other brands that posted on YouTube prior to the game include Jaguar, Toyota, and Volkswagen.

The site celebrated the 10-year anniversary of YouTube by selecting the 20 most iconic advertisements. Along with infographics, a video, and a quiz, the site presented highlights from its first 10 years online. It attempted to capture 300 hours of video in one minute. YouTube has become the place to go to see product commercials and branded messages. As previously mentioned, some of these branded videos go viral.

Viral Marketing and Branding

Not everything can go viral. "Only a specific type of product or business or piece of content will go viral—it not only has to be worth spreading, it has to provoke a desire in people to spread it" (Holiday, 2014, p. 32). Viral marketing supports the passing along of information by customers. "It's effective because it can be crafted once and left up to individual consumers to spread the message themselves" (Wright, 2006, p. 48). Viral messages can spread very quickly on the Internet.

Jonah Berger (2013) identifies six principles for explaining why some ideas catch on and others do not. These ideas include "*Social Currency* and are *Triggered, Emotional, Public, Practically Valuable*, and wrapped into *Stories*" (p. 25). He uses the acronym STEPPS to describe them. Social currency relates to the fact that hearing information from other people affects an individual's thinking. The most powerful marketing is personal recommendation. One reason why social media are so popular is that they allow people to share opinions and ideas with each other.

Word of mouth is a method for making a good impression. There are two types of word of mouth: immediate and ongoing. Immediate is sharing information soon after you hear about it. In contrast, ongoing is spreading the news in the weeks or months that follow. The Net Generation has "twice as large a circle of word-of-mouth influence than the rest of the population due to their higher degree of Internet and mobile connectedness" (Moffitt & Dover, 2011, p. 29). In addition, the cars they buy and designer dresses they wear make an impact on other people. This is a form of social currency—that is, gaining a desired impression from others. People want to look good and show off their achievements. Branded products can be used to do this.

The second principle explaining why things catch on is triggers. Triggers act as reminders to call attention to the brand. The best triggers are ones that have a direct relationship to the product. For instance, when NASA had a triumph on Mars, it made people think of the Mars candy bar, and sales increased. Obviously, the relationship is in the name. Placing a healthy eating message on a cafeteria tray will have a better impact than a catchy slogan sung in a song. Think about how a trigger can be used in everyday situations to spark acknowledgment of the brand. Moreover, "by acting as reminders, triggers not only get people talking, they keep them talking" (Berger, 2013, p. 79). The first and second principles are interrelated, because triggers are the foundation of word of mouth. Triggers encourage people to talk to each other.

The third principle is emotion. One emotion that generates interest in people is awe. Awe can make us think about things we do not generally encounter in our everyday lives. Awe-inspiring articles are more likely to be circulated around the Internet. Some of the most viral YouTube videos inspire awe, such as the Mentos and Coke video described earlier. Positive and amusing messages are also noticed. The ones least likely to motivate are negative and sad. Sharing also occurs with information that is associated with anger and anxiety. There are several instances of individuals receiving poor customer service and then posting videos about the experience on YouTube. In most cases, the company changed its policies in response to the public customer complaint. For example, a dissatisfied Comcast customer videotaped a Comcast technician falling asleep during a service call. The technician went to sleep after being placed on hold during a call to his own company. The image was partnered with the song "I Need Some Sleep" to create a re-mixed video. Within the space of 2 weeks the video was viewed over 200,000 times, and Comcast was forced to address the situation. Apple Computer has also had to change some of its policies because of unhappy consumer videos posted to YouTube.

Principle number four is public. Have you ever noticed that some of the email messages you receive include a notice written at the bottom, "sent from my iPhone"? Every time you see that message it is a reminder of the brand. This is a strategy instituted by Hotmail to use electronic media messages as brand reminders. The products advertise themselves every time they are used. Google has also frequently asked users to have their friends join the service. These messages are visual social proof that the product is a good one, because people are using it. Another tactic for making brands public is to give away quality shopping bags with the company's logo. These bags are sure to be used again—especially designer bags because of their social currency. Brands often find clever methods for publicizing their name and logo.

The fifth principle is practical value. Social value is about how sharing information makes people look. Giving someone a piece of advice that will make his or her life easier is always appreciated. An example of a practical viral video is Ken Craig's "Clean Ears Every Time." Ken's daughter-in-law videotaped him showing his trick for shucking corn to eliminate corn silk. Though she was recording the trick for her own reference, the daughter-in-law later placed it on YouTube, where it became an instant success. You don't need to be famous to go viral. You just need valuable information that helps people save time or money. This principle may also be the easiest to apply to viral marketing.

Finally, stories are important. Applying stories to brands was discussed in Chapter 4. Stories are an important strategy for sharing information. They relate directly to other principles in the STEPPS process. Stories promote social currency, which can evoke emotions. They provide practical information that is valuable. What may seem like idle chatter can actually be a branding tactic to build awareness. In this process, the brand's central benefit should be a key element of the narrative. Stories help brands to be more memorable for consumers.

User-Generated Marketing

To involve customers in the branding process, a number of different companies have run contests to create commercials for different products. "Frito-Lay has run successful contests in many countries where consumers created commercials that aired during the Super Bowl or developed new products with impressive creative and payout performance" (Moffitt & Dover, 2011, p. 14). Similarly, Dove solicited ads from consumers that turned user-generated content into advertising content that was broadcast on YouTube. Finalists in the competition won tickets for the Academy Awards, and the spot was broadcast during the program (see Neff, 2006a).

Apple Computer places photographs taken on iPhones onto billboards. The campaign has presented pictures from 77 individuals in 70 cities and 24 countries across the globe. "All of the photos were noncommissioned, found images. Apple combed through tens of thousands of photos to choose the ones for the campaign" (Nudd, 2015a, p. 2). Similarly, Red Bull appealed to consumers by encouraging them to create art with their cans. Pabst Blue Ribbon beer ran a similar PBRArt competition and received more than

500 entries. The winning design appeared on a limited number of the company's cans. Pabst plans to run another competition (see Griner, 2015).

Coca-Cola even got into the act by creating a commercial from short video clips made by fans. The clips came from fans all around the world. These activities led to sponsored brand engagement that was shared through social networks. By getting customers involved with marketing and advertising efforts, companies can gain valuable insights into their products.

Consumer involvement can also be generated through Instagram or Twitter. By using hashtags #, participants can post their photos. Benefit cosmetics ran a theme for a contest on "inner beauty." It encouraged positivity among young women and offered prizes ranging from $200 to $600 (see Ciambriello, 2014). One strategy for engaging consumers with branding experiences is to hold a user-generated contest. Generating activities that involve consumers directly with branding practices has become a method for consumer engagement.

Summary

The Internet creates a new interactive marketplace wherein conversation is becoming the economy of business. Digital technologies enable brands to sell directly to customers without an intermediary. This enables brands to create a dialogue with consumers, which can lead to the development of new and improved products.

The digital environment creates new methods for communication. Telling the brand story through the network is central to online success. Consumers can become engaged with branding activities through user-generated contests. All of these branding activities can generally be viewed on YouTube. Moreover, word of mouth spreads the news about these branded campaigns through the network and beyond.

Exercises

1. Locate viral videos on YouTube. Analyze the videos to report how they fit with the principles of how things catch on.
2. Locate a current newspaper, magazine, or Internet article that discusses branding on the Internet. How does the technology help to promote the brand and why?

3. Find three brands and research their websites and online presence. What is their brand story?
4. Pick a product and try to design a viral video or design a user-generated consumer contest.

References

Anderson, M. (2005, March 7). Dissecting "subservient chicken." *Adweek*. Retrieved December 5, 2006, from http://www.adweek.com/news/advertising/dissecting-subservient-chicken-78190

Berger, J. (2013). *Contagious: Why things catch on*. New York: Simon & Schuster.

Chen, Q., & Wells, W.D. (1999, September/October). Attitude toward the site. *Journal of Advertising Research*, 27–37.

Ciambriello, R. (2014, January 16). With new contest, cosmetics brand rewards inner beauty over selfies. *AdWeek*. Retrieved January 20, 2014, from http://www.adweek.com/adfreak/new-contest-cosmetics-brand-rewards-inner-beauty-over-hot-selfies-155008

Ferraro, A. (1998). Electronic commerce: The issues and challenges to creating trust and a positive image in consumer sales on the World Wide Web. *First Monday*, 3(6). Retrieved March 5, 2015, from http://firstmonday.org/ojs/index.php/fm/article/view/601

Griner, D. (2015, March 19). This Pabst Blue Ribbon fan art will appear on 6 million cans. *AdWeek*. Retrieved April 26, 2015, from http://www.adweek.com/adfreak/pabst-blue-ribbon-fan-art-will-appear-6-million-cans-163558

Holiday, R. (2013). *Growth hacker marketing*. New York: Penguin.

Jiwa, B. (2014). *Marketing a love story*. Australia: The Story of Telling Press.

Johnson, L. (2015, July 16). Brands start hosting real-time video chats on Facebook. *Adweek*. Retrieved July 26, 2015, from http://www.adweek.com/news/technology/brands-start-hosting-real-time-video-chats-facebook-165944

Kalakota, R., & Whinston, A.B. (1996). *Frontiers of electronic commerce*. Indianapolis, IN: Addison-Wesley.

Lee, B.-K., Hong, J.-Y., & Lee, W.-N. (2004). How attitude toward the web site influences consumer brand choice and confidence while shopping online. *Journal of Computer-Mediated Communication*, 9(2). doi: 10.1111/j.1083–6101.2004.tb00282.x

Lee, W.-N., & Choi, S.M. (2005). The role of horizontal and vertical individualism and collectivism in online consumers' response toward persuasive communication on the web. *Journal of Computer-Mediated Communication*, 11(1), article 15.

Levine, M. (2003). *A branded world*. Hoboken, NJ: John Wiley & Sons.

Matwick, C. (2002). Understanding the online consumer: A topology of online relational norms and behavior. *Journal of Interactive Marketing*, 16(1), 40–55.

Moffitt, S., & Dover, M. (2011). *Wiki brands*. New York: McGraw-Hill.

Neff, J. (2006a, December 14). Dove latest to solicit ads from consumers. *Advertising Age*. Retrieved December 20, 2006, from adage.com/print?article_id=11381

Neff, J. (2006b, December 4). Marketers' websites outdraw those of major media players. *Advertising Age*. Retrieved December 10, 2006, from http://adage.com/article/news/mar keters-websites-outdraw-major-media-players/113556/

Nudd, T. (2015a, March 2). Apple is putting users' beautiful iPhone 6 photos on billboards and print ads. *AdWeek*. Retrieved March 3, 2015, from http://www.adweek.com/adfreak/apple-putting-users-beautiful-iphone-6-photos-billboards-and-print-ads-163235

Nudd, T. (2015b, August 14). Target loved the guy who trolled its haters, judging by this genius Facebook post. *AdWeek*. Retrieved August 15, 2015, from http://www.adweek.com/adfreak/target-loved-guy-who-trolled-its-haters-judging-genius-facebook-post-166408

Oser, K. (2004a). Nike assays blog as marketing tool. *Advertising Age, 75*(24), 26.

Oser, K. (2004b). Targeting influencers: More marketers test blogs to build buzz. *Advertising Age, 75*(37), 3–4.

Postman, N. (1985). *Amusing ourselves to death*. New York: Penguin.

Rushkoff, D. (1999). *Coercion: Why we listen to what they say*. New York: Riverhead Books.

Schlosser, A.E., Shavitt, S., & Kanfer, A. (1999). Survey of Internet users' attitudes toward Internet advertising. *Journal of Interactive Marketing, 13*(3), 34–54.

Sheehan, K.B., & Morrison, D.K. (2009). Beyond convergence: Confluence culture and the role of the advertising agency in a changing world. *First Monday, 14*(3). Retrieved March 4, 2015, from http://firstmonday.org/article/view/2239/2121

Shields, M. (2014, February 5). Many brands who held back Super Bowl ads struggle on YouTube. *AdWeek*. Retrieved February 26, 2014, from http://www.adweek.com/videowatch/many-brands-who-held-back-super-bowl-ads-struggle-youtube-155458

Thorbjørnsen, H., Supphellen, M., Nysveen, H., & Pedersen, P.E. (2002). Building brand relationships online: A comparison of two interactive applications. *Journal of Interactive Marketing, 6*(3), 17–34.

Travis, D. (2000). *Emotional branding*. Roseville, CA: Prima Venture.

Wolin, L.D., & Korgaonkar, P. (2003). Web advertising: Gender differences in beliefs, attitudes and behavior. *Internet Research, 13*(5), 375–385.

Wright, J. (2006). *Blog marketing*. New York: McGraw-Hill.

Zyman, S. (2000). *Building brandwidth: Closing the sale online*. New York: Harper Collins.

· 1 1 ·

BRANDS AND CULTURAL CONCERNS

Today clever branding has become nothing more than an exercise in loading a product with the social values consumers want.
—Daryl Travis, 2000, pp. 16–17

A number of issues have been addressed about the relationship and presentation of branding to people. An example is how American brands have spread to other cultures around the world. As these brands are disseminated, a countercultural movement has developed to alter the meaning of different brands. Culture jamming is a method that groups use to challenge the idea of branding. Publications such as Adbusters create an alternative conversation to commercialism. Brands are altered in their discussions. Additionally, advertising practices that create cultural concerns are presented, such as behavioral targeting, contextual advertising, abuse of user-generated content and sex in advertising. The impact of and protest against brands will be described in this chapter, along with a discussion of how brands are socially responsible citizens. There are both positive and negative aspects to the relationship between brands and culture.

For some scholars, advertising and branded messages are problematic. For example, Naomi Klein (1999) argued "that as more people discover the brand-name secrets of the global logo web, their outrage will fuel the next big political movement, a vast wave of opposition squarely targeting transnational corporations, particularly those with very high name-brand recognition" (p. xviii). In contrast to this view, branding today is even more prevalent, given the Internet and its applications such as YouTube, which celebrates branded messages.

Scholars have contended that an underlying message in all advertising images is the endorsement and perpetuation of commodity values, and these values are central to a capitalist ideology. This view is highly critical of advertising and brands. For instance, Malcom Barnard (1995) stated that the function of an advertisement is to create desire. However, the desire being created is directed toward "false ideals and in a way that obscures the real structure of society. So ads intend to make us feel we are lacking, they engender desire in us, and they direct our desire towards consumer goods" (p. 34). Though academics have been extremely critical of advertising and branding, their cultural presence appears to be growing.

In looking at the relationship between branding and culture, others argue that advertising symbols can be removed from the commodity context to be used for the creation of social messages. Separated from its commercial function, the rhetorical structure of an advertisement is "indifferent" to the emotional and ideological values of commerce. Isolated advertising elements can be "recycled" and applied to cultural messages. This is often seen in the user-generated, remixed videos that appear on YouTube. Thus, this latter perspective appears to be a current academic trend.

Today, branding is about the image of a company rather than the creation of a product. This has led to the buying and branding of products rather than the manufacture of goods. Klein (1999) contends that the increased use of branding requires an endless parade of brand images and the creation of fresh spaces to market these ideas. Along with the rise in branding came the idea that brands are not a product, but a way of life. For some companies, "branding was not just a matter of creating value for a product. "It was about thirstily soaking up cultural ideas and iconography that their brands could reflect by projecting these ideas and images back on the culture" (p. 29). Engaging consumers with branding experiences through the Internet supports this notion. The Internet spreads branded messages.

Culture Jamming

Using brands for the creation of cultural messages, culture jammers re-purpose or re-define the brand message to communicate a social one. The phrase "culture jamming" was created in 1984 by a San Francisco band named Negativland. It refers to the activity of altering advertising billboards to create new types of social communication. The practice includes cutting and pasting graffiti onto modern billboards. A number of different brands have been the target of these pranks.

"The most sophisticated culture jams are not stand-alone ad parodies but interceptions—counter-messages that hack into a corporation's own method of communication to send a message starkly at odds with the one that was intended" (Klein, 1999, p. 281). For instance, pasting the face of serial killer Charles Manson over an image for Levi's jeans attempts to design a disruptive message about labor practices. It was believed that Chinese prisoners assembled Levi's jeans, and Manson helps to illustrate this because he is a prisoner.

Another popular culture jam was to turn the now-retired Joe Camel into Joe Chemo and hook up the image to an IV machine. The cartoon character was accused of luring children into cigarette smoking. Similarly, Apple Computer's billboards have been altered in a number of ways, such as morphing the rainbow Apple logo into a human skull.

In addition to advertising billboards, some jammers also engage in a combination of theater and activism. For instance, the Guerrilla Girls paraded outside the Whitney Museum in New York City wearing guerrilla masks to protest the male-dominated art world. On a more subversive level, hackers will break into corporate websites and leave their own messages behind. Culture jammers are concerned about the role of corporate life in culture. As argued here, branding is pervasive in contemporary society. Culture jammers believe that "free speech is meaningless if the commercial cacophony has risen to the point that no one can hear you" (Klein, 1999, p. 284). The prevalence of branding dominates the landscape, making it difficult for other voices to be heard.

As a result, culture jammers communicate their message through billboards, zine publishing, pirate radio, activist video, and community activism. A key publication for culture jammers is *Adbusters*, which recycles elements of advertisements to create messages that are critical of advertising itself. The magazine claims it is a global network of artists, activists, writers, pranksters, students, and educators who want to advance social activism in the twenty-first century. It is a non-profit organization that is reader supported rather than advertising assisted. The organization wants to bring down current power structures and create a new way of living. It criticizes capitalism and supports projects such as "Buy Nothing Day" to protest shopping days, especially after

Thanksgiving. Brands often represent the power structures that they want to topple.

Brands that *Adbusters* regularly targets include McDonald's, Nike, Absolut, and Visa. The *Adbusters* website (www.adbusters.org) is used as a focal point for culture jammers. The magazine also questions today's aesthetics. It inquires about whether or not people are designing a terrifying future. For instance, the magazine is concerned about the contribution of corporations to global environmental pollution. Moreover, it is concerned about the "mental" environment of our planet. The goal of the magazine is to spark a paradigm shift in public thinking.

Though the Internet may be crowded with branded images, it also makes the creation and circulation of advertising parodies much easier. In addition, corporate websites are links to culture jammers located around the world. Digital technologies enable culture jammers to design images that look like actual advertising campaigns, but with altered messages. Using digital tools, jammers can reproduce the slick look of an advertisement itself. Thus, it is difficult to distinguish a real advertisement from one that has been designed by activists.

Digital Media and Anti-Corporate Activists

Anti-Corporate Activist movements occur on a global level. For example, they have taken place in Prague, Quebec, Genoa, Puerto Alegre, Seattle, and Barcelona. These events are organized by way of digital media, including email, online forums, and websites. At the demonstrations, activists broadcast real-time reports through laptops, sending information through the Internet. In addition, they shoot hours' worth of digital documentary footage of their events, which can then be used to create Internet videos.

The speed, flexibility, and global reach of digital networks enable people to express and share social movements. Internet communication facilitates global connectedness while also increasing local ties. This effect is called "glocalization." Using the Internet as their infrastructure, anti-corporate activists can coordinate both local and global, on- and offline activities. "The horizontal networking logic facilitated by new digital technologies not only provides an effective method of social movement organizing, it also represents a broader model for creating alternative forms of social, political, and economic organization" (Juris, 2005, p. 192).

As an example, Internet technology helps to build horizontal ties; it supports the free and open circulation of information; and it fosters democratic decision making and self-directed networking. These forms of social behavior are in stark contrast to the idea of corporate control. Brands need to entice consumers to become loyal to their them, because devoted customers translate into improved sales. By contrast, activists warn consumers about the unethical business practices of brands. Brand-based activism has spearheaded anti-sweatshop campaigns against brands such as Nike, Ralph Lauren, Victoria's Secret, Calvin Klein, and The Gap. These movements try to discourage people from buying products manufactured under oppressive conditions. Unfair practices by brands are a central reason for cultural concern.

Commercial Exploitation of User Data

Another topic of concern—and an important social issue—is the use of personal data for advertising purposes. Digital technologies enable brands to collect highly specific and personal data about people. Today, search engines are in the advertising business because three of the major search engine providers have acquired advertising companies. This represents a shift from a focus on improving the quality of search results to an application of contextual advertising. Contextual advertising is targeted advertising, and it uses keywords to display advertisements on web pages. For example, if a user is searching the word "fashion," the advertising on the page will display fashion topics. In other words, the content of the advertising relates to the subject of the website being viewed.

Applying personalization to contextual advertising enables brands to tailor advertising specifically to individual interests. By targeting advertising to the interests of people, it becomes much more cost effective. Moreover, contextual advertising can create a feeling of connectivity between the brand and the consumer, because the message appears more personalized. On the other hand, the use of personal data by search engines raises serious questions about the exploitation of a user's data.

Privacy issues are a concern because the point of interaction between people and institutions can be monitored and recorded. This surplus information can be used to construct consumer profiles for the purpose of delivering targeted commercial messages. Companies want to encourage the buying behavior of their clients and build rapport. Personal information can be collected because computing power and storage capability is increasing, with the result that companies are capable of analyzing ever-expanding amounts of data.

As better computer methods for predicting consumer behavior are developed, the result will be better selling techniques. "Instead of choosing target groups based on costly demographic research, this type of advertising made it possible for advertisers to communicate directly with users the moment they expressed a certain interest" (Rohle, 2007, p. 5). This has developed into behavioral targeting, which describes methods for analyzing consumer behavior to determine when a person is most receptive to a certain type of advertising. Behavioral targeting techniques are used to analyze data to predict online buying behavior. "By combining contextual advertising and behavioral targeting, all user activities including searching, browsing and shopping, can be accompanied by precisely targeted advertisements" (p. 5). An individual's information needs to correspond with the advertising message. The social issue is how personal data being collected by brands are used to target individual people and whether or not this information is being misused.

Exploitation of User-Generated Content

The use and misuse of online information extends to user-generated content. Depending on how it is used, such content can vary in significance. User-generated content is produced for the Internet by individuals rather than mass-media organizations. It can take the form of videos, photographs, and online conversation. Petersen (2008) argues that, although the Internet generates pleasure, it also exploits users. People take pictures and upload them to software programs such as Flickr or Facebook for their friends and family to view. Once an image is placed online, magazines and tourist guides may become interested in publishing it. Additionally, user content can become part of the participatory citizen media movement, which is exemplified by citizen journalism.

Citizen journalists frequently contribute pictures and videos to news outlets with large audiences, such as CNN news reports. Petersen (2008) contends that "a single photo can have many different significances and create different forms of value (economic, social, and affective) due to the different relations which it is a part of" (p. 2). Further, digital technologies make it easy for images to be moved between programs and platforms for widespread distribution.

Digital technology also supports creativity. Design software is commonly available for use by the average person. This raises the issue of labor. In today's automated society, knowledge rather than labor is the foundation of wealth. Labor is marginalized. For instance, when Google purchased Deja News, an archive of Usenet, Google incorporated all of its user-generated content into its system. "Google's appropriation of all the free labor that is stored in Usenet postings and discussions is an example of how a distributed network of participation turns into a closed architecture of exploitation" (Petersen, 2008, p. 4). When companies appropriate cost-free content created by individuals, the question of exploitation can be raised. People need to be aware of how their user-generated content can be utilized by brands and others. Exploitation of user-generated materials is one example of a social issue associated with brands.

Sex in Advertising

Another social issue that brands face is the use of sex in advertising. Sex in advertising is the depiction of sexually provocative or erotic imagery and language in commercial messages. These images are used to arouse interest in a product, service, or brand. Fashion designers have a long history of using sex in their advertising campaigns. For example, in the 1980s, Calvin Klein created a number of sexually oriented print advertisements to sell its brand.

Two of the key issues related to sex and advertising are (1) how advertising uses sex to sell products, and (2) the ways in which advertising depicts sexual behavior. The use of sex in advertising has a long history, and the definition of what is acceptable has changed over time. Cultural attitudes toward sex influence how brands use it in their promotional materials.

The erotic appeal of advertisements has generated newspaper stories, editorials, and letters. Advertisers and brands keep pushing the limits of what is acceptable and what is not. Sex in advertising is often depicted by means of clothing—or the lack thereof. In addition, sex is shown as the contact between couples, such as a sexual embrace, or it can be based on sexual language and words. It has been concluded that "using sex in advertising has frequently, but not always, increased consumer interest and often aided in selling products and building strong brand identities" (O'Barr, 2011, p. 9).

Consumers respond differently to sexual material. Some respond with their pocketbooks, while others are offended.

As social concepts of sex change, advertisements reflect these differences. For instance, widespread discussion of gay marriage has led brands to begin to incorporate gay relationships into their advertisements. Life insurance, beer, and over-the-counter medications have all depicted gay relationships. In terms of sexual roles, advertisers for laundry detergent and diapers now show men rather than women doing these chores. How consumers react to sex in advertising depends upon the person. However, brands are warned to use sex only for appropriate products. For example, using nudity to sell lawn mowers probably would not work. Brands need to be aware of the types of social messages they promote.

Social Responsibility

Brands themselves support social and cultural messages because authenticity is a business value that is embraced by customers. This often takes the form of cause/charity events and sponsorships. Corporate social responsibility can be a high priority for companies. "Cone Research found that 88 percent of millennial consumers (aged eighteen to twenty-four) and 79 percent of all consumers would switch from one brand to another (all else being more or less equal in quality and price) if the other brand were associated with a good cause" (Moffitt & Dover, 2011, p. 193). For this reason, many brands become involved in social causes.

Malone and Fiske (2013) refer to social responsibility as the principle of worthy intentions. This occurs when a company puts its customers' interests ahead of its own. Customers respond to the company's worthy intentions with trust and loyalty, thus helping brands to become admired and long lasting. Starbucks is a company that understands worthy intentions. It has created the "Green Apron Book" that fits into the pocket of a Starbucks apron. The book describes five ways in which employees should behave: being welcoming, genuine, considerate, knowledgeable, and involved.

Instructing employees to be kind and considerate to customers adds to the notion of worthy intentions. Similarly, Zappos has a customer-loyalty team that is thoroughly responsive to customer desires. For example, one employee spent 9 hours and 37 minutes on the telephone with a customer, though it is unclear whether or not the call generated any sales. "When you call Zappos, perhaps with questions about a pair of shoes or gloves, you are guaranteed to speak with someone who only has worthy intentions" (Malone & Fiske, 2013, p. 95). Spending time with customers is rewarded with their loyalty.

Social responsibility can also involve employee engagement. For example, Häagen-Dazs's employees became involved in the issue of a decline in the number of honeybees, and their concern led to an increase in sales. Companies have also set up grant programs. For instance, PepsiCo set up the Pepsi Refresh Project, giving away $20 million to improve communities. The company was also interested in extending its program into education. Another company involved with philanthropic work is Hershey. A large portion of Hershey's profits is allocated to funding the Milton Hershey School in Pennsylvania, a boarding school for underprivileged children. Customers respect these types of worthy projects.

Coca-Cola and Social Responsibility

Coca-Cola has been involved in a number of projects designed to deal with social issues, including an advertising campaign called "Crossroads," for the Latin American market, that explored two teenage boys, one of whom was gay. For the campaign, Oscar winner Dustin Lance Black created several different films that challenged young people to choose compassion and kindness over cruelty. The films invited them to ponder what real friends would do in difficult social situations. At a crucial moment in one film, a boy goes to the refrigerator for a Coke. Gianatasio (2015) states: "one could argue that by placing itself at the precise moment of truth, Coke strengthens its connection to the cause, and affirms that its commitment is very much the real thing" (p. 2). Product placement in films is another method of brand awareness. The product can be part of a scene or somewhere in the background.

In addition to social causes, Coca-Cola also has a commitment to the outdoors. The company created a "happiness machine," a bio cooler that dispensed soft drinks. It did not need electricity or batteries to cool the beverage. Instead, ancient technology was used that had a plant atop the machine, which produced evaporation and a mirror to convert gas to liquid. Designed for use in South America, where electricity is not readily available, it works well in hot climates.

Critics have questioned whether or not it was insensitive to bring an unhealthy beverage to thirsty populations. However, the project was not about bringing water or food to the needy. "Instead, this [was] about bringing people a modest luxury that's normally out of reach, so such arguments don't really hold water" (Gianatasio, 2014a, p. 2). With help from the International Physics Centre in Bogota, Colombia, Coke helped to develop a solution to the problem of a lack of electricity. Moreover, the solution was environmentally friendly.

Environmental Advertising

The cooler described above is a technology that does not compromise the environment. In fact, it is designed to work in places that are off the electrical grid. In the past, Coca-Cola and the World Wildlife Fund have created billboards with fukien tea plants to absorb air pollution. Other branded projects that help the physical environment have included Peruvian billboards that generate clean air and water.

The Japanese cosmetics brand Shokubutsu Hana and TBWA\SMP helped to clean up the Pasig River in the Philippines. They created an 88-foot billboard made of grass that absorbs toxins. The billboard can help to clean up thousands of gallons a day. Shokubutsu Hana states on its website that the effort represents the company's belief in "'healthy beauty brought about by the restorative power of nature' and commitment to 'provide not only a clean message but also a clean future'" (Gianatasio, 2014b, p. 2). The company plans to place other billboards on polluted rivers. Here we have examples of brands being good corporate citizens by aiding the physical environment. But despite the fact that some brands engage in socially responsible actions, scholars are still critical of commercial messages.

Cultural Heterogeneity

Efforts to aid society are in stark contrast to concerns over the effect of global brands on local cultures. Scholars such as McAllister (1998) are concerned that the factual usefulness of advertising messages designed to help consumers make informed buying decisions might be replaced with images of American popular culture. This change could encourage cultural imperialism and erode diversity. Further, it has been argued that global brands tend to convey an overall message about the dominance of American products. It is argued that American corporations "want cultural uniformity, specifically the uniformity of everyone drinking Coke, or using IBMs, or riding in Budget rent-a-cars" (McAllister, 1998, p. 57). The concern is that the brand's values will overshadow local cultural ones.

McAllister (1998) is further concerned about how global branding strategies could be turning the globe into a large monoculture, a place where everyone eats at the same fast-food restaurants, wears the same jeans, and watches the same movies and television programs. Thompson and Arsel (2004) refer to this as a hegemonic brandscape, which refers to the hegemonic influence of brands on local culture. Brandscapes impact both the economic and social structures of a culture. Thompson and Arsel (2004) are particularly concerned about the influence of Starbucks on local coffee shops. "Starbucks has become a cultural icon for all the rapacious excesses, predatory intentions, and cultural homogenization that social critics attribute to globalizing corporate capitalism" (p. 2). Starbucks is also a center of attention for culture jammers and anti-Starbucks slogans. Moreover, Starbucks is a symbol of the effects of branded globalization on everyday cultural life.

Following the pattern of global advertising, the Internet also tends to promote American ideals and values. As communication networks merge into a global village, questions are being raised about whether the world is turning into a huge monoculture. More important, this monoculture tends to be dominated by American ideologies. However, it is questionable whether additional cultures will allow this to happen. The relationship between brands and society can vary from culture to culture.

Branding and Culture

When we examine the meanings embedded in branded messages (see Chapter 3), an understanding of the relationship between brands and culture can be identified. Katherine T. Firth (1998) refers to this as undressing the advertisements to understand the role advertising and branding play in the formation of culture. Society will at times have a negative reaction to a brand's message. For example, Bic pens made women furious in South Africa with a recent advertisement placed in social media. The offending copy read: "Look Like a Girl...Think Like a Man." Internet users did not like the associations being made and criticized the brand. "Bic made things worse by trying to defend itself in one half-apology before deleting that (further angering people who'd commented on it) and posting a second apology" (Nudd, 2015, p. 2).

In fact, this is not the first time the brand has been ridiculed for poor taste in copy. It was criticized a few years ago for its "Bic for Her" slogan.

Cultures do not always respond well to a brand's message. However, further research may be needed to fully understand the cultural meaning of an advertisement. Firth (1998) proposed a form of textual advertising analysis based on literary and artistic methods of criticism. The technique uses three stages of reading: the surface meaning (rhetorical approach), the advertiser's intended meaning (Lasswell model), and the ideological meaning (branded meaning) (see Chapter 3). Understanding an advertisement is similar to peeling an onion. Each layer must be discovered before the surface of the onion is revealed. The first layer is the surface meaning or overall impression that a reader receives from an advertisement. One way to understand the surface meaning of an advertisement is to list all of the objects, people, and copy.

The second level is the advertiser's intended meaning, or the sales message that is represented. In marketing terminology, this is called the strategy behind the ad and is the preferred meaning. Strategies generally fall into two categories: product oriented or consumer oriented. Product-oriented approaches are selling messages that focus on the product itself, and they tend to be more logical. For example, they communicate a unique product feature, and the selling claim could be summarized as, "You should purchase a _____________ because it's the only one that _____________." In contrast, consumer-oriented strategies attempt to sell the personality of the brand (Chapter 4), or they relate the product to a lifestyle or an attitude. This approach relies on emotional (Chapter 5) instead of rational reasons for buying a product.

Finally, the third layer is the cultural or ideological meaning. It relies on the cultural knowledge and the background of the reader examining the message. Advertisements make sense to us when we associate them with our shared cultural belief system. For example, Americans believe in free speech, progress, democracy, and individualism. These concepts are integral to American society, and people tend to forget that they are not universal attitudes. "Because we are so deeply embedded in our own set of cultural beliefs, it is often difficult for us to see the ideas that buttress and support the social system within which we live" (Firth, 1998, p. 9). Thus, it can be difficult to understand the deeply embedded cultural values that brands tap into.

Subtle ideological values are expressed in advertisements. For instance, before the U.S. Civil Rights Movement, African Americans were generally seen in subservient roles in advertisements—as maids and bellhops. Women have also been stereotyped in subservient ways. Brands often use stereotypical images in advertisements to make cultural connections. However, as cultural values change, advertisers must adapt to the changes.

Another way to examine the ideological concepts displayed in advertisements is to look at the associations being depicted between the individuals featured in the ad. Particularly, how does the image show men and women in relation to each other? Often, cultural ideologies are difficult to perceive, and we must look more closely at the social relationships being displayed in the image. To understand relationships between people, Firth (1998) suggested asking the following questions: "Who is in charge? Who holds the power? Who is weak? Who is dominant and who is subordinate…?" (p. 9). Asking these questions will facilitate a better understanding of the cultural roles communicated in an advertisement.

As culture changes, brands alter the human relationships depicted in advertisements. For example, women generally performed cooking chores because they were depicted as stay-at-home moms. Now some food commercials show dad and the kids making dinner because mom is still working. Men are now doing household work, including changing diapers, that was once viewed as "women's work" in commercials. As culture changes, advertisements adjust to fit the times.

Summary

The widespread use of digital networks has led to an increase in branded messages. Moreover, online programs such as YouTube celebrate brands and distribute their communications widely. In addition to promoting brands, the Internet can be used by culture jammers and citizens who are critical of brand activities. Activist groups can use the network's tools to organize anti-brand demonstrations.

The Internet raises a number of cultural issues about the relationship between brands and society. These include how digital data is used by brands for commercial purposes. Contextual advertising and targeted behavioral marketing raise concerns about privacy and the misuse of information. Further, the misuse of user-generated content by branded companies is an issue that has also been raised.

Brands' relationships to culture have both positive and negative attributes. On the positive side, brands confront social topics such as prejudice and the environment. They attempt to bring about positive social change. On the negative side, brands have been accused of creating a hegemonic brandscape and monoculture. In traditional advertising, brands are criticized for using sex and stereotyping in their selling approaches. The role of brands in culture is a topic of wide debate that centers on a variety of different issues.

Exercises

1. Argue whether or not the use of branded user-generated contests is a misuse of people's labor. Are these contests fair to individuals or do they exploit them?
2. How are brands socially responsible? Provide three examples.
3. What types of messages do brands communicate?
4. What is the relationship between brands and culture? Pick one culture to discuss.
5. Use the Firth method to analyze a print advertisement. What are the three different messages?

References

Barnard, M. (1995). Advertising: The rhetorical perspective. In C. Jenkins (Ed.), *Visual culture* (pp. 26–41). New York: Routledge.

Firth, K.T. (1998). *Undressing the ad.* New York: Peter Lang.

Gianatasio, D. (2014a, June 8). No power? No problem. Coke creates bio cooler for off the grid. *AdWeek.* Retrieved June 10, 2014, from http://www.adweek.com/adfreak/no-power-no-problem-coke-creates-bio-cooler-villages-grid-158173

Gianatasio, D. (2014b, June 4). Beauty brand's floating billboard cleans a polluted river by absorbing toxins. *AdWeek.* Retrieved June 5, 2014, from http://www.adweek.com/adfreak/beauty-brands-floating-billboard-cleans-polluted-river-absorbing-toxins-158114

Gianatasio, D. (2015, July 9). Ad of the day: Coca-Cola unveils crown jewel of its "Crossroads" series on teen friendship. *AdWeek.* Retrieved July 10, 2015, from http://www.adweek.com/news/advertising-branding/ad-day-coca-cola-unveils-crown-jewel-its-crossroads-series-teen-friendship-165807

Juris, J.S. (2005). The new digital media and activist networking within anti-corporate globalization movements. *Annals of the American Academy of Political and Social Science, 597*(189), 189–207.

Klein, N. (1999). *No logo.* New York: Picador.

Malone, C., & Fiske, S.T. (2013). *The human brand.* San Francisco, CA: Jossey-Bass.

McAllister, M.P. (1998). Sponsorship, globalization, and the Summer Olympics. In K.T. Firth (Ed.), *Undressing the ad* (pp. 35–64). New York: Peter Lang.

Moffitt, S., & Dover, M. (2011). *Wiki brands*. New York: McGraw-Hill.

Nudd, T. (2015, August 12). Bic apologizes for Women's Day ad that mostly just made women furious. *AdWeek*. Retrieved August 13, 2015, from http://www.adweek.com/adfreak/bic-apologizes-womens-day-ad-mostly-just-made-women-furious-166358

O'Barr. W.M. (2011). Sex and advertising. *Advertising & Society Review, 12*(2). Retrieved August 3, 2015, from http://muse.jhu.edu/journals/advertising_and_society_review/v0

Petersen, S.M. (2008). Loser generated content: From participation to exploitation. *First Monday, 13*(3). Retrieved August 7, 2015, from http://firstmonday.org/article/view/2141/1948

Rohle, T. (2007). Desperately seeking the consumer: Personalized search and the commercial exploitation of user data. *First Monday, 12*(9). Retrieved August 3, 2015, from http://firstmonday.org/issues/issue12_9/rohle/index.html

Thompson, C.J., & Arsel, Z. (2004). The Starbucks brandscape and consumers' (anticorporate) experiences of glocalization. *Journal of Consumer Research, 31*(3). Retrieved August 2, 2015, from http://www.jstor.org/stable/10.1086/425098

Travis, D. (2000). *Emotional branding*. Roseville, CA: Prima Venture.

· 1 2 ·
SOCIAL BRANDING

When so much of the wealth that underpins personal and family well-being derives from the commercial success of brands, it is curious that brands' overall social impact is generally regarded in a negative light.
—Steve Hilton, 2003, p. 47

Brands have traditionally been associated with commercialism and the concept of selling a product or service. Rarely are they examined for their social benefits. Brands have cultural power, economic clout, and a global reach. Moreover, the concept of branding has been applied to politics, non-profit organizations, and geographic locations. Branding is an integral part of our economic lives, social responsibility, social progress, and culture. This chapter will examine the social benefits of branding.

The widespread use of branding concepts has been applied to a variety of social issues. According to Steve Hilton (2003), brands support social progress by:

- creating customer loyalty, which promotes reliable companies
- fostering innovation that generates revenue from new and improved products
- providing systems for consumer protection

- creating demands for corporate social responsibility
- providing a role for social responsibility
- developing a sense of social cohesion through shared participation

In these ways, branding contributes to an assortment of social benefits. Socially, brands help to produce wealth, which translates into the development of social well-being. They also generate the wealth that sustains social progress, including health, education, and living standards. Today, a consumer society would be impossible without the use of branding.

Customer protection and customer loyalty are also associated with the concept of brands. As argued in Chapter 6, consumers need to believe that one company's offerings are better than another's. It is the company's responsibility to make sure that its products maintain good value. News about poor-quality products can make or break a brand. Therefore, it is in the best interests of the company to maintain high standards. The Tylenol example described in Chapter 4 is an illustration of how a corporation should react in a safety situation. In addition to recalling all of its potentially tainted products, Johnson & Johnson developed new tamper-proof packaging. These efforts bolstered Tylenol's reputation as of one of the most trusted brands on the market and, at the same time, illustrated how brands help to protect consumers and provide consumer safety.

Brand personalities need to be respected, and it is the company's responsibility to maintain high standards. If a goal of branding is to sell products, it is equally important to maintain good quality. Thus, consumers receive the benefit of knowing that what they have purchased is of value; otherwise they would not support the brand.

Brand Expansion

Once a brand is established in the marketplace as a beneficial product, it can use its identity to diversify. As discussed in Chapter 7, corporations can expand their core products into other areas. Sodas that add flavors to their main product are an example of how this works. However, brand expansion can also be innovative. Hilton (2003) stated: "Behind every great brand lies a valuable social benefit delivered through innovation" (p. 51). Brands develop products and services for Third World countries that are not always brought to the attention of Western markets. According to Hilton, "In Brazil, Unilever's

Ala brand detergent was created specifically to meet the needs of low-income consumers who wanted an affordable but effective product for laundry that is often washed by hand in river water" (p. 50).

Brands have created low-cost tooth powder and enhanced foods with vitamins, products that help to establish the brand in Third World nations. The benefits can go beyond the product itself. Improved products can help to upgrade the health of citizens, reducing the need for emergency hospitalization and medical care.

Environmental advertising, as described in Chapter 11, is another example of the social value of brands. Confronting issues of social concern—such as air pollution or the lack of electricity—are ways of meeting the needs of populations.

Developing or adapting products to address the requirements of poorer nations is an example of how Maslow's hierarchy of need is instituted on a practical level (see Chapter 4). People must fulfill their basic needs before they can purchase goods and products beyond their means. The act of identifying a need and filling it demonstrates how brands can be good corporate citizens. Value, choice, convenience, and functionality are all benefits that brands can offer to consumers.

Historically, the development of brands has enabled companies to expand their operations from a local to a global reach. As companies expand, they create more jobs, which in turn enables people to participate in a consumer society. Moreover, as customers buy brands, they help to develop an industrial infrastructure. This, in turn, leads to more employment. This is especially true when brands build local plants in poorer nations. The economy improves for everyone.

Social Benefits: The Promise of Branding

It is said that behind every brand lies a social benefit. The benefit is generally a result of the brand's innovative work. For example, Procter & Gamble markets Pampers, a brand of diapers for babies. The company's promise is that the diapers keep babies dryer. A dry baby is a happy baby. Pampers make both babies and mothers happy with this selling proposition.

Apple Computer promises that people will "think different," an appeal directed toward people who are more creative. The intuitive design of Apple's software makes some people believe that using a Macintosh is much easier than operating a Windows-based machine. In addition, the selling proposition appeals to people who don't want to follow traditional patterns.

Walmart's social brand mission is to lower the cost of living. Many products can be purchased for a lower price at Walmart than at other retail stores. The company's ability to buy large quantities of merchandise reduces the retail price of many household items. As a result, people get more for their money when they shop at Walmart. Brands live up to their promises and, in this way, provide social benefits.

Branding Critics

Branding critics question the hegemonic brandscape (see Chapter 11). They complain that branded products hinder the success of local products. However, there is another way to look at this. No matter where you are in the world, purchasing a bottle of Coca-Cola will fulfill the promise of quenching your thirst. Principles that apply to big corporations do not apply to small businesses. This is especially true of food standards. For instance, the standards of a McDonald's in India would follow the company's global corporate guidelines. A local food vendor has no such restrictions.

People concerned about how their food is prepared would be better off at a branded restaurant. In some countries, tourists have been warned to stay away from local eating establishments because of the questionable quality of the food. Brands are very conscious about health and safety regulations. Moreover, they are under pressure to behave as responsible corporate citizens. Companies that despoil the environment, hurt local communities, cover up health risks, and exploit their workers destroy their reputation in the marketplace. Once a reputation is lost, it is next to impossible to regain. When companies build brands, they need to protect them.

Moreover, some companies will champion different social causes. Chapter 9 described how Benetton's advertising depicted social conflicts as a way of bringing these issues to the public's attention. Nike supports environmental causes, and McDonald's has pioneered new standards for animal welfare. In the 1990s, Nike was criticized for its sweatshop practices; today the company fights for better working conditions and human rights in Third World countries. According to Doane (2003):

> Consumers can probably put more trust, for example, in a Nike shoe than a non-branded shoe from their local store, not just because of better quality, but also because

of the knowledge that Nike has to ensure higher standards of working conditions for those who make its shoes because it is under the eye of the global watchdog. (p. 186)

Branding is a concept that has been developed primarily by corporations, and at considerable expense—millions of dollars are spent on creating a brand image. When a social problem with a brand is discovered, steps must be taken to correct the company's image. Companies invest time, money, and resources into brand development, and once a brand is established, its image needs to remain consistent. It has been argued that in maintaining an image, corporations do not always consider the complexity of social issues. As a result, brands are still open to criticism.

Some topics of concern include:

- People do not always know who owns a brand.
- Do corporate responsibility programs really work?
- Can a company promote investment while engaging in social causes?

Larger corporations often purchase smaller brands, actions that consumers are not always aware of. For example, a large corporation now owns the ice cream company begun by Ben and Jerry.

Many large corporations—from pharmaceutical companies to major oil conglomerates—have initiated Corporate Social Responsibility (CSR) programs. A question raised about these efforts is: How much of the news is based on public relations and how much stems from actual social concern? Social responsibility programs have a voluntary code of conduct, which raises the question of whether or a not a company can be promoting social causes and also working on its bottom line. Can a commercial entity also be a good corporate citizen? To answer these questions, specific companies need to be examined.

Today, branding applies not just to products. In the current media environment, branding is not only part of the corporate world. Politicians, non-profit organizations, nations, and geographical locations also use branding as a strategy for identification and recognition.

Political Branding

It is argued that exposure to political advertising is informative. For over 50 years, politicians have been using television advertising. The televised Nixon/Kennedy debates in 1960 demonstrated the power of the image in shaping public opinion. Nixon, with his five-o'clock shadow, was not received well visually. In contrast, the youthful Kennedy came across in a very positive way. Interestingly enough, people who heard the debate on radio thought Nixon was a better speaker than Kennedy. Seeing can create a different impression than hearing. Chapter 5 described how brands work on an unconscious level. We can like something without being conscious of why.

Political branding is designed to make a candidate more appealing to the public. Moreover, branding attempts to create a relationship with a citizen and to build loyalty (Chapter 6). A key aspect of relationship building and loyalty programs is branding. "This aspect of relationship marketing has clear parallels with the political process, which relies heavily on the intangible aspects of party and candidate appeal, their 'image' or 'reputation'" (Needham, 2005, p. 347). Needham argues that branding is an important element in political campaigns for three reasons: internal values, external presentation, and consumer perception. She states:

> Reputation is a blend of internal values and consumer perception, but gives little insight into external presentation. Image is a combination of external presentation and consumer perception, but does not have a values component. (p. 347)

Branding combines these three elements to create a positive reputation and image for a candidate. Additionally, instead of information-intensive advertising, effective branding provides a few pieces of information about the person. Moreover, branding is designed to differentiate candidates. Branding creates a unique personality (see Chapter 4). As previously argued, "An effective brand is reassuring, a guarantee of standardization and replicability" (Needham, 2005, p. 348). This is done through the creation of simple brand messages. Both Bill Clinton and Tony Blair used branding effectively.

Other politicians have used digital media effectively to brand themselves. A study by Wulan, Suryadi, and Prastyo (2014) examined the 2014 presidential election in Indonesia and how Twitter was used to develop personal branding. They stated: "Through current developed information technology, political actors deliver a pack of messages that helps differentiate themselves from the existing political competitors" (p. 2). In the course of sending Twitter messages, the candidates were able to develop their own personal brand. The researchers found that through computer-mediated communication, people were able to develop both positive and negative impressions of political candidates' personal brands. This demonstrates that digital media can be used for the development of branded messages.

Political branded messages can be communicated through popular media. Warner (2007) argued that *The Daily Show with Jon Stewart* is an example of how culture jamming uses humor and parody to interrupt political branded messages (see Chapter 11). A concern about the use of branding in the public arena is the fact that it is based on emotional persuasion rather than logical appeal. Democracy depends on a rational discussion by diverse participants. It is argued that branding undermines lengthy conversations with its emotional shortcuts. Warner stated that brand hegemony "works to the detriment of the tenets of democratic theory both by talking over viable voices and conversations in the public sphere and by operating through calculated emotional appeals" (p. 18). Does the use of political branding undermine a healthy democracy? This is a topic that needs to be debated.

Non-profit Branding

Although political branding may be a topic of concern, most people do not have a problem when brands associate with non-profit causes. "Because of growing public concern over environmental and social issues, corporations have begun to affiliate their products with a range of popular causes, including social and ecological issues" (Farache, Perks, Wanderley, & de Sousa Filho, 2008, p. 2). This has led to the creation of cause-related marketing (CRM), which occurs when a company's marketing strategy forms a partnership with a non-profit organization. Corporations that work with non-profits are better regarded by consumers.

Cause-related marketing began in 1982 with an American Express campaign that donated some of its profits to art organizations. "It is commonly accepted that cause-related marketing is a communications tool for increasing customer loyalty and building reputation" (Brønn & Vrioni, 2001, p. 207). The effort was a success, and other companies tried the same approach. A key reason for using cause-related marketing is to improve a corporation's brand image and generate positive publicity. "It appears to be a new way of adding value to brands so as to satisfy growing consumer demands for demonstrations of social commitment" (Farache et al., 2008, p. 4). However, when firms are perceived as exploiters of causes and charities, publicity can turn negative. To stop this from happening, companies need to be socially responsible.

Since 1999, non-profit organizations have been using the Internet to spread their messages. "Developing public-private partnerships with commercial organisations is undoubtedly an effective non-profit strategy in order to better achieve mission statements" (Boeder, 2002, p. 14). The Internet can be a strategic tool in helping non-profits to achieve their goals and build online communities (see Chapter 10).

Branding can also be used to achieve public policy goals. This can be done through the unique use of taglines and brand names. The use of public policy branding can be traced back to Teddy Roosevelt and the Rough Riders, or Franklin Delano Roosevelt's concept of the "New Deal." Another example is the 1994 Republican Party's use of the phrase "Contract with America."

> One of the planks in the Contract with America platform was the elimination of the estate tax. Sufficient popular support for this goal which would ultimately benefit only 2 percent of the population was garnered largely by changing the tax name or "brand name" from estate tax to death tax. Luntz found through testing that a death tax was perceived by a larger percentage of voters to be inherently unfair. The brand of the death tax carried an emotional weight that could help change positions on the issue. (Pyles, 2008, 444)

A goal of public policy branding is to create a memorable and lasting emotional impression. This enables public policy groups to create a common language that can be understood across a wide variety of groups. The effective use of language can have a powerful emotional effect that can be used by non-profit organizations as well. "It is increasingly important for nonprofit leadership to create and maintain distinct brand identities that clearly differentiate themselves in the marketplace and lead to higher levels of brand equity" (Becker-Olsen & Hill, 2006, p. 73). Branding is relevant to non-profits because they help differentiate, define, and provide a social context for causes. Moreover, "potential donors often are aware of various causes without recognizing the unique character of charities that benefit these causes" (p. 74). This is frequently done through sponsorship programs with another corporation that is already branded.

Destination (Place) Branding

A new type of branding that does not rely on corporate support is destination branding. It involves branding a place in the same way that products or services are branded. Places want to brand themselves to attract visitors, promote jobs, gain prestige, and develop urban planning. "Countries, regions and cities began applying to their 'product' certain marketing techniques previously developed for consumer goods" (Caldwell & Freire, 2004, p. 50). Building a positive brand image for a location is a key marketing tool for attracting tourists and a goal of destination branding.

A difference between traditional and destination branding is that the brand image for the consumer needs to connect the city branding with the cultural geography. Another difference is the point of view. Destination branding needs to focus on the consumer's orientation. "We think of the place from the viewpoint of the end user; in terms of the way they sense, understand, use and connect to the place" (Kavaratzis & Ashworth, 2005, p. 510). Using branding as part of a location's communication program can provide cultural benefits for the place. "A proper and thorough communication process stemming from a country towards the rest of the world fosters a burgeoning environment for cultural discovery, touristic exploration, social interactions and networking" (Bivolaru, Andrei, & Purcaroiu, 2009, p. 110). An example of a nation that changed its branded image is Japan.

> Only 40, or even 30, years ago "Made in Japan" was a decidedly negative concept, as most western consumers had based their perception of "brand Japan" on their experience of shoddy, second-rate products flooding the market. The products were cheap, certainly, but they were basically worthless. In many respects, the perception of Japan was much as China's has been in more recent years. (Anholt, 2003, p. 216)

Additionally, governments want to shape the design of a place's identity. "The fundamental geographical idea of sense of place must include the deliberate creation of such senses through place marketing" (Kavaratzis & Ashworth, 2005, p. 506). Through place or destination marketing, "brands can be characterised as having two dimensions: representational (attributes linked to the individual's self-expression) and functional (utilitarian aspects of the destinations—sun, reefs, sky, culture, and so on)" (Caldwell & Freire, 2004, p. 52). Moreover, people differentiate between contending offers by the amount of representationality and functionality communicated by a particular brand. As a result, brands should be placed in a technical capacity and personality dimension. This is illustrated through the Brand Box Model developed by De Chernatony and McWilliam (1989).

The model was originally developed for physical and service products and was applied to destination branding by Caldwell and Freire (2004). This model has two dimensions to help clarify the strength of a brand: representationality and functionality. Representationality is based on the concept that consumers use brands to help them to express something about themselves. Functionality is built on the idea that consumers associate certain attributes with different brands. As in product branding, people develop an emotional and functional attachments to a location.

The Last Word on Brands

Brands are indicators of economic health. Branded companies create jobs and produce quality products for consumers to purchase. Consumers stand to gain high quality, lower prices, and product innovation. For instance, Starbucks increases coffee consumption outside the home. It also inspires competition in the marketplace. Seattle's Best Coffee and Tully's coffee are examples. Moreover, the presence of Starbucks forces rivals to improve their services.

Consumers control brands through their purchasing power.

> In the West, if our Gap jeans fray or our Mercedes car breaks down, we know exactly where to go to complain. We may not get a perfect response, which may lead us to shop elsewhere next time, but if we are regular customers the best brands will fall over themselves to put the problem right. (Ahmad, 2003, p. 174)

Brands and the companies behind them are neither good nor evil; they are merely structures designed to look after money. When corporations behave badly, governments can regulate them. Today, "Globalisation is a stepping-stone to prosperity. Countries that open themselves up to trading their products and ideas freely with other countries raise everyone's standard of living" (Ahmad, 2003, p. 177). While brands can raise a country's standard of living, they can also saturate people with marketing campaigns. At times it is difficult for people to see the value that brands have. However, there is no doubt that brands are embedded in American culture. As people study branding and marketing concepts, they become less susceptible to advertising messages because they understand the marketing process.

Summary

Brands create social benefits for countries, consumers, and workers. They create wealth and support social well-being. Brands look after consumers and provide consumer protection. They are innovative and develop products for Third World nations. This approach often follows Maslow's hierarchy of needs, because corporations find a need and fill it. Further, brands must fulfill their promises to consumers to protect their success.

In this way, corporations are acting as good corporate citizens. Corporate Social Responsibility programs and Cause Related Marketing are strategies that help brands to establish their social reach. Today, the use of branding is not limited to corporations; politicians, non-profit organizations, cities, nations, and regions also use it. Branding is an integral part of globalization, and its influence has increased with the use of digital media. It is so widespread in society that it is a topic worthy of study and debate.

Exercises

1. Pick one of your favorite brands. Research it to see if it has a corporate social responsibility program. What social benefits does the company provide?
2. Discuss whether or not your opinion about a company would be influenced by its social concerns.
3. Pick a recent election. Describe the branded images of the different candidates. How are they similar or different?
4. Find a corporation with a social cause. How do the products or services relate to the non-profit organization? If they don't relate, why?
5. Does the use of political branding undermine a healthy democracy? Debate this issue.
6. Develop a branded image for your location. What symbols could be used to indicate your place?

References

Ahmad, S. (2003). Globalization and brands. In R. Clifton & J. Simmons (Eds.), *Brands and branding* (pp. 171–184). London: Economist & Profile Books.

Anholt, S. (2003). Branding places and nations. In R. Clifton & J. Simmons (Eds.), *Brands and branding* (pp. 213–226). London: Economist & Profile Books.

Becker-Olsen, K.L., & Hill, R.P. (2006). The impact of sponsor fit on brand equity: The case of non-profit service providers. *Journal of Service Research*, 9(1), 73–83.

Bivolaru, E., Andrei, R., & Purcaroiu, G.V. (2009). Branding Romania: A Pestel framework based on a comparative analysis of two country brand indexes. *Management & Marketing*, 4(4), 101–112.

Boeder, P. (2002). Non-profits on E: How non-profit organisations are using the Internet for communication, fundraising, and community building. *First Monday*, 7(7). Retrieved February 8, 2016, from http://firstmonday.org/ojs/index.php/fm/article/view/969/890

Brønn, P.S., & Vrioni, A.B. (2001). Corporate social responsibility and cause-related marketing: An overview. *International Journal of Advertising*, 20, 207–222.

Caldwell, N., & Freire, J.R. (2004). The differences between branding a country, a region and a city: Applying the Brand Box Model. *Brand Management*, 12(1), 50–61.

De Chernatony, L., & McWilliam, G. (1989). The strategic implications of clarifying how marketers interpret brands. *Journal of Marketing Management*, 5(2), 153–171.

Doane, D. (2003). An alternative perspective on brands: Markets and morals. In R. Clifton & J. Simmons (Eds.), *Brands and branding* (pp. 185–197). London: Economist & Profile Books.

Farache, F., Perks, K.J., Wanderley, L.S., & de Sousa Filho, J.M. (2008). Cause related marketing: consumers' perceptions and benefits for profit and non-profit organisations. *Brazilian Administration Review*, 5(3), 1–13. Retrieved February 8, 2016, from http://dx.doi.org/10.1590/S1807-76922008000300004

Hilton, S. (2003). The social value of brands. In R. Clifton & J. Simmons (Eds.), *Brands and branding* (pp. 47–64). London: Economist & Profile Books.

Kavaratzis, M., & Ashworth, G.J. (2005). City branding: An effective assertion of identity or a transitory marketing trick? *Tijdschrift voor Economische en Sociale Geografie*, 96(5), 506–514.

Needham, C. (2005). Brand leaders: Clinton, Blair and the limitations of the permanent campaign. *Political Studies*, 53, 343–361.

Pyles, N. (2008). Building political will: Branding the nuclear-free world movement. *Nonproliferation Review*, 15(3), 441–457.

Warner, J. (2007). Political culture jamming: The dissident humor of *The Daily Show with Jon Stewart*. *Popular Communication*, 5(1), 17–36.

Wulan, B.A., Suryadi, S., & Dwi Prasetyo, B.D. (2014). Student perception towards personal branding of political leaders on Twitter ahead of presidential Election 2014. *Wacana*, 17(1), 1–6.

CONCLUSION

Further, because of the interaction of brands with society, and since so many socially influential brands are in the not-for-profit sector, the future of brands is also inextricably linked to the future of society.
—Rita Clifton, 2003, p. 227

Branding is a global process. Since the American Civil War, the use of symbols to identify products and services has become prevalent in contemporary society. To understand the role that brands play in culture, their messages can be analyzed using traditional communication models.

Rhetorical models of communication can be used as a method for uncovering branded communication. However, when utilizing the rhetorical method, several different readings are required. The Laswell Model of communication is another method for uncovering branded messages. The method speaks to the persuasive aspect of marketing communication. The goal of a branded message is to encourage consumers to purchase a product or service, and marketers utilize a variety of different methods for encoding their communication with both emotional and logical appeals.

Creating branded messages requires research and careful thought. The amount of thought included in the branding process is reflected in the complexity of understanding the messages. Several different readings are often required to comprehend the entire impact of brand communication. This is because branded messages are designed to work on emotional and logical mental levels. Finding emotional appeals that resonate with an individual's lifestyle helps to build brand loyalty.

Brands want to develop relationships with their customers. The introduction of interactive digital media has enabled marketers to communicate directly with consumers. Thus, brands can create the feeling of an interpersonal exchange, which helps to encourage customers to think favorably about a product or service. In today's marketing environment, brands need to have conversations with their customers. Another factor that makes brands appealing is their personality. People tend to envision brands in terms of human traits. As a result, it is important for a brand to always communicate the same personality traits.

These personality traits should also reflect the brand's core values. Moreover, it is important that a company be honest about its products and services. All of these factors are reflected in the story that is told about the company and product. That story needs to relate to the lives of consumers. By relating directly to a person's life, brands build loyalty and support.

In some cases, an individual can go beyond loyalty to identify with a brand. This can happen when consumers personalize branded products. Postmodern consumers want to express themselves through a product. Today technology makes it possible for a brand to directly communicate with its customers and for consumers to become brands.

Concepts from marketing, especially those associated with branding, have been applied to individuals. This is called personal branding, which is connected to an individual's image and reputation. Selfies shared through cell phones, Facebook, and the Internet are part of this phenomenon. Difficulties in the contemporary job market have encouraged people to view themselves as a brand. Digital technologies have made the ability to brand oneself even easier.

Interactive digital technology introduces new methods of branding and communicating with consumers. Through the Internet, many individuals form brand communities. These communities provide activities and socialization for group members.

Internet communication has positive and negative consequences for brands. Consumers can post both rave reviews and complaints. Once a complaint goes viral, the brand needs to act quickly to address it, and how a company responds will determine how much damage is done to the brand itself. In some cases, a positive response to a negative comment or situation can add to the trustworthiness of the brand. As new technologies emerge, companies will find new ways to brand their services:

> In order to regain appeal for their brands, marketers will have to learn to adopt new tactics that are only gradually catching on, such as guerrilla marketing (one-off events designed to be startling enough that people talk about them), sponsoring events and product placement in hit shows like *Sex in the City*. bmw's series of mini-movies from famous directors and starring bmw cars are one example of how to do things differently. (Ahmad, 2003, p. 181)

Brands play a large role in today's social environment. Branding is so pervasive that it fills our natural and mediated environments. Scholars and activists have criticized its role in society. They argue that brands communicate messages of false desire and capitalism. Others argue that advertising symbols can be removed from a commercial context and understood as social messages. Branding is about reflecting social concepts back to consumers.

A social concept associated with digital media is the collection of personal data. Social media, blogs, and discussion lists enable advertisers to record the personal preferences of individuals. By placing these people into specific groups, advertising can be targeted to the group. For instance, individuals discussing weddings online will be targeted with wedding products. Advertising using this method is much more cost effective for brands.

Many brands strive to go further than simply avoiding controversy and want to be viewed as good corporate citizens. This can be achieved by being socially responsible. Brands that place their customers first will gain a reputation of having worthy intentions. Social branding is now being applied to non-profits, political campaigns, and places. Although we are surrounded by branded messages, understanding them requires research.

The future of branding is linked to the future of society. Branded messages are ubiquitous within global culture and are an integral part of its economy. Major brands will probably still exist in 25 years; however, they will need to maintain their emotional and technological appeal. Branding skills will develop as new types of digital media emerge. Global markets will contribute products and services to consumer culture. As a result, new and innovative brands from around the world will become household words.

References

Ahmad, S. (2003). Globalization and brands. In R. Clifton & J. Simmons (Eds.), *Brands and branding* (pp. 171–184). London: Economist & Profile Books.

Clifton, R. (2003). Future of brands. In R. Clifton & J. Simmons (Eds.), *Brands and branding* (pp. 227–241). London: Economist & Profile Books.

GLOSSARY

Accidental symbol is when there is no intrinsic relationship between the symbol and that which it represents.

Advertising is a paid-for message totally under the control of a company.

Arbitrary graphics are abstract symbols that have no visual resemblance to the object.

Archetypes are universal symbols that represent inherent patterns from the structure of the unconscious.

Behavioral targeting is a term that describes methods for analyzing consumer behavior to determine when a person is most receptive to a certain type of advertising message.

Blogs are websites comprising posts or content written by an individual that are typically organized into categories and sorted in reverse chronological order.

Brand attachment is how much people consider the brand to be an extension of themselves.

Brand attitude measures how much people like a brand.

Brand awareness is the degree to which a brand is familiar to potential customers.

Brand community is a specialized, non-geographically bound community based on a structured set of social relationships among admirers of a brand.

Brand extension is the addition of a new product to a line of merchandise.

Branding is the process of creating an identity for a product by utilizing a distinctive symbol or name.

Brandscape refers to the hegemonic influence of brands on local culture.

Cause-related marketing (CRM) occurs when a company's marketing strategy forms a partnership with a non-profit organization.

Cognitive dissonance occurs when people feel discomfort because of two conflicting belief systems.

Collaborative filtering takes place when search engines keep track of a user's searches and automatically repeat the search options as a form of personalization.

Concept-related graphics capture the essence of an object and stylize it.

Connotation in language means the secondary association of a word. Connotative signs refer back visually to the referent.

Consciousness is the mental activity in which our state of being is preoccupied with external reality.

Contextual advertising is targeted advertising that uses keywords to display advertisements on web pages.

Conventional symbol is when there is an inherent relationship between the symbol and that which it represents.

Corporate social responsibility (CSR) programs are programs that corporations develop to support a social cause.

Creative brief is the document that describes the thinking behind the advertisement.

Denotation is the primary association a word has for a certain linguistic group. In pictures, denotation is an arbitrary symbol assigned to an object or business.

Destination branding refers to branding a place in the same way that products or services are branded.

Disintermediation presumes that there is nothing between the merchandiser and a client except a direct and personal connection from one computer to another.

E-commerce refers to engaging in business transactions and sustaining business relationships through computer networks.

Ethos (speaker) is the source's credibility or the character of the speaker.

Gestalt theory argues that visual perception is the result of organizing visual elements or shapes into groups.

Glocalization is using the Internet as an infrastructure to coordinate both local and global activities.

Graphic revolution refers to the advances made in the technological ability to reproduce, transmit, and disseminate images through media such as photographs, television, and the Internet.

Halftone is a term used to describe the intermediate tones between light and dark in a photographic image.

Iconic signs resemble the objects they represent.

Iconography is the study of symbols.

Iconology is the study of symbols in relation to a specific historical period.

Image-related graphics have a relationship to the object.

Indexical signs make a logical connection to the concepts they represent.

Infographics is information combined with graphics.

Laswell Model is a model of communication that was originally developed to study propaganda and is frequently used to examine advertising messages.

Lithography is a printing process that uses stone with water and oil to create images. An image is drawn with oil and then treated to etch parts of the stone away.

Logos are the visual symbols a brand or company uses to identify itself to consumers.

Logos (argument) is the logical nature of the message being presented by the speaker to the audience.

Lovemarks are a marketing concept used instead of brands, because love is needed to rescue brands. It is brand loyalty beyond reason

Maslow Hierarchy of Needs is a model that includes five basic levels of human motivational needs.

Metaphors describe something in terms of something else.

Metonym is a figure of speech in which one thing stands for another.

Monoculture is a culture in which everyone eats at the same fast-food restaurants, wears the same jeans, and watches the same movies and television programs.

Multiple intelligences theory argues for the existence of seven different human intelligences. These intelligences work together to allow people to develop their intellectual and social skills.

Myths are stories that attract human consciousness by communicating human emotions or cultural ideals.

Neuromarketing studies consumer responses to marketing stimuli through techniques such as EEG (electroencephalogram), brain sensors, MRI imaging, and galvanic skin response.

Nonnotational symbol systems cannot be broken down into smaller parts.

Notational symbol systems can be broken down into smaller components that have meaning.

Pathos (audience) is an appeal to the emotions and how the audience feels about the message being communicated.

Personal branding is using marketing to create a brand for oneself.

Personality determines the tone and attitude of the brand message.

Personalization consists of customizing a feature of a product or service so that the customer benefits from greater convenience, lower cost, or some other advantage.

Photoengraving uses light-sensitive, resistant material that is applied to the surface of a metal plate. Images are etched on the unshielded areas.

Pictorial symbols are images that clearly represent the object or idea portrayed.

Pseudo-events are staged events used by public relations and advertising companies to bring attention to products and services.

Public relations are not paid-for messages and are under the control of the publication sharing the story, rather than the company itself.

Public signs are graphics that indicate services and facilities such as restrooms.

Rebus is an image that sounds like the letter or word it represents.

Rhetorical model was developed in ancient times to study the art of persuasion.

Semiotics is the study of signs and symbols.

Sign is something that symbolizes another thing.

Slogan. See **Tag line.**

Soul branding is the process of linking corporate behaviors to higher social values.

Subliminal advertising refers to distributing advertising messages below the threshold of consciousness.

Symbolic forms are systems of knowledge, perception, and experience, including myths, arts, sciences, history, and religion.

Symbolic signs have no representational or logical relationship to the object or concept they symbolize.

Symbols represent something else. Barry (1997) argues that a difference between signs and symbols is the idea that signs relate to experiential connections, and symbols have abstracted associations.

Tag line (also called a **slogan**) is a short phrase that is used with the brand name or logo.

Target audience is the group of people who are in a position to buy or use a product or service.

Tribal marketing is a term used to refer to branding communities.

Unconscious is the mental experience in a state of existence in which we have shut off communication with the outer world.

Universal symbol is one in which the association between the symbol and that which is symbolized is not coincidental but intrinsic.

User-generated content is when individual people rather than mass media organizations produce content for the Internet.

Value is the worth that consumers receive when they purchase a product or service.

Viral marketing supports the passing along of information from one customer to another.

Visual appeal is a novel technical aspect of the image that violates what viewers expect. This violation functions both to create interest in the image and to decontextualize it.

Visual intelligence is a quality of mind advanced to the point of critical perceptual awareness in visual communication.

Voice in advertising is the brand's image expressed though language, such as a headline.

Zaltman Metaphor Elicitation Technique (ZMET) uses qualitative research methods to bring out the metaphors, constructs, and mental models that drive customers' thinking and behavior.

INDEX

Susan B. Barnes, *General Editor*

Visual communication is the process through which individuals in relationships, organizations, and cultures interpret and create visual messages in response to their environment, one another, and social structures. This series seeks to enhance our understanding of visual communication, and explores the role of visual communication in culture. Topics of interest include visual perception and cognition; signs and symbols; typography and image; research on graphic design; and the use of visual imagery in education. On a cultural level, research on visual media analysis and critical methods that examine the larger cultural messages imbedded in visual images is welcome. By providing a variety of approaches to the analysis of visual media and messages, this book series is designed to explore issues relating to visual literacy, visual communication, visual rhetoric, visual culture, and any unique method for examining visual communication.

For additional information about this series or for the submission of manuscripts, please contact Dr. Barnes at *susanbbarnes@gmail.com.*

To order other books in this series, please contact our Customer Service Department:

> (800) 770-LANG (within the U.S.)
> (212) 647-7706 (outside the U.S.)
> (212) 647-7707 FAX

Or browse online by series at www.peterlang.com.